Face Geometry and Appearance Modeling

Human faces are familiar to our visual systems. We easily recognize a person's face in arbitrary lighting conditions and in a variety of poses, detect small appearance changes, and notice subtle expression details. Can computer vision systems process face images as well as human vision systems can?

Face image processing has potential applications in surveillance, image and video search, social networking, and other domains. A comprehensive guide to this fascinating topic, this book provides a systematic description of modeling face geometry and appearance from images, including information on mathematical tools, physical concepts, image processing and computer vision techniques, and concrete prototype systems.

This book will be an excellent reference for researchers and graduate students in computer vision, computer graphics, and multimedia as well as application developers who would like to gain a better understanding of the state of the art.

DR. ZICHENG LIU is a Senior Researcher at Microsoft Research, Redmond. He has worked on a variety of topics including combinatorial optimization, linked figure animation, and microphone array signal processing. His current research interests include activity recognition, face modeling and animation, and multimedia collaboration. He has published more than 70 papers in peer-reviewed international journals and conferences and holds more than 40 granted patents.

DR. ZHENGYOU ZHANG is a Principal Researcher with Microsoft Research, Redmond, and manages the multimodal collaboration research team. He has published more than 200 papers in refereed international journals and conferences and coauthored *3-D Dynamic Scene Analysis: A Stereo Based Approach (1992); Epipolar Geometry in Stereo, Motion and Object Recognition (1996); Computer Vision (1998)*; and *Face Detection and Adaptation (2010)*. He is an IEEE Fellow.

Face Geometry and Appearance Modeling
Concepts and Applications

ZICHENG LIU
Microsoft Research, Redmond

ZHENGYOU ZHANG
Microsoft Research, Redmond

CAMBRIDGE UNIVERSITY PRESS
Cambridge, New York, Melbourne, Madrid, Cape Town,
Singapore, São Paulo, Delhi, Tokyo, Mexico City

Cambridge University Press
32 Avenue of the Americas, New York, NY 10013-2473, USA

www.cambridge.org
Information on this title: www.cambridge.org/9780521898416

First published 2011

Printed in the United States of America

A catalog record for this publication is available from the British Library.

Library of Congress Cataloging in Publication Data
Liu, Zicheng, 1965–
    Face geometry and appearance modeling : concepts and applications / Zicheng Liu,
    Zhengyou Zhang.
        p.   cm.
    Includes bibliographical references and index.
    ISBN 978-0-521-89841-6 (hardback)
    1. Computer vision.   2. Computer graphics.   3. Image processing.   I. Zhang,
    Zhengyou, 1965–   II. Title.
    TA1634.L58 2011
    006.4′2–dc22   2011002438

ISBN 978-0-521-89841-6 Hardback

Cambridge University Press has no responsibility for the persistence or accuracy of URLs
for external or third-party Internet Web sites referred to in this publication and does not
guarantee that any content on such Web sites is, or will remain, accurate or appropriate.

Contents

1

Introduction

Face image processing has been a fascinating topic for researchers in computer vision, computer graphics, and multimedia. Human face is so interesting to us partly because of its familiarity. We look at many different faces every day. We rely on our face as a communication channel to convey information that is difficult or impossible to convey in other means. Human faces are so familiar to our visual system that we can easily recognize a person's face in arbitrary lighting conditions and pose variations, detect small appearance changes, and notice subtle expression details. A common question in many researchers' minds is whether a computer vision system can process face images as well as a human vision system.

Face image processing has many applications. In human computer interaction, we would like the computer to be able to understand the emotional state of the user as it enriches interactivity and improves the productivity of the user. In computer surveillance, automatic face recognition is extremely helpful for both the prevention and investigation of criminal activities. In teleconferencing, face image analysis and synthesis techniques are useful for video compression, image quality enhancement, and better presentation of remote participants. In entertainment, face modeling and animation techniques are critical for generating realistic-looking virtual characters. Some video games even allow players to create their personalized face models and put "themselves" in the game.

The last decade has been an exciting period for face image processing with many new techniques being developed and refined. But the literature is scattered, and it has become increasingly difficult for a person, who is new in this field, to search for published papers and to get a good understanding of the state of the art. The goal of this book is to provide a systematic treatment of the technologies that have been developed in this field. We hope that it will serve as a good reference for practitioners, researchers, and students who are interested in this field.

Face image processing is a broad field. It is virtually impossible to cover all the topics in this field in a single book. This book mainly focuses on geometry and appearance modeling, which involves the representation of face geometry and reflectance property and how to recover them from images. Face geometry and appearance modeling is a core component of the face image processing field. In general, any face image processing task has to deal with pose and lighting variations, which can be addressed by applying 3D geometry and appearance modeling techniques. Some of these applications are described in the last part of the book.

In this chapter, we give a literature review and describe the scope of the book and the notation scheme.

1.1 Literature review

Human perception of faces has been a long-standing problem in psychology and neuroscience. Early works can be traced back to Duchenne [49, 50] and Darwin [42]. Duchenne [49, 50] studied the connection between an individual facial muscle contraction and the resulting facial movement by stimulating facial muscles with electrodes to the selected points on the face. Darwin [42] studied the connections between emotions and facial expressions. In 1888, Galton [69] studied how to use iris and finger prints to identify people. In the past decade, there has been a lot of study on what features humans use to recognize faces and objects and how the features are encoded by the nervous system [17, 56, 70, 89].

Early research on computational methods for face recognition can be traced back to Bledsoe [20], Kelly [109], and Kanade [106, 107]. Kanade's thesis [106] is a pioneer work on facial image analysis and feature extraction. In these works, the classification was usually done by using the distances between detected face feature points.

Early 1970s was also the time frame when the first computational method for face image synthesis was developed. In 1972, Parke [162] developed a polygonal head model and generated mouth and eye opening and closing motions. After that, Parke [163] continued his research by collecting facial expression polygon data and interpolating between the polygonal models to generate continuous motion.

In 1977, Ekman and Friesen [52] developed the Facial Action Encoding System (FACS). This scheme breaks down facial movement into Action Units (AUs) where each AU represents an atomic action, which is resulted from the contraction of either a single muscle or a small number of muscles. FACS has been extensively used for both analysis and synthesis tasks.

In early 1980s, as part of the effort to develop a system for performing the actions of American Sign Language, Platt and Badler [170] developed a physically based representation for facial animation. In their representation, face skin deformation was caused by the contraction of muscles, and a mechanism was developed to propagate muscle contractions to the skin surface deformation.

In 1985, Bergeron and Lachapelle [13] produced the famous animated short film *Tony de Peltrie*. They photographed a real person performing 28 different facial expressions. These images were marked manually, and the feature point motions were used to drive their face model. Their work demonstrated the power of facial expression mapping.

In 1986 and 1987, Pearce et al. [165] and Lewis and Parke [124] developed speech-driven animation systems that used phoneme recognition to drive lip movement. In 1987, Waters [233] developed a muscle model for generating 3D facial expressions. Compared to the work of Platt and Badler [170], Waters's model is more flexible in that it avoids hard-coding the mapping from a muscle contraction to the skin surface deformation. This technique was adopted by Pixar in the animated short film *Tin Toy* [115].

In 1988, Magnenat-Thalmann et al. [140] proposed to represent a face animation as a series of abstract muscle action procedures, where each abstract muscle action does not necessarily correspond to an actual muscle.

The 1990s witnessed an exciting period of rapid advancement in both face image analysis and synthesis fields. In 1990, range scanners such as the ones manufactured by Cyberware, Inc., became commercially available. Such scanners were extremely valuable for data collection. In the same year, Williams [239] developed a performance-driven facial animation system. He obtained a realistic 3D face model by using a Cyberware scanner. For tracking purposes, a retroreflective material was put on the live performer's face so that a set of bright spots can be easily detected on the face. The motions of the spots were then mapped to the vertices of the face model.

Terzopoulos and Waters [208, 209, 210] developed a physically based model to not only synthesize but also analyze facial expressions. They used a technique called snakes [108] to track facial feature contours, and estimated the muscle control parameters from the tracked contours. The recovered muscle control parameters can then be used to animate a synthetic face model. Lee et al. [121, 122] developed a system for cleaning up laser-scanned data, registering, and inserting contractile muscles.

Since 1990, there has been a tremendous amount of work on image-based face modeling and animation. In the following, we review the literature along five different but interconnected threads: statistical models and subspace representation, geometry modeling, appearance modeling, animation, and the modeling of eyes and hair.

1.1.1 Statistical models and subspace representation

In 1987, Sirovich and Kirby [112, 199] proposed to use eigenvectors (called eigenpictures) to represent human faces. In 1991 in their seminar paper [216], Turk and Pentland proposed to use this representation for face recognition, and they call the eigenvectors "eigenfaces." Their work not only generated much excitement in face recognition but also made Principal Component Analysis an extremely popular tool in designing statistic models for image analysis and synthesis. In 1992, Yuille et al. [251] developed a template-based technique for detecting facial features. Their technique can be thought of as an extension to the snakes technique [108] in that the local elastic models in the snakes are replaced by the global deformable templates. In 1995, Cootes et al. [38] proposed to use a statistic shape model, called Active Shape Model (ASM), as a better deformable template. An active shape model is constructed by applying Principal Component Analysis to the geometry vectors of a set of face images. ASM was later extended to the Active Appearance Model (AAM) [37], which consists of a statistic shape model as well as a statistic texture model. In 1997, Vetter and Poggio [220] introduced linear object classes for synthesizing novel views of objects and faces. In 1999, Blanz and Vetter [19] further extended this idea and introduced a morphable model for 3D face reconstruction from a single image. They used the University of South Florida (USF) dataset of 200 Cyberware scanned faces to construct a statistic shape model and a statistic texture model. Given an input face image, the shape and texture model coefficients can be recovered through an analysis-by-synthesis framework. Since then, both the USF dataset and the notion of the linear object classes have become very popular. Linear space representations are described in Chapters 2 and 3. The face-modeling technique of Blanz and Vetter [19] will be described in Section 7.2.

The study of subspace representation of face images under varying illuminations also started to attract much attention in the same period. In 1992, Shashua [194] proposed that, without considering shadows, the images of a Lambertian surface in a fixed pose under varying illuminations live in a three-dimensional linear space. In 1994, Hallinan [82] made a similar observation and proposed to use a low-dimensional representation for image synthesis. In 1995, Murase and Nayar [153] proposed to use low-dimensional appearance manifolds for object recognition under varying illumination conditions.

In 1997, Belhumeur et al. [12] extended Murase and Nayar's appearance manifold method to the case of multiple light sources and shadowing and proposed the illumination cone representation. In 2001, Lee et al. [119] showed that there exists a configuration of nine point light source directions so that the nine images taken under these light sources can be used as the basis for the illumination subspace. In the same year, Ramamoorthi and Hanrahan [177] and Basri and Jacobs [8] independently discovered that nine spherical harmonic basis functions are sufficient to approximate any irradiance map of an object under arbitrary illumination conditions. After that, spherical harmonics became a popular tool for illumination modeling [227, 228, 236, 255, 258]. Spherical harmonics will be described in Section 3.3.

One of the early works on bilinear models was by Brainard and Wandell [24] who tried to isolate the effect of varying illumination from that of varying the surface reflectance. In 1992, D'Zmura [51] proposed to use the bilinear model to recover the surface color (albedo) from images obtained under different illuminations. Around the same period, Tomasi and Kanade [212] published their factorization technique to recover shape and motion from an image sequence. In 1997, Freeman and Tenenbaum [64] proposed techniques to learn bilinear models from training observations and demonstrated how the learned bilinear models can be used for various analysis and synthesis tasks. In 2002, Vasilescu and Terzopoulos [218] proposed a multilinear representation, called TensorFace, to model face images with variations in multiple modes such as identity, expression, illumination, and head pose. In 2005, they [219] introduced a multilinear independent component analysis framework that generalizes the traditional ICA (Independent Component Analysis) to the multilinear case. Bilinear models are described in Sections 2.4.1 and 7.4.

1.1.2 Geometry modeling

In early 1990s, many researchers started to become interested in 3D face reconstruction from images. In 1991, Leclerc and Bobick [117] developed a shape-from-shading technique to reconstruct the 3D face geometry from images where they used stereo processing to initialize the shape-from-shading solver. In 1994, Devernay and Faugeras [46] developed a technique to recover the 3D structure by first computing differential properties from disparity maps, and they applied the technique to face images. In 1996, Proesmans et al. [171] developed a structure-light-based system for acquisition of 3D face geometries. In the same year, Ip and Yin [96] developed a system to construct 3D face model from two orthogonal views.

In 1998, Fua and Miccio [67, 68] developed a system to fit an animated face model to noisy stereo data. Given a video sequence, they treat consecutive frames as stereo pairs or triplets. They assumed that both the intrinsic and extrinsic camera parameters were known a priori. The obtained stereo data was used as input for 3D model fitting. In 1999, Fua [66] extended the system so that it does not require calibration data. Given a video sequence for which the calibration motions are not known, they used a generic face model to regularize the bundle adjustment so that they were able to recover camera motions between successive frames. After that, they generated stereo data and fit a face model as in [67].

In 2000 and 2001, Liu et al. [134, 135, 193, 268] developed a system to construct an animated 3D face model from a video sequence. They used a linear space representation to reduce the number of unknowns in the bundle adjustment process. Their system was so robust that they did many live demos at various events including ACM Multimedia 2000, ACM1:Beyond Cyberspace, CHI 2001, ICCV 2001, and the 20th Anniversary of the PC, where they set up a booth to construct face models for visitors. In 2001, Chen and Medioni developed a stereovision-based face-modeling system using a precalibrated and synchronized camera pair. In 2004, Dimitrijevic et al. [47] developed a structure-from-motion-based system to reconstruct 3D face models from uncalibrated image sequences. Their bundle adjustment technique is similar to [193] in that they also employed a linear space face geometry representation in their bundle adjustment formulation. Unlike [193], they used laser-scanned data (USF dataset) to construct their basis. The system developed by Liu et al. [268] will be described in Section 5.1.

In 2006, Golovinskiy et al. [74] developed an example-based approach to synthesize geometric details. They acquired high-resolution face geometries for people of different ages, genders, and races. The geometric details are extracted and represented with displacement maps. Statistical models of the displacement maps are obtained and used to synthesize plausible geometric details of a new face.

In 2007, Amberg et al. [3] developed a model-based stereo system to recover the 3D face geometry as well as the head poses from two or more images taken simultaneously. Like [193] and [47], they also used linear space geometry representation in their model and motion estimation. But they did not use feature point correspondences. Instead, they used the image intensity difference as the objective function. Note that using image intensity difference would not work well if the head is turning (i.e., using a single camera) due to the illumination changes caused by the head rotation.

1.1.3 Appearance modeling

Another line of work that started at the end of 1990s was the reflectance and illumination recovery of face images. In 1997, Marschner and Greenberg [142] developed an inverse lighting system for face relighting. Given a camera model, the face geometry and albedo, and a set of basis lights, their system produces (either synthesizes or captures) a set of basis images for the face under the basis lights. Given a new photograph, their system searches for a linear combination of the basis images to match the photograph. The linear coefficients are essentially the lighting coefficients. In 1999, Marschner et al. [144] developed an image-based system to measure the Bidirectional Reflectance Distribution Functions (BRDF). They assumed that the surface area of an object is curved and all the points on the measured object have the same BRDF. In 2000, Debevec et al. [43] developed a system to capture spatially varying reflectance properties of a human face's skin area. It requires a 2D array of light sources and a number of synchronized cameras, and the light sources and the cameras need to be calibrated. In 2005, Weyrich et al. [237, 238] developed a system to capture and measure a more general bidirectional surface scattering distribution function, which takes into account the translucent component of the skin reflectance. These systems will be described in Section 6.1.

In 2000, Zhao and Chellappa [270] developed a symmetric shape-from-shading technique to handle illumination variations in face recognition. The estimated shape information was used to generate a prototype image under a canonical lighting condition, and the prototype image is used for face recognition.

In 2001, Nishino et al. [157] developed a technique to recover illumination and reflectance from a small set of uncalibrated images by leveraging specular reflections. This technique will be described in Section 6.3.

In 2003, Wen et al. [236] proposed to use spherical harmonics to reconstruct a pseudo irradiance environment map from a single face image where the face geometry was assumed to be known (a generic face mesh was used in their experiment). The pseudo irradiance environment map can then be used to modify the lighting conditions of the face image. In the same year, Zhang and Samaras [255] proposed to recover the nine spherical harmonic basis images from a set of example images in a bootstrap manner. The technique of Wen et al. will be described in Section 6.2.

A physiologically based skin color and texture synthesis technique was proposed in 2003 by Tsumura et al. [214]. Given an input image of a face, they first remove the shading and then extract the hemoglobin and melanin information using independent component analysis. Based on the extracted hemoglobin and melanin information, they are able to synthesize the texture changes in pigment caused by aging or application of cosmetics. This technique will be described in Section 9.2.

In 2005, Zhang et al. [258] developed a 3D spherical harmonic basis morphable model. The model was built from a set of example face meshes such as the USF dataset. For each face mesh, nine spherical harmonic basis images were computed. In this way, they obtained a matrix of spherical harmonic basis images, which was used as the basis for a bilinear representation of the space of all the shaded faces under arbitrary illumination conditions. In the same year, Lee et al. [118] developed a bilinear illumination model to reconstruct a shape-specific illumination subspace. It requires a large dataset collected in a controlled environment in order to capture the wide variation of the illumination conditions. In 2007, Wang et al. [227, 228] proposed a spatially varying texture morphable model. They divide the image into multiple subregions and have a separate texture morphable model for each subregion. The spatial coherence between subregions is modeled as a Markov random field. Their technique is capable of handling harsh lighting conditions that cause cast shadows and saturations, as well as partial occlusions. The technique of Lee et al. will be described in Section 7.4. The techniques of Zhang et al. and Wang et al. will be described in Sections 7.3 and 7.5, respectively.

1.1.4 Animation

Toward the end of 1990s, encouraged by the success of image-based rendering work, many researchers investigated example-based techniques to generate photorealistic facial animations. In 1997, Bregler et al. [26] developed a video-rewrite system that synthesizes lip-synchronized face animations from speech. This technique was later extended by Brand [25], Ezzat et al. [53], and Joshi et al. [104]. In 1998, Guenter et al. [80] developed a system with six synchronized cameras to capture 3D facial expressions. In the same year, Pighin et al. [168] used convex combinations of the geometries and textures of a person's example facial expressions to generate new facial expressions for the same person. Basically the geometries and textures of a person's example expressions form the basis of the person's expressions. This representation was also used for facial expression tracking [169]. In 2001, Liu et al. [130] proposed a technique, called the expression ratio image, to map one person's expression details to a different person's face. Noh and Neumann [159] developed the expression cloning technique to map the geometric motions of one person's expression to a different person. In 2004, Sumner and Popovic [204] developed a technique to transfer detailed geometric deformations between two 3D face meshes. In 2006, Zhang et al. [259] developed a technique to synthesize photorealistic facial expression details from feature point motions. In 2007, Song et al. [200] developed a general framework for facial expression transfer. Their technique works on both 3D meshes and 2D images. Some of the facial animation techniques will be described in Chapter 8. Video-rewrite technique will be described in Section 11.1.

1.1.5 Eyes and hair

1.1.5.1 Eyes

The amount of research work on modeling face organs such as eyes and mouth has been relatively small. In 1994, Sagar et al. [185] proposed an anatomy-based eye model for surgical simulation. In 2002, Lee et al. [120] developed an eye movement model based on eye-tracking data of face-to-face conversations. In 2003, Itti et al. [100] developed a neurobiological model of visual attention including the eye and head movement. Based on eye gaze tracking data, a visual attention model was built to predict the gaze direction for any given visual stimuli (e.g., an image). A model for the eye and head movement was also developed to generate animations for avatars.

1.1.5.2 Hair

In comparison, hair modeling has received a lot more attention. Ward et al. [230] provided a nice literature survey on the hair modeling.

One of the earlier works on furry surface rendering was published in 1989 by Kajiya and Kay [105]. They proposed a volumetric texture representation, called texel, to render furry surfaces. They generated some impressive rendering results of a teddy bear model. In 1991, LeBlanc et al. [116] proposed an explicit hair geometry model by representing an individual hair strand with a 3D cylinder. In this way, they were able to leverage existing rendering pipelines to quickly generate hair images. In the same year, Rosenblum et al. [181] developed a technique that uses a mass-spring system to control the motion of a hair strand. In 1992, Anjyo et al. [99] developed a technique for modeling hair style and dynamic behavior. They derived simple differential equations that coarsely approximate physics while capturing the aesthetic features of human hair. In the same year, Watanabe and Suenaga [232] presented a technique to group the individual hairs into wisps for more efficient rendering and animation. In 1993, Daldegan et al. [39] developed an integrated system that combines hair modeling, rendering, animation, and collision detection. They used the wisp model to reduce the complexity of collision detection.

In 1995, Stam [202] proposed to use motion vector field for hair modeling by tracing particles through the vector field. The trajectory of the particle
determines the shape of the hair strand. In 1997, Goldman [73] accelerated
Kajiya and Kay's method [105] by using an aggregated lighting model. In
1999, Chen et al. [31] developed a hair rendering system using a trigonal
prism wisp model. In 2000, Kong and Nakajima [113] proposed a jittering
and pseudo shadow technique to improve the realism of hair rendering. Kim
and Neumann [110] developed a technique to simulate hair-hair interactions by
using a bounding volume that encloses the hair surface. Hadap and Magnenat-
Thalmann [81] used fluid flow to model hairstyle by tracing particle trajectories
along the vector field of the fluid flow. Essentially, the vector field of the fluid
flow acts as a global controller over the hairstyle.

In 2001, Yu [250] used a 3D vector field for hairstyle modeling. They introduced a set of vector field primitives for both global and local control of
hairstyles. In 2002, Chang et al. [29] developed a system to model the interactions of the hair strands by applying dynamics simulation on a sparse set of
guide strands, and a dense hair model is obtained by interpolating the sparse
guide strands. In the same year, Kim and Neumann [111] developed a multiresolution hair modeling system that allows hairstyle editing. At the coarsest
level, the hairs are created with a small set of hair clusters. These clusters can
be refined by subdividing the clusters. The system allows editing at any level.
Grabli et al. [76] developed an image-based technique to recover the geometry of the hair strands from images taken at a fixed view point under various
lighting conditions.

In 2003, Marschner et al. [141] measured light scattering from hair fibers and
proposed a hair shading model that is more accurate than the model proposed
by Kajiya and Kay [105]. Bertails et al. [58] proposed use of an adaptive wisp
tree to allow dynamic splitting and merging of hair clusters over time. Ward
and Lin [231] developed a level-of-detail representation to adaptively group
and subdivide hair during dynamics simulation.

In 2004, Paris et al. [161] developed an image-based technique to capture the
hair geometry by extending the system of [76] to allow multiple view points.
In this way, they were able to capture the geometry of the entire hair surface.

In 2005, Wei et al. [234] proposed another image-based approach to capture
the hair geometry. Compared to the previous work [76, 161], their system does
not require special setup for the controlled illumination. A user can simply
use a handheld camera to capture hair images under uncontrolled illumination
conditions.

In 2006, Bertails et al. [14] proposed to use Kirchhoff's equations for elastic rods to describe the motion of hair strands. The equations are solved by

representing a hair strand as a piecewise helical rod. In the same year, Moon and Marschner [148] proposed an efficient physically based technique to simulate the multiple scattering of hair based on volumetric photon mapping.

In 2008, Moon et al. [149] improved their previous technique [148] and developed a much faster volumetric rendering method to compute multiple scattering solutions.

In 2009, McAdams et al. [145] developed a hybrid approach to simulate the dynamics of hair interactions where large-scale interactions are handled with a fluid solver while local hair-hair interactions are handled with Lagrangian self-collision. Wang et al. [225] developed an example-based approach for hair geometry synthesis. Given an input hairstyle, their system can generate a new hairstyle, which has a statistically similar hair strand arrangement and geometric details. Based on their synthesis method, they developed a hair-editing technique that can perform hair detail transfer between different hairstyles.

1.2 Scope of the book

This book focuses on the modeling of 3D face geometry, reflectance and illumination from images, and applications. It does not cover 2D face processing techniques. Some of the 2D techniques are critical components for 3D face processing systems. For example, an image-based 3D face modeling system typically depends on face detection (outputs a rectangle that locates the face) and face feature alignment (outputs the feature point positions). So far, the best face detector is based on the Viola–Jones face detector [222], which is a 2D method in the sense that it does not directly or indirectly perform any 3D analysis. The reader is referred to [254] for the latest development on face detection. Two commonly used techniques for face alignment are Active Shape Models [38] and Active Appearance Models [37]. Both are 2D methods as well. These techniques are not covered in this book.

In the past decade, face recognition has attracted a lot of interest due to its potential in surveillance, image and video search, and social network applications. Face recognition by itself is a large field. Some of the geometry and appearance modeling techniques described in the book can be used for face recognition to handle pose and illumination variations, and we will discuss these applications later in the book. But face recognition is by no means the theme of this book. Recently two edited books focused on face recognition [127, 271] provide nice collections of state-of-the-art techniques in this area.

The book is divided into three parts. Part I describes commonly used representations for face geometry, reflectance, and illumination. These representations serve as the foundation for the face modeling techniques described in Part II. Part I consists of two chapters. Chapter 2 provides an overview to the geometric representations. It first describes the commonly used representations for general geometric modeling such as triangle meshes and parametric surfaces. After that, it describes the linear space representation for faces of different people, and furthermore, it describes the bilinear space representation for faces of different people with different facial expressions. Chapter 3 provides an overview on the appearance representations that involve the reflectance and lighting. It describes various illumination models that are used in computer graphics and computer vision community. In addition, this chapter describes low-dimensional space representations for lighting environment such as spherical harmonic basis for irradiance environment maps and low-dimensional space representations for face albedo.

Part II discusses face modeling techniques. Chapter 4 provides an overview on the systems that use active sensors such as laser scanners, structured light systems, and structured light stereo systems. The iterative closest point (ICP) technique and its extension to the parametric surface, called deformable iterative closest point, are introduced in this chapter. ICP technique is useful for image-based modeling (Chapter 5) and pose tracking (Chapter 10). Chapter 5 describes techniques that reconstruct face geometry from images. It focuses on techniques that use two or more views. These techniques usually do not model the reflectance and illumination.

Chapter 6 discusses appearance-modeling techniques. These techniques usually assume that the face geometry is known or can be approximated by a generic face model. The goal is to reconstruct the skin reflectance and the lighting. Chapter 7 describes techniques that reconstruct face geometry, albedo, and illumination. These techniques typically work with a single input image and rely on shading information to resolve the geometry. Low-dimensional space representations for face geometry, albedo, and illumination are essential for these techniques.

Part III describes various applications that benefit from some of the face-modeling techniques. The applications are grouped into four categories: face animation, appearance editing, model-based tracking and gaze correction, and human computer interaction. Face animation is discussed in Chapter 8. This chapter gives an overview on various animation techniques including pre-designed action units, physically based approaches, morph-based approaches, and facial expression mapping. It provides more detailed descriptions on facial expression mapping techniques.

Appearance editing is discussed in Chapter 9. It describes image-based techniques to modify the appearance of a face image. The techniques include geometrical detail transfer without explicitly reconstructing geometry, physiologically based technique that extracts the hemoglobin and melanin components from an image and modifies them to generate new images of different melanin texture or different hemoglobin levels, virtual lighting technique that learns from professional photographers to make the skin tone look appealing, and active lighting technique that uses computer-controlled lights to automatically adjust the lighting.

Model-based tracking and gaze correction is discussed in Chapter 10. This chapter first introduces the pose estimation techniques that are essential to pose tracking. It then describes monocular head pose tracking, stereo head pose tracking, and multicamera head pose tracking where the relative camera geometries are not known a priori. Finally this chapter describes a gaze correction technique that aims at improving the eye contact during video conferencing.

Chapter 11 describes two applications in human computer interaction: conversational agent and face-based human interactive proof (HIP). There are two different ways to animate the avatar in a conversational agent system. The first is the video-rewrite-based system, which is capable of generating photorealistic facial animations but is not flexible. The second is the 3D-model-based system which is more flexible in terms of generating facial expressions and head motions, but the image quality is usually not as good as that of the video-rewrite technique. Human interactive proof (also called CAPTCHA) is a method that exploits the intelligence gap between computers and humans to tell a computer program (bot) from a human. Text-based HIP has been widely used in internet services, but as the optical character recognition (OCR) technology advances, it has become difficult to design text-based HIPs that are difficult for computers yet easy for humans. This chapter describes a face-based HIP that exploits the gap between computer programs and human users in face feature detection.

1.3 Notation

We adopt a notation scheme similar to what was used in [61]. Points, lines, and planes are denoted by Roman or Greek letters in italic font (e.g., P, Δ, Π). Coordinate vectors of 3D points are denoted by uppercase letters in typewriter font (e.g., P, Q). Coordinate vectors of 2D image points and other generic vectors are denoted by lowercase letters in bold font (e.g., $\mathbf{p}$, $\mathbf{q}$). A vector that joins two points P and Q is often denoted by $\overrightarrow{PQ}$. Matrices are denoted by uppercase letters in bold font (e.g., $\mathbf{U}$). A tensor is denoted by uppercase letters in sans serif font (e.g., A).

We use $\Re$ to denote the field of real numbers. The space of all n-tuples of real numbers forms an n-dimensional vector space over $\Re$ and is denoted by $\Re^n$.

The dot product of two vectors $\mathbf{a} = (a_1,\ldots,a_n)^T$ and $\mathbf{b} = (b_1,\ldots,b_n)^T$ in $\Re^n$ is defined by

$$\mathbf{a} \cdot \mathbf{b} = a_1 b_1 + \cdots + a_n b_n.$$

The cross product of two vectors $\mathbf{a} = (a_1,a_2,a_3)^T$ and $\mathbf{b} = (b_1,b_2,b_3)^T$ in $\Re^3$ is defined by

$$\mathbf{a} \times \mathbf{b} = \begin{pmatrix} a_2 b_3 - a_3 b_2 \\ a_3 b_1 - a_1 b_3 \\ a_1 b_2 - a_2 b_1 \end{pmatrix}.$$

The cross product can be represented by a matrix times a vector as

$$\mathbf{a} \times \mathbf{b} = [\mathbf{a}]_\times \mathbf{b} = \begin{pmatrix} 0 & -a_3 & a_2 \\ a_3 & 0 & -a_1 \\ -a_2 & a_1 & 0 \end{pmatrix} \begin{pmatrix} b_1 \\ b_2 \\ b_3 \end{pmatrix},$$

where

$$[\mathbf{a}]_\times = \begin{pmatrix} 0 & -a_3 & a_2 \\ a_3 & 0 & -a_1 \\ -a_2 & a_1 & 0 \end{pmatrix}.$$

We denote the homogeneous coordinates of a vector $\mathbf{x}$ by $\widetilde{\mathbf{x}}$, i.e., the homogeneous coordinates of an image point $\mathbf{p} = (u,v)^T$ are $\widetilde{\mathbf{p}} = (u,v,1)^T$, and those of a 3D point $P = (x,y,z)^T$ are $\widetilde{P} = (x,y,z,1)^T$. A camera is described by a pinhole model, and a 3D point P and its image point $\mathbf{p}$ are related by

$$\lambda \widetilde{\mathbf{p}} = \mathbf{APM}\widetilde{P}, \tag{1.1}$$

where λ is a scale, and $\mathbf{A}$, $\mathbf{P}$, and $\mathbf{M}$ are given by

$$\mathbf{A} = \begin{pmatrix} \alpha & \gamma & u_0 \\ 0 & \beta & v_0 \\ 0 & 0 & 1 \end{pmatrix}, \quad \mathbf{P} = \begin{pmatrix} 1 & 0 & 0 & 0 \\ 0 & 1 & 0 & 0 \\ 0 & 0 & 1 & 0 \end{pmatrix}, \quad \text{and} \quad \mathbf{M} = \begin{pmatrix} \mathbf{R} & \mathbf{t} \\ \mathbf{0}^T & 1 \end{pmatrix}.$$

The elements of matrix $\mathbf{A}$ are the intrinsic parameters of the camera, and matrix $\mathbf{A}$ maps the normalized image coordinates to the pixel image coordinates (see e.g. [55]). Matrix $\mathbf{P}$ is the perspective projection matrix. Matrix $\mathbf{M}$ is the 3D rigid transformation (rotation $\mathbf{R}$ and translation $\mathbf{t}$) from the object/world coordinate system to the camera coordinate system. For simplicity, we also denote the nonlinear 3D-2D projection function (1.1) by function ϕ such that

$$\mathbf{p} = \phi(\mathbf{M}, P). \tag{1.2}$$

Here, the internal camera parameters are assumed to be known. In case the internal camera parameters are not known, we can add A to the right hand size of (1.2).

When two images are concerned, a prime ′ is added to denote the quantities related to the second image. When more images are involved, a subscript is used to specify an individual image.

The fundamental geometric constraint between two images is known as the *epipolar constraint* [55, 263]. It states that in order for a point $\mathbf{p}$ in one image and a point $\mathbf{p}'$ in the other image to be the projections of a single physical point in space, or, in other words, in order for them to be matched, they must satisfy

$$\tilde{\mathbf{p}}'^T \mathbf{A}'^{-T} \mathbf{E} \mathbf{A}^{-1} \tilde{\mathbf{p}} = 0 \,, \tag{1.3}$$

where $\mathbf{E} = [\mathbf{t}_r]_\times \mathbf{R}_r$ is known as the essential matrix, $(\mathbf{R}_r, \mathbf{t}_r)$ is the relative motion between the two images, and $[\mathbf{t}_r]_\times$ is a skew symmetric matrix such that $\mathbf{t}_r \times \mathbf{v} = [\mathbf{t}_r]_\times \mathbf{v}$ for any 3D vector $\mathbf{v}$.

Let A denote a tensor and $\mathbf{U}$ a matrix. We use $\mathsf{A} \times_i \mathbf{U}$ to denote the mode-i product of tensor A and matrix $\mathbf{U}$. For example, if $\mathsf{A} = \{a_{i_1 i_2 i_3}\}_{I_1 \times I_2 \times I_3}$ is a 3-mode tensor, and $\mathbf{U} = \{u_{j_1 j_2}\}_{I_2 \times J}$ is a matrix, then the mode-2 product $\mathsf{A} \times_2 \mathbf{U} = \{b_{i_1 j_2 i_3}\}_{I_1 \times J \times I_3}$ is another 3-mode tensor where

$$b_{i_1 j_2 i_3} = \sum_{k=1}^{I_2} a_{i_1 k i_3} u_{k j_2} \,.$$

We use $\odot$ to denote the component-wise multiplication. Given two $m \times n$ images I_1 and I_2, $I_1 \odot I_2$ is an $m \times n$ image with $(I_1 \odot I_2)(i,j) = I_1(i,j)^* I_2(i,j)$.

PART I

Face representations

2

Shape models

This chapter describes various geometric representations which are commonly used in face modeling. Triangular meshes and parametric surfaces are popular geometric representations for general shape modeling. Linear space representations are particularly useful for faces because people's faces have similar topology, and there are semantically meaningful point-to-point correspondences between different people's faces. One main advantage of the linear space representation is that it greatly reduces the dimensionality (i.e., the degree of freedom). Given a set of example face meshes, one can use Principal Component Analysis to obtain the basis of the face space. This chapter also describes bilinear models, which are used for representing the space of facial expressions of different people. As an extension to the linear representation, the principal components of a bilinear model can be obtained through bilinear singular value decomposition.

2.1 Mesh

Triangular mesh is the most common geometric representation for face shapes. A triangular mesh consists of a set of vertices and a set of triangles. The triangles define how the vertices are connected to form the surface. The connectivity of the vertices is also called the topology of the mesh.

Figure 2.1 shows an example of a triangular mesh of a face. It has approximately 190 vertices and 310 triangles. Its vertex coordinates are defined with respect to a coordinate system, called *model coordinate system*. For example, one can choose to place the origin of the coordinate system somewhere behind the nose. The x-axis goes from left to right, the y-axis goes from bottom to top, and the z-axis is along the frontal direction. In Figure 2.1 for visualization purposes, the model coordinate system is drawn at the bottom left corner so that the axis lines do not interfere with the mesh.

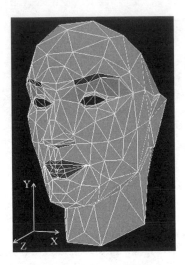

Figure 2.1. A manually designed face mesh. Its vertex coordinates are defined with respect to a model coordinate system. The mesh consists of approximately 190 vertices and 310 triangles.

In face geometry modeling, many people often predesign the topology of a face mesh while leaving the coordinates of the vertices as variables to be estimated.

2.1.1 Face features

Face features such as mouth, eyes, eyebrows, and nose are important visual cues, and there are usually creases separating face features. When designing a face mesh, people often put vertices along face feature boundaries.

For animation purposes, the mouth and eyes need to be cut out. Separate eyeball models can be placed behind the eye cut-out region to allow eyeball movement. Separate teeth and tongue models may be placed behind the mouth cut-out region for speech animation as well as facial expressions.

2.2 Parametric surfaces

One drawback with the mesh representation is that the mesh is not smooth along the edges. Parametric surface representations are used to create smooth surfaces. A 3D surface can be represented by three bivariate parametric functions, one for each of the three spatial dimensions. Typically these functions are quadratic or cubic polynomials.

One popular class of parametric surface is B-spline surfaces. It has the form

$$P(u,v) = (x(u,v), y(u,v), z(u,v))^T = \sum_{i=0}^{m} \sum_{j=1}^{n} C_{i,j} f_i(u) g_j(v), \qquad (2.1)$$

where $f_i(u)$ and $g_j(v)$ are the basis functions and $C_{i,j}$ are the control points. For face modeling application, the basis functions are typically predesigned while the control points are the unknowns to estimate.

The most commonly used basis functions are piecewise polynomials that are constructed from a set of knot values. B-spline curves and surfaces have been extensively used in the CAD industry. For a systematic treatment of B-spline curves and surfaces, the readers are referred to [7, 54, 167].

2.3 Linear space representation

In the past decade, we have seen rapid adoption of using linear space to represent face geometry after the publication of the seminar paper by Blanz and Vetter [19]. A linear space representation is also called a morphable model, a term first coined by Blanz and Vetter [19]. In this book, we use both the term *linear space representation* and the term *morphable model* depending on the context.

The advantage of the linear space representation is that the number of unknowns is significantly reduced. In linear space representation, the unknowns are the coefficients of the basis shapes in the database which is typically much smaller than the number of vertex coordinates in a mesh representation.

2.3.1 Linear space of face meshes

One type of basis used for the linear space representation is a set of existing face meshes, which are typically obtained by using laser scanners. The meshes scanned by laser scanners are usually dense and have accurate geometric details. Before they can be used as basis, the meshes need to be cleaned up and aligned so that all the meshes have the same number of vertices, and furthermore, there is a correspondence between the vertices of different meshes. The alignment can be done semiautomatically by first manually marking a number of face feature points such as eye corners, eyebrow boundaries, nose tip, and mouth corners. From the feature point correspondences, one can then generate a rough alignment between two meshes through interpolation. The alignment can be refined by computing a flow field between the two meshes that minimizes the texture and shape differences [19].

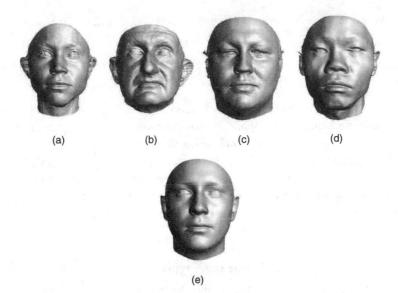

(a)　　　　　　　(b)　　　　　　　(c)　　　　　　　(d)

(e)

Figure 2.2. Examples of face meshes used for linear space representation. (a), (b), (c), and (d) are examples of laser-scanned face meshes from University of South Florida (USF) HumanID 3D database. (e) is the average of 100 faces in the USF HumanID 3D database.

Let $V_i = (X_i, Y_i, Z_i)^T$, $i = 1,...,n$, denote the vertices of a face mesh. Its geometry is represented by a vector

$$\mathcal{S} = (V_1^T,...,V_n^T)^T = (X_1, Y_1, Z_1,..., X_n, Y_n, Z_n)^T. \qquad (2.2)$$

Suppose there are $m + 1$ face meshes that are obtained by using laser scanner or some other means. Let $\mathcal{S}^j$ denote the geometry of the jth mesh, $j = 1,...,m+1$. These faces generate a linear space of face geometries:

$$F = \left\{ \sum_{j=1}^{m+1} \alpha_j \mathcal{S}^j : \sum_{j=1}^{m+1} \alpha_j = 1 \right\}. \qquad (2.3)$$

Let $\mathcal{S}^0$ denote the average face geometry, that is, $\mathcal{S}^0 = \frac{1}{m+1} \sum_{j=1}^{m+1} \mathcal{S}^j$. Denote $\delta \mathcal{S}^j = \mathcal{S}^j - \mathcal{S}^0$, $j = 1,...,m+1$. Note that these vectors are linearly dependent. We perform Principal Component Analysis on the vectors $\delta \mathcal{S}^1,...,\delta \mathcal{S}^{m+1}$. Let $\sigma_1^2,...,\sigma_m^2$ denote the eigenvalues with $\sigma_1^2 \geq \sigma_2^2 \geq \cdots \geq \sigma_m^2$. Let $\mathcal{M}^1,...,\mathcal{M}^m$ denote the corresponding eigenvectors. Then any face $\mathcal{S} \in F$ can be represented as the average face $\mathcal{S}^0$ plus a linear combination of the eigenvectors, that is,

$$\mathcal{S} = \mathcal{S}^0 + \sum_{j=1}^{m} c_j \mathcal{M}^j. \tag{2.4}$$

We call c_j the model coefficients. The prior probability for model coefficients $c_1, ..., c_m$ is given by

$$Pr(c_1, ..., c_m) = e^{-\frac{1}{2}\sum_{j=1}^{m} \frac{c_j^2}{\sigma_j^2}}. \tag{2.5}$$

2.3.2 Linear space of deformation vectors

Instead of using scanned meshes, an alternative approach is to manually design the average mesh $\mathcal{S}^0$ and the deformation vectors $\delta \mathcal{S}^j$. Figure 2.1 is the average mesh used in [268]. They designed 65 deformation vectors. Each deformation vector corresponds to an intuitive way of deforming the face.

Figure 2.3 shows some examples of deformation vectors, where (a) shows a neutral face rendered with texture map, (b) is the side view, (c) is the effect of applying the "nose-big" deformation vector, (d) is the effect of applying the "mouth-narrow" deformation vector, (e) is the effect of applying the "jaw-wide" deformation vector, (f) is the effect of applying "face-flat" deformation vector, (g) is the effect of applying "head-narrow" deformation vector, and (h) is the effect of applying "more-female" deformation vector.

Similar to (2.4), any face can be represented as the average face plus a linear combination of the deformation vectors. If we use the same symbols $\mathcal{M}^1, ..., \mathcal{M}^m$ to denote the deformation vectors, we have the same equation to represent a face $\mathcal{S} \in F$, that is,

$$\mathcal{S} = \mathcal{S}^0 + \sum_{j=1}^{m} c_j \mathcal{M}^j. \tag{2.6}$$

For face modeling purpose, the deformation vectors are used in almost the same way as the eigenvectors. The only difference is that for eigenvectors, we have a prior probability for the model coefficients (see (2.5)). For deformation vectors, we instead have a valid range for each model coefficient. More specifically, for each deformation vector $\mathcal{M}^j$, we predesign a lower bound l_j and an upper bound u_j. During model fitting, we add constraints that coefficient c_j satisfies $l_j \leq c_j \leq u_j$.

2.3.3 Semantic coordinate

Note that only the 3D coordinates of a point on the face model depends on the model coefficients C, while its semantic meaning is independent of C. For

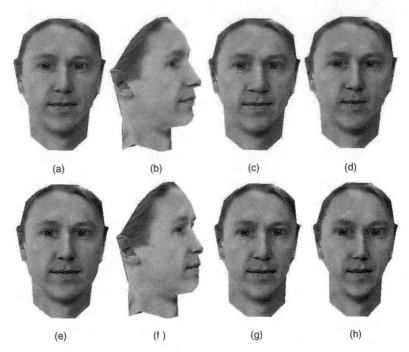

(a)   (b)   (c)   (d)

(e)   (f)   (g)   (h)

Figure 2.3. Examples of face deformation vectors: (a) a neutral face; (b) side
view; (c) making nose bigger; (d) making mouth narrower; (e) making jaw wider;
(f) making face flatter; (g) making head narrower; (h) making face more female
looking.

example, if vertex number 50 happens to be the left mouth corner. Regardless of
the model coefficients C, vertex number 50 will always be the left mouth corner.
Intuitively, the semantic meaning of vertex number 50 is the left mouth corner.
In general, any point on the face model is in one of the mesh triangles. Let P
denote a point on the face model, and let V_{i_1}, V_{i_2}, and V_{i_3} denote the vertices of
the triangle which P belongs to. Then there exist barycentric coordinates $\alpha \geq 0$,
$\beta \geq 0$, $\gamma \geq 0$ with $\alpha + \beta + \gamma = 1$ such that

$$P = \alpha * V_{i_1} + \beta * V_{i_2} + \gamma * V_{i_3}. \tag{2.7}$$

Let e_i, $i = 1, ..., 3N$, denote a $3N$-dimensional vector where $e_i(j) = 0$ for all
$j \neq i$ and $e_i(i) = 1$. For example,

$$
\begin{aligned}
e_1 &= (1, 0, 0, 0, 0, 0, ..., 0, 0, 0)^T, \\
e_2 &= (0, 1, 0, 0, 0, 0, ..., 0, 0, 0)^T, \\
e_3 &= (0, 0, 1, 0, 0, 0, ..., 0, 0, 0)^T.
\end{aligned}
\tag{2.8}
$$

Thus

$$V_1 = \begin{pmatrix} X_1 \\ Y_1 \\ Z_1 \end{pmatrix} = \begin{pmatrix} e_1^T \\ e_2^T \\ e_3^T \end{pmatrix} \mathcal{S}. \qquad (2.9)$$

In general,

$$V_i = \begin{pmatrix} e_{3i-2}^T \\ e_{3i-1}^T \\ e_{3i}^T \end{pmatrix} \mathcal{S}. \qquad (2.10)$$

Denote $\mathbf{E}_i = \begin{pmatrix} e_{3i-2}^T \\ e_{3i-1}^T \\ e_{3i}^T \end{pmatrix}$, which is a $3 \times 3N$ matrix. (2.10) becomes

$$V_i = \mathbf{E}_i \mathcal{S}. \qquad (2.11)$$

From Equation (2.7), we have

$$P = (\alpha * \mathbf{E}_{i_1} + \beta * \mathbf{E}_{i_2} + \gamma * \mathbf{E}_{i_3}) \mathcal{S}. \qquad (2.12)$$

Denote $\mathbf{B} = \alpha * \mathbf{E}_{i_1} + \beta * \mathbf{E}_{i_2} + \gamma * \mathbf{E}_{i_3}$. (2.12) becomes

$$P = \mathbf{B} \mathcal{S}. \qquad (2.13)$$

We call $\mathbf{B}$ the semantic coordinate of P. So a semantic coordinate is a $3 \times 3N$ matrix, and any point on the face model can be represented by its semantic coordinate times the geometry vector of the face model. Note that the semantic coordinate of a point on the face model is independent of the model coefficients C.

2.4 Expression space representation

2.4.1 Bilinear model

In Section 2.3, we used a linear space to represent face geometries of different people. In this section, we describe a bilinear model to represent the space of face geometries of different people with different expressions.

The bilinear model requires some training data to construct the basis. The training data typically consists of a set of face meshes of different people with different expressions. For example, Yin et al. [248] developed such a dataset called BU-3DFE. It consists of 3D laser scans of various people's facial expressions. There are 100 subjects of which 56 are females and 44 are males. For each

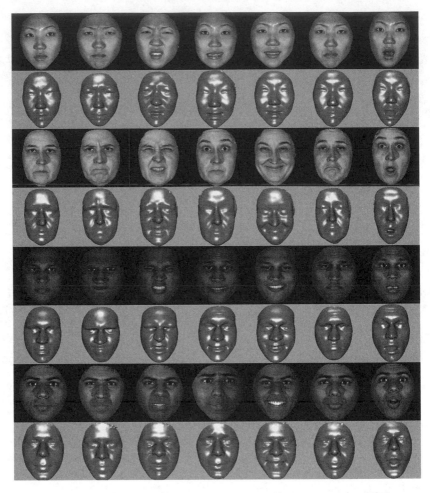

Figure 2.4. Examples of BU-3DFE dataset. There are 7 expressions for each subject: neutral, angry, disgust, fear, happy, sad, and surprise. Courtesy of Yin et al. [248].

subject, there are seven facial expressions: neutral, angry, disgust, fear, happiness, sad, and surprise. Each facial expression except the neutral is divided into four intensity levels. For each subject, each expression type, and each intensity level, they captured a color image as well as a laser-scanned mesh. Figure 2.4 shows some of the samples in the dataset where each row corresponds to a subject and each column corresponds to an expression type. Only a single intensity level is shown.

Let I_1 denote the number of people and I_2 the number of facial expressions. Let $\mathcal{S}_{i_1 i_2}$ denote the geometry vector of person i_1 with expression i_2, where $i_1 = 1, ..., I_1$ and $i_2 = 1, ..., I_2$. Denote $\mathcal{S}^0$ to be the average of the I_1 neutral faces, and

$$\delta \mathcal{S}_{i_1 i_2} = \mathcal{S}_{i_1 i_2} - \mathcal{S}^0. \tag{2.14}$$

Let $\mathcal{S}$ denote the geometry vector of any new face with any expression. $\mathcal{S}$ is represented as $\mathcal{S}^0$ plus a bilinear combination of the examples $\delta \mathcal{S}_{i_1 i_2}$, that is,

$$\mathcal{S} = \mathcal{S}^0 + \sum_{i_1=1}^{I_1} \sum_{i_2=1}^{I_2} \alpha_{i_1} \tau_{i_2} \delta \mathcal{S}_{i_1 i_2}, \tag{2.15}$$

where $\{\alpha_{i_1}\}_{i_1=1}^{I_1}$ are identity coefficients while $\{\tau_{i_2}\}_{i_2=1}^{I_2}$ are expression coefficients.

(2.15) is called a bilinear model. The geometry of an expression face is determined by two sets of coefficients $\{\alpha_{i_1}\}_{i_1=1}^{I_1}$ and $\{\tau_{i_2}\}_{i_2=1}^{I_2}$. If we fix $\{\alpha_{i_1}\}_{i_1=1}^{I_1}$ and vary $\{\tau_{i_2}\}_{i_2=1}^{I_2}$, we generate different facial expressions for the same person. On the other hand, if we fix $\{\tau_{i_2}\}_{i_2=1}^{I_2}$ while varying $\{\alpha_{i_1}\}_{i_1=1}^{I_1}$, we generate different identities all with the same expression.

Similar to linear models, we can also compute the principal components of $\delta \mathcal{S}_{i_1 i_2}$, and use the principal components as the basis. This is useful for removing data redundancy, reducing dimensionality, and making the numerical systems (e.g., in modeling fitting) better conditioned.

In the case of linear model, the principal components can be computed by using the well-known Singular Value Decomposition (SVD). In the case of bilinear model, we need a bilinear singular value decomposition method. Denote

$$\delta \mathcal{S}_{i_1 i_2} = \begin{pmatrix} a_{i_1 i_2 1} \\ a_{i_1 i_2 2} \\ \vdots \\ a_{i_1 i_2 I_3} \end{pmatrix}. \tag{2.16}$$

Then $\mathbf{A} = \{a_{i_1 i_2 i_3}\}_{I_1 \times I_2 \times I_3}$ is a three-way array, called an order-3 tensor.

It has been shown that any order-3 tensor has a generalized singular value decomposition as follows:

$$a_{i_1 i_2 i_3} = \sum_{j_1=1}^{I_1} \sum_{j_2=1}^{I_2} \sum_{j_3=1}^{I_3} b_{j_1 j_2 j_3} u^1_{i_1 j_1} u^2_{i_2 j_2} u^3_{i_3 j_3}, \tag{2.17}$$

where $\{u^1_{i_1 j_1}\}_{I_1 \times I_1}$, $\{u^2_{i_2 j_2}\}_{I_2 \times I_2}$, and $\{u^3_{i_3 j_3}\}_{I_3 \times I_3}$ are orthogonal matrices, and $\{b_{j_1 j_2 j_3}\}_{I_1 \times I_2 \times I_3}$ is an order-3 tensor that satisfies the following "all-orthogonality" property: for all $\alpha \neq \beta$,

$$\sum_{i_1 i_2} b_{i_1 i_2 \alpha} b_{i_1 i_2 \beta} = 0, \tag{2.18}$$

$$\sum_{i_2 i_3} b_{\alpha i_2 i_3} b_{\beta i_2 i_3} = 0, \tag{2.19}$$

$$\sum_{i_1 i_3} b_{i_1 \alpha i_3} b_{i_1 \beta i_3} = 0. \tag{2.20}$$

Denote

$$\begin{aligned}
\mathbf{B} &= \{b_{j_1 j_2 j_3}\}_{I_1 \times I_2 \times I_3}, \\
\mathbf{U}^1 &= \{u^1_{i_1 j_1}\}_{I_1 \times I_1}, \\
\mathbf{U}^2 &= \{u^2_{i_2 j_2}\}_{I_2 \times I_2}, \\
\mathbf{U}^3 &= \{u^3_{i_3 j_3}\}_{I_3 \times I_3}.
\end{aligned} \tag{2.21}$$

(2.17) is sometimes written as a matrix form:

$$\mathbf{A} = \mathbf{B} \times_1 \mathbf{U}^1 \times_2 \mathbf{U}^2 \times_3 \mathbf{U}^3, \tag{2.22}$$

where $\times_1, \times_2, \times_3$ are the so-called mode-1, mode-2, mode-3 products, respectively.

Let $\mathcal{U}^3_j$ denote the jth column vector of the matrix $\mathbf{U}^3$, that is,

$$\mathcal{U}^3_j = \begin{pmatrix} u^3_{1j} \\ u^3_{2j} \\ \vdots \\ u^3_{I_3 j} \end{pmatrix}, \tag{2.23}$$

and denote

$$\mathcal{B}_{j_1 j_2} = \sum_{j_3=1}^{I_3} b_{j_1 j_2 j_3} \mathcal{U}^3_{j_3}. \tag{2.24}$$

(2.16) and (2.17) yield

$$\delta \mathcal{S}_{i_1 i_2} = \sum_{j_1=1}^{I_1} \sum_{j_2=1}^{I_2} u_{i_1 j_1}^1 u_{i_2 j_2}^2 \begin{pmatrix} \sum_{j_3=1}^{I_3} b_{j_1 j_2 j_3} u_{1 j_3}^3 \\ \vdots \\ \sum_{j_3=1}^{I_3} b_{j_1 j_2 j_3} u_{I_3 j_3}^3 \end{pmatrix}$$

$$= \sum_{j_1=1}^{I_1} \sum_{j_2=1}^{I_2} u_{i_1 j_1}^1 u_{i_2 j_2}^2 \sum_{j_3=1}^{I_3} b_{j_1 j_2 j_3} \begin{pmatrix} u_{1 j_3}^3 \\ \vdots \\ u_{I_3 j_3}^3 \end{pmatrix}. \tag{2.25}$$

From (2.23) and (2.24), we have

$$\delta \mathcal{S}_{i_1 i_2} = \sum_{j_1=1}^{I_1} \sum_{j_2=1}^{I_2} u_{i_1 j_1}^1 u_{i_2 j_2}^2 \mathcal{B}_{j_1 j_2}. \tag{2.26}$$

(2.15) and (2.26) yield

$$\begin{aligned} \mathcal{S} &= \mathcal{S}^0 + \sum_{i_1=1}^{I_1} \sum_{i_2=1}^{I_2} \alpha_{i_1} \tau_{i_2} \delta \mathcal{S}_{i_1 i_2} \\ &= \mathcal{S}^0 + \sum_{i_1=1}^{I_1} \sum_{i_2=1}^{I_2} \alpha_{i_1} \tau_{i_2} \sum_{j_1=1}^{I_1} \sum_{j_2=1}^{I_2} u_{i_1 j_1}^1 u_{i_2 j_2}^2 \mathcal{B}_{j_1 j_2} \\ &= \mathcal{S}^0 + \sum_{j_1=1}^{I_1} \sum_{j_2=1}^{I_2} (\sum_{i_1} \alpha_{i_1} u_{i_1 j_1}^1)(\sum_{i_2} \tau_{i_2} u_{i_2 j_2}^2) \mathcal{B}_{j_1 j_2} \end{aligned} \tag{2.27}$$

Denote

$$\begin{aligned} \tilde{\alpha}_{j_1} &= \sum_{i_1} \alpha_{i_1} u_{i_1 j_1}^1, \\ \tilde{\tau}_{j_2} &= \sum_{i_2} \tau_{i_2} u_{i_2 j_2}^2. \end{aligned} \tag{2.28}$$

(2.27) can be rewritten as

$$\mathcal{S} = \mathcal{S}^0 + \sum_{j_1=1}^{I_1} \sum_{j_2=1}^{I_2} \tilde{\alpha}_{j_1} \tilde{\tau}_{j_2} \mathcal{B}_{j_1 j_2}. \tag{2.29}$$

Comparing (2.29) with (2.15), we can see that (2.29) is also a bilinear representation except that it uses a different basis: $\mathcal{B}_{j_1 j_2}$, which plays the same role as the principal components in the one-dimensional principal component analysis framework. $\{\tilde{\alpha}_{j_1}\}_{j_1=1}^{\tilde{I}_1}$ and $\{\tilde{\tau}_{j_2}\}_{j_2=1}^{\tilde{I}_2}$ are called model coefficients. An analysis problem typically involves solving for the model coefficients.

One could choose to use a smaller number of components in (2.29) for dimensionality reduction. Suppose we use $\tilde{I}_1$ components in mode-1 (identity) and use $\tilde{I}_2$ in mode-2 (expression), (2.29) becomes

$$S = S^0 + \sum_{j_1=1}^{\tilde{I}_1} \sum_{j_2=1}^{\tilde{I}_2} \tilde{\alpha}_{j_1} \tilde{\tau}_{j_2} B_{j_1 j_2}. \tag{2.30}$$

2.4.2 Linear model

In this section, we show that the bilinear model of (2.15) can be simplified to a linear model if we assume that the geometric deformation resulted from a facial expression is person independent. Under this assumption, we can represent $\delta S_{i_1 i_2}$ as a sum of two terms: identity term δS_{i_1} and expression term δS_{i_2}, that is,

$$\delta S_{i_1 i_2} = \delta S_{i_1} + \delta S_{i_2}. \tag{2.31}$$

Substituting (2.31) into (2.15), we obtain

$$
\begin{aligned}
S &= S^0 + \sum_{i_1=1}^{I_1} \sum_{i_2=1}^{I_2} \alpha_{i_1} \tau_{i_2} \delta S_{i_1 i_2} \\
&= S^0 + \sum_{i_1=1}^{I_1} \sum_{i_2=1}^{I_2} \alpha_{i_1} \tau_{i_2} (\delta S_{i_1} + \delta S_{i_2}) \\
&= S^0 + \sum_{i_1=1}^{I_1} \alpha_{i_1} (\sum_{i_2=1}^{I_2} \tau_{i_2}) \delta S_{i_1} + \sum_{i_2=1}^{I_2} \tau_{i_2} (\sum_{i_1}^{I_1} \alpha_{i_1}) \delta S_{i_2}
\end{aligned} \tag{2.32}
$$

Denote

$$
\begin{aligned}
\hat{\alpha}_{i_1} &= \alpha_{i_1} \sum_{i_2=1}^{I_2} \tau_{i_2}, \\
\hat{\tau}_{i_2} &= \tau_{i_2} \sum_{i_1=1}^{I_1} \alpha_{i_1}.
\end{aligned} \tag{2.33}
$$

(2.32) can be written as

$$S = S^0 + \sum_{i_1=1}^{I_1} \hat{\alpha}_{i_1} \delta S_{i_1} + \sum_{i_2=1}^{I_2} \hat{\tau}_{i_2} \delta S_{i_2}. \tag{2.34}$$

This is a linear representation where $\{\hat{\alpha}_{i_1}\}_{i_1=1}^{I_1}$ and $\{\hat{\tau}_{i_2}\}_{i_2=1}^{I_2}$ are the model coefficients.

There are two advantages of using a linear model. First, it results in linear equations, which are easier to solve. Second, it requires much less training data to construct the basis. Its disadvantage is that it does not handle person-dependent expression deformations.

3

Appearance models

The appearance of an object depends not only on its geometry but also the lighting environment and its reflectance property. Such relationships are characterized by illumination models. In computer graphics, people have developed various illumination models for image synthesis. Some of the illumination models are very useful for face geometry and appearance modeling. In this chapter, we will first give a brief overview on the illumination models. We then describe subspace representations of diffuse lighting and face albedos, which are useful tools for the recovery of face geometry, albedo, and lighting.

3.1 Illumination models

3.1.1 Bidirectional reflectance distribution function

For any point on an surface, its reflectance property can be categorized by a four-dimensional function $\rho(L, V)$, where L is the incoming light direction and V is the reflected light direction (see Figure 3.1). $\rho(L, V)$ is called a Bidirectional Reflectance Distribution Function (BRDF). We usually represent L with its spherical angles θ_i and ϕ_i, and V with θ_r and ϕ_r. Thus, ρ can be written as a function of the four angles as $\rho(\theta_i, \phi_i, \theta_r, \phi_r)$. Strictly speaking, we have a different BRDF for each wavelength. In practice, we usually use a BRDF for each (R, G, B) color channel.

The amount of light incident on a surface is called *irradiance*, which is the power of the radiant energy that falls on a unit surface area. It is measured in Watts per square meter, that is, W/m^2. The amount of the light emitted from a surface is called *radiance*, which is the power per unit foreshortened area radiated into a unit solid angle. It is measured in Watts per square meter per steradian, that is, W/(Sr · m^2). Let $I_r(V)$ denote the reflected radiance along direction V. Let $E_i(L)$ denote the incident irradiance along direction L. Then

31

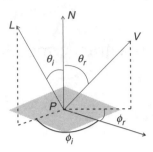

Figure 3.1. Bidirectional Reflectance Distribution Function.

$$\rho(\mathrm{L},\mathrm{V}) = \frac{I_r(\mathrm{V})}{E_i(\mathrm{L})}. \tag{3.1}$$

The BRDF ρ has unit 1/Sr.

The drawback of directly using BRDF to model surface reflectance is that there are too many parameters. One popular way to simplify the model is to consider the bidirectional reflectance as composed of diffuse and specular components, which we describe in the following sections.

3.1.2 Diffuse reflection

Some surfaces reflect light equally in all directions. As a result, these surfaces appear equally bright from all viewing angles. This type of reflectivity is called diffuse reflection, also known as Lambertian reflection. Figure 3.2 shows a point P on a surface where N is the normal at P. Assume there is a single point light source. Let L denote the normalized direction from P to the light source, and I_L denote the intensity of the light source. The reflected intensity at P is

$$I = I_L\, \rho\, (\mathrm{N}\cdot\mathrm{L})$$
$$= I_L\, \rho\cos\theta, \tag{3.2}$$

where ρ is the material's *diffuse reflection coefficient* at P. We sometimes call ρ the *albedo*. In this equation, we implicitly assume that θ is no larger than 90°. If θ is larger than 90°, we assume the light source has no effect on the point P. This situation is called self-occluding. We sometimes say P is in the *attached shadow*. To handle attached shadow explicitly, we can use the following equation:

$$I = I_L\, \rho\, \max(0,\cos\theta). \tag{3.3}$$

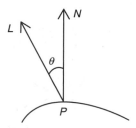

Figure 3.2. Diffuse reflection. P is a point on the surface. N is the surface normal at P. L is the direction from P to the light source.

If we use (r, g, b) color space, (3.3) holds per color channel. Let $\lambda \in \{r, g, b\}$ denote a color channel, we have

$$I_\lambda = I_{L,\lambda}\, \rho_\lambda\, \max(0,\, \cos\theta). \tag{3.4}$$

If the point light source is sufficiently far from the object, the light direction is almost the same for all the points P on the object. Thus, L is independent of P. In this case, we call the light source a *directional light source*.

3.1.3 Specular reflection

Specular reflection is used to model a shiny surface. When we look at a shiny surface, the highlights are caused by specular reflection. Specular reflections are view dependent, and the reflected color is in general the color of the incident light instead of the color of the surface material. Phong [166] developed a popular illumination model for specular reflection. As shown in Figure 3.3, we use R to denote the direction of reflection that mirrors L about N. Denote V as the viewing direction, and α the angle between V and R. Phong illumination model assumes that the specular reflectance is the strongest along the reflection direction R and falls off as α increases. More specifically, according to Phong's model, the observed intensity at P from view direction V is defined as

$$\begin{aligned} I_\lambda &= I_{L,\lambda}\left(k_d\rho_\lambda(N\cdot L) + k_s O_\lambda(V\cdot R)^n\right)\\ &= I_{L,\lambda}\left(k_d\rho_\lambda\cos\theta + k_s O_\lambda\cos^n\alpha\right). \end{aligned} \tag{3.5}$$

In this equation, n is the material's *specular reflection exponent*, k_d and k_s are the diffuse and specular coefficients, which are nonnegative and satisfy $k_d + k_s = 1$, and O_λ is the object's specular color. The first term $I_{L,\lambda}(k_d\rho_\lambda\cos\theta)$ is the diffuse reflection component, and the second term $I_{L,\lambda}k_s O_\lambda\cos^n\alpha$ is the specular reflection component.

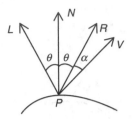

Figure 3.3. Specular reflection. P is a point on the surface. N is the surface normal at P. L is the direction from P to the light source. V is the direction from P to the view point. R is the reflection direction.

3.1.3.1 Torrance–Sparrow model

The Torrance–Sparrow model [213] improves the specular reflection component in Phone's model. It is a physically based model for surface reflection where a surface is assumed to be composed of a collection of mirror like microfacets, each a perfectly smooth reflector. According to Torrance–Sparrow's model, the observed intensity at a point P from view direction V is defined as

$$
\begin{aligned}
I_\lambda &= I_{L,\lambda}\left(k_d\rho_\lambda(N \cdot L) + k_s\frac{F_\lambda DG}{\pi(N \cdot V)}\right) \\
&= I_{L,\lambda}\left(k_d\rho_\lambda \, \cos(\theta_i) + k_s\frac{F_\lambda DG}{\pi\cos(\theta_r)}\right),
\end{aligned}
\tag{3.6}
$$

where D is a microfacet distribution function, G is a geometrical attenuation factor, and F_λ is the Fresnel term. The microfacet distribution function D can be modeled by using a Gaussian distribution function as the following:

$$
D = e^{-\frac{\beta^2}{\sigma^2}},
\tag{3.7}
$$

where β is the angle between N and the *halfway vector* H which is the bisecting direction between V and L (see Figure 3.4), and σ is the standard deviation, which determines the specular reflectivity of the surface. The geometrical attenuation factor G takes into account the shadowing between the microfacets. If we assume the microfacets form a V-shaped groove that is symmetric about the (average) surface normal N, the attenuate factor can be derived as [21]

$$
G = \min\left\{1, \frac{2(N \cdot H)(N \cdot V)}{V \cdot H}, \frac{2(N \cdot H)(N \cdot L)}{V \cdot H}\right\}.
\tag{3.8}
$$

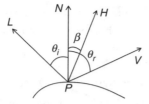

Figure 3.4. Torrance–Sparrow model.

The Fresnel term gives the proportion of the incident light that is reflected as opposed to being absorbed. It is a function of the incidence angle on the microfacet and the material's index of infraction. The reader is referred to [59] for the details.

3.1.4 Multiple light sources

When there are multiple light sources, we simply add the contributions from all the light sources. Suppose there are m light sources. If we use the Phone's illumination model for each light source, the total intensity at P for color channel λ is equal to

$$I_\lambda = \sum_{i=1}^{m} I_{L_i\lambda}(k_d\rho_\lambda\,(\mathrm{N}\cdot\mathrm{L}_i) + k_s\,O_\lambda(\mathrm{V}\cdot\mathrm{R}_i)^n). \qquad (3.9)$$

This formula can be used to approximate an area light source by dividing the area light source into multiple subregions and treating each subregion as a point light source.

3.1.5 Global illumination

In addition to light sources, a lighting environment may also contain surfaces that reflect and/or refract lights. An object in such an environment will be illuminated not only by light sources directly but also by the reflected lights indirectly (secondary reflections). In fact, in real-world environments the indirectly reflected lights play an important role on an object's appearance. An illumination method that takes into account the reflected lights is called *global illumination*. In contrast, a method that only considers lighting directly coming from light sources is called *local illumination*.

There are two classes of global illumination algorithms: recursive ray tracing and radiosity. The descriptions of these algorithms are beyond the scope of this book. The interested readers are refereed to [60]. Global illumination methods generate more realistic images, but they are computationally expensive.

3.2 Irradiance environment map

One effective approach for generating realistic images under an arbitrarily complex lighting environment (either real or simulated) is the *environment maps*. The assumption is that the object is small compared to its distance from the lighting environment. Under this assumption, the illumination at any given point on the object is independent of its position. The environment observed from the object center is stored as a panoramic image where the color at each pixel represents the incoming lighting along a certain direction. The panoramic image is called an environment map or *illumination map* [147].

Blinn and Newell [22] first used environment maps to generate realistic reflections of distant objects. Miller and Hoffmann [147] and Greene [78] introduced *reflection maps*, also called *prefiltered environment maps* to precompute the diffuse and specular reflection components into two separate maps. The diffuse reflection components are indexed by surface normals while the specular reflection components are indexed by reflection directions (i.e., R in Figure 3.3).

The reflection map for the diffuse components is also called an *irradiance environment map* since what is stored at each pixel is the (total) incident irradiance for a particular surface normal direction. Let L_i, $i = 1, ..., m$, denote the discretized 3D unit vectors. Let I_{L_i} denote the intensity of the light ray along direction L_i (I_{L_i} is basically the environment map). The incident irradiance $E(N)$ for surface normal N is

$$E(N) = \sum_{i=1}^{m} I_{L_i} \max(0, N \cdot L_i). \tag{3.10}$$

Note that this equation holds per color channel. We omit the color channel index to simplify the expression.

For any given point P on the object, let $\rho(P)$ denote its albedo and $N(P)$ denote its normal. The reflected radiance at P is

$$I = \rho E(N). \tag{3.11}$$

3.3 Spherical harmonics

Ramamoorthi and Hanrahan [178] and Basri and Jacobs [9] discovered that the irradiance $E(N)$ can be well approximated by using a small number of spherical

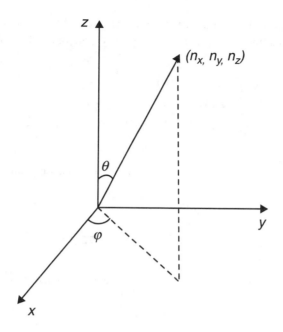

Figure 3.5. Spherical coordinates.

harmonic bases. They showed that with nine spherical harmonic bases, the average approximation error is no more than 1%.

Denote $N = \begin{pmatrix} n_x \\ n_y \\ n_z \end{pmatrix}$. Since N is on a unit sphere, we can parameterize it using spherical coordinates as follows (Figure 3.5):

$$n_x = \sin\theta \, \cos\phi,$$
$$n_y = \sin\theta \, \sin\phi, \qquad (3.12)$$
$$n_z = \cos\theta,$$

where $0 \le \theta \le \pi$ and $0 \le \phi \le 2\pi$. Therefore, $E(N)$ is a function of θ and ϕ, and we denote $E(\theta,\phi) = E \begin{pmatrix} n_x \\ n_y \\ n_z \end{pmatrix}$.

It has been shown in the spherical harmonics theory that any real function defined over a unit sphere can be represented as a linear combination of (possibly infinitely many) spherical harmonic basis functions. For an introduction to the theory of spherical harmonics, the reader is referred to [139]. The spherical harmonic basis functions $Y_{l,m}$, $l \geq 0, -l \leq m \leq l$, are defined as follows:

$$
Y_{l,m} = \begin{cases}
N_{l,0} P_l^0(\cos \theta), & \\
\sqrt{2} N_{l,m} P_l^m(\cos \theta) \cos(m\phi) & if \ \ m > 0, \\
\sqrt{2} N_{l,m} P_l^{-m}(\cos \theta) \sin(m\phi) & if \ \ m < 0,
\end{cases}
\tag{3.13}
$$

where $N_{l,m} = \sqrt{\frac{(2l+1)}{4\pi} \frac{(l-m)!}{(l+m)!}}$ and $P_l^m(x)$ are associated Legendre polynomials defined as

$$
P_l^m(x) = \frac{(-1)^m}{2^l l!} (1 - x^2)^{m/2} \frac{d^{l+m}}{dx^{l+m}} (x^2 - 1)^l.
\tag{3.14}
$$

The explicit expressions of the first nine basis functions are

$$
\begin{aligned}
Y_{0,0}(\theta,\phi) &= \sqrt{\tfrac{1}{4\pi}} \\
Y_{1,-1}(\theta,\phi) &= \sqrt{\tfrac{3}{4\pi}} n_y & &= \sqrt{\tfrac{3}{4\pi}} \sin \theta \sin \phi \\
Y_{1,0}(\theta,\phi) &= \sqrt{\tfrac{3}{4\pi}} n_z & &= \sqrt{\tfrac{3}{4\pi}} \cos \theta \\
Y_{1,1}(\theta,\phi) &= \sqrt{\tfrac{3}{4\pi}} n_x & &= \sqrt{\tfrac{3}{4\pi}} \sin \theta \cos \phi \\
Y_{2,-2}(\theta,\phi) &= \sqrt{\tfrac{15}{4\pi}} n_x n_y & &= \sqrt{\tfrac{15}{4\pi}} \sin^2 \theta \sin \phi \cos \phi \\
Y_{2,-1}(\theta,\phi) &= \sqrt{\tfrac{15}{4\pi}} n_y n_z & &= \sqrt{\tfrac{15}{4\pi}} \sin \theta \cos \theta \sin \phi \\
Y_{2,0}(\theta,\phi) &= \sqrt{\tfrac{5}{16\pi}} (3 n_z^2 - 1) &= \sqrt{\tfrac{5}{16\pi}} (3 \cos^2 \theta - 1) \\
Y_{2,1}(\theta,\phi) &= \sqrt{\tfrac{15}{4\pi}} n_x n_z & &= \sqrt{\tfrac{15}{4\pi}} \sin \theta \cos \theta \cos \phi \\
Y_{2,2}(\theta,\phi) &= \sqrt{\tfrac{15}{16\pi}} (n_x^2 - n_y^2) &= \sqrt{\tfrac{15}{16\pi}} (\sin^2 \theta \cos^2 \phi - \sin^2 \theta \sin^2 \phi)
\end{aligned}
\tag{3.15}
$$

According to [9, 178], $E(N)$ can be effectively represented as a linear combination of the first nine basis functions:

$$
E(N) = \sum_{l=0}^{2} \sum_{m=-l}^{l} L_{l,m} Y_{l,m}(N),
\tag{3.16}
$$

where $L_{l,m}$ are called the *illumination coefficients*. For notational convenience, we sometimes use $h_1, h_2, ..., h_9$ to denote the first nine basis functions, and write Equation (3.16) as

$$E(\mathrm{N}) = \sum_{i=1}^{9} l_i h_i(\mathrm{N}), \qquad (3.17)$$

where l_i are the illumination coefficients. Thus,

$$I = \rho \sum_{i=1}^{9} l_i h_i(\mathrm{N}). \qquad (3.18)$$

In this way, the estimation of an arbitrarily complex lighting environment is reduced to the estimation of the nine illumination coefficients. This property is extremely useful for face appearance modeling as described later in this book.

3.4 Morphable model of face albedo

This section describes the linear space representation of face albedo. In the literature of face geometry and appearance modeling, people often use the term face texture in place of face albedo.

Let $V_i = (X_i, Y_i, Z_i)^T$, $i = 1, ..., n$, denote the vertices of a face mesh; let (R_i, G_i, B_i) denote the R, G, B color values of the face albedo at vertex V_i. Let T denote the albedo (a.k.a. texture) vector

$$T = (R_1, G_1, B_1, ..., R_n, G_n, B_n)^T. \qquad (3.19)$$

Similar to the linear space representation of face geometry in Section 2.3.1, one can use a set of precaptured face albedos as the basis to span the space of face albedos. Suppose there are $m + 1$ exemplar face albedos. Let ρ^j denote the albedo vector of the jth face, $j = 1, ..., m + 1$. These examples generate a linear space of face albedos:

$$F_A = \left\{ \sum_{j=1}^{m+1} \alpha_j \rho^j : \sum_{j=1}^{m+1} \alpha_j = 1 \right\}. \qquad (3.20)$$

Let ρ^0 denote the average face albedo, that is, $\rho^0 = \frac{1}{m+1} \sum_{j=1}^{m+1} \rho^j$. Denote $\delta \rho^j = \rho^j - \rho^0$, $j = 1, ..., m + 1$. We perform Principal Component Analysis on the vectors $\delta \rho^1, ..., \delta \rho^{m+1}$. Let $\zeta_1^2, ..., \zeta_m^2$ denote the eigenvalues with $\zeta_1^2 \geq \zeta_2^2 \geq \cdots \geq \zeta_m^2$. Let $T^1, ..., T^m$ denote the corresponding eigenvectors.

Then any face albedo $\rho \in F_A$ can be represented as the average face albedo ρ^0 plus a linear combination of the eigenvectors, that is,

$$\rho = \rho^0 + \sum_{j=1}^{m} \beta_j \mathcal{T}^j. \tag{3.21}$$

We call β_j the albedo (also called texture) coefficients.

The prior probability for albedo coefficients $\beta_1, ..., \beta_m$ is given by

$$\Pr(\beta_1, ..., \beta_m) = e^{-\frac{1}{2} \sum_{j=1}^{m} \frac{\beta_j^2}{\zeta_j^2}}. \tag{3.22}$$

PART II

Face modeling

4

Shape modeling with active sensors

Active sensors are the most reliable equipment to obtain accurate geometries of any objects including faces. An active sensor system typically consists of a light emitter (e.g., laser or projector) and a light receiver (camera). The reason that it is called an active sensor is because it actively emits lights. There are different types of active sensors including laser scanners, structured light systems, and structured light stereo systems. So far, the laser scanners are the most commonly used and most accurate active sensors. Recently, structured light systems have started to gain interest because they are capable of capturing continuous motions. Active sensors are popular tools for researchers to obtain ground truth data or to capture example faces or facial expressions as training data.

4.1 Laser scanners

So far, laser scanners are the most accurate and reliable equipment to obtain face geometry. It works by projecting a laser onto the face (or any object to be scanned), and a camera is used to detect the laser light on the face. The distance can then be determined based on the pixel location of the detected laser light. Laser scanners usually do not work well on shiny surfaces, and they do not work well on dark materials such as hair.

The main drawback of laser scanning is that laser scanners are expensive and most people do not have access to them. The point cloud data obtained from laser scanning usually have holes and spikes. Some postprocessing is needed to remove the spikes and fill in the holes. To use the data for animation purposes, one needs to register the data, that is, to create a correspondence between the points and a predesigned face model. Lee et al. [121, 122] developed a system to clean up and register data generated from laser scanners. The obtained model is then animated by using a physically based approach.

4.1.1 Mesh registration through model fitting

One effective method for mesh registration is to fit a parametric face model to the point cloud. In the following, we will describe a mesh-fitting method based on the linear space representation. The same technique can be used for other parametric face representations such as B-spline surfaces.

As in (2.4), a face model S is represented as a linear function of the coefficients $C = (c_1, \ldots, c_n)^T$. Let $P_1, \ldots, P_n$ denote the 3D points obtained from the laser scanner. To fit a face model to the 3D points, we need to compute a global transformation in addition to the model coefficients C. The global transformation consists of a scaling factor s, a rotation matrix $\mathbf{R}$, and a $3D$ translation vector $\mathbf{t}$. Denote

$$\hat{S}(C, s, \mathbf{R}, \mathbf{t}) = s\mathbf{R}S + \mathbf{t}, \tag{4.1}$$

that is, $\hat{S}(C, s, \mathbf{R}, \mathbf{t})$ is the face model S after applying the global transformation.

Let $d(P_i, \hat{S})$ denote the distance from P_i to $\hat{S}$, which is defined as the smallest distance from P_i to any point on the face mesh $\hat{S}$. The model-fitting problem is formulated as

$$\min_{s, \mathbf{R}, \mathbf{t}, C} \left(\sum_{i=1}^{n} d^2(P_i, \hat{S}) \right). \tag{4.2}$$

Let G_i denote the point on the face that has the shortest distance from P_i, that is, $||P_i - G_i||^2 = d^2(P_i, \hat{S})$. Let $\mathbf{B}_i$ denote the semantic coordinate (Section 2.3.3) of G_i. Basically $\mathbf{B}_i$ is the registration of P_i on the face model. (4.2) can be rewritten as

$$\min_{s, \mathbf{R}, \mathbf{t}, C, \mathbf{B}_1, \ldots, \mathbf{B}_n} \left(\sum_{i=1}^{n} ||P_i - \mathbf{B}_i \hat{S}||^2 \right). \tag{4.3}$$

This nonlinear optimization problem can be solved in an iterative manner as shown in Algorithm 1. The algorithm is an extension of the conventional iterative closest point (ICP) technique [15, 261], which is described in Section 10.1.5. The conventional iterative closest point method registers a point cloud with a parametric surface by computing a global scaling, rotation, and translation, but it does not allow the parametric surface to deform. In comparison, Algorithm 1 allows the parametric surface to deform. We call the algorithm *deformable iterative closest point*, or *deformable ICP*.

At each iteration loop, the first step is the projection. We fix $s, \mathbf{R}, \mathbf{t}$, and C, and for each point P_i finds its closest point G_i on the face model. Then we set $\mathbf{B}_i$ to be the semantic coordinate of G_i. The second step updates the global transformation while fixing C and $\mathbf{B}_i$, $i = 1, \ldots, n$. This becomes the problem of finding the scaling, rotation, and translation for a given set of 3D point correspondences. This problem can be solved by using the well-known quaternion-based technique described in [91]. The third step performs projection again to update $\mathbf{B}_i$. At the fourth step, we fix $s, \mathbf{R}, \mathbf{t}$, and $\mathbf{B}_i$, and solve for C to minimize (4.3). Since $\hat{S}$ is a linear function of C, the objective function in (4.3) is a quadratic function of C and can be solved by using a least square method.

Algorithm 1 Deformable ICP for face model fitting

Initialization: Set $C = \mathbf{0}$. Set the global transformation to be
a user-specified initial transformation.
Iterative minimization:

(1) **Projection:** Fix $s, \mathbf{R}, \mathbf{t}, C$, and compute $\mathbf{B}_i$ by finding the closest point G_i on the face model for each point P_i, $i = 1, \ldots, n$. Set $\mathbf{B}_i$ to be the semantic coordinate of G_i.
(2) **Updating the global transformation:** Fix C and $\mathbf{B}_i$, and solve for $s, \mathbf{R}$ and $\mathbf{t}$.
(3) **Projection:** Same as step (1).
(4) **Updating C:** Fix $s, \mathbf{R}, \mathbf{t}$, and $\mathbf{B}_i$. Solve for C.

The performance of the deformable ICP algorithm depends on a reasonable initialization of the global transformation. If the initial transformation is too far off, the iterative minimization will likely be stuck in a local minimum and results in a bad registration.

To obtain a good initialization, one can detect a number of face feature points (e.g., nose tip, eye corners, mouth corners) on the point cloud. Since a laser scanner usually outputs a color image together with the 3D point cloud, one could use both the color image and the 3D point cloud for automatic feature point detection.

In addition to initializing the global transformation, the detected face feature points can also be used during the iterative optimization process. Denote the Q_j, $j = 1, \ldots, Q$, to be the detected face feature points. Let $\mathbf{D}_j$ denote the semantic coordinate of the point on the face model that corresponds to face feature point Q_j. We can then modify Equation (4.3) as

$$\min_{s, \mathbf{R}, \mathbf{t}, C, \mathbf{B}_1, \ldots, \mathbf{B}_n} \left(\sum_{i=1}^{n} ||P_i - \mathbf{B}_i \hat{S}||^2 + w \sum_{j=1}^{Q} ||Q_j - \mathbf{D}_j \hat{S}||^2 \right), \qquad (4.4)$$

where w is a weighting parameter indicating how much we trust the detected face feature points. An algorithm similar to Algorithm 1 can be used to solve this minimization problem. The only difference is that at the steps of updating the global transformation and the model coefficients C, we have more constraints from the detected face feature points Q_j.

4.2 Structured light systems

Figure 4.1 is a diagram of a structured light system. It consists of a camera and a light source. C is the projection center of the camera (assuming a pinhole camera model). C' is the position of the light source. Π is the image plane of the camera. Π' is the pattern that is projected onto the object. e and e' are epipoles. X is a point on the object. x is the projection of X on the image plane Π. Given any pixel **x** on the image plane Π, its correspondence on the pattern plane Π' must lie on a line shown as l' in Figure 4.1. l' is called the epipolar line for image point **x**. To determine the depth of X, we need to determine the position of the correspondence $\mathbf{x}'$. This is done with the help of a sequence of projected patterns (see Figure 4.2). As we can see, the epipolar line l' is divided into multiple segments by the vertical stripes of a pattern. For each projected pattern, we record one bit information at **x** indicating whether it is white or black. If there are n patterns, we will obtain a sequence of binary bits of length n: $b_1,...,b_n$ where b_i is either 0 or 1. Based on $b_1,...,b_n$, we can determine which column $\mathbf{x}'$ is in. The intersection of the column and the epipopar line l' is the position of $\mathbf{x}'$.

One type of pattern scheme is called natural binary code. The top row of Figure 4.2 shows four patterns of the natural binary code scheme. Each 4-bit sequence uniquely identifies one of the 16 columns. The bottom row of Figure 4.2 is the so-called Gray code scheme, which was invented by Gray [77]. Compared to the binary code pattern, the Gray code pattern has the advantage

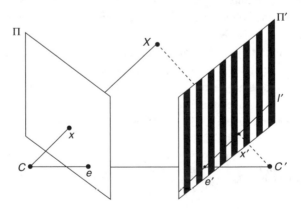

Figure 4.1. Structured light system. C: projection center of the pinhole camera. C': structured light source.

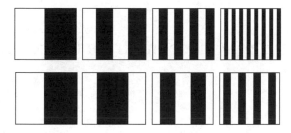

Figure 4.2. Structured light patterns. Top row: natural binary code patterns. Bottom row: gray code patterns.

that for the same code length (which determines the spatial resolution), the required pattern resolution is lower.

Both the binary code scheme and the Gray code scheme require projecting a sequence of patterns to the object. The object has to stay static during this procedure. Therefore they are not suited for capturing deforming surfaces such as facial expressions. To address this problem, people have proposed to use a single pattern [23]. The readers are referred to [48, 187] for details on various code schemes.

One problem with using visible light sources is that they are intrusive. To address this problem, people have proposed to use invisible light sources such as infrared lights. The readers are referred to [xxx] for a survey on invisible structured light systems.

xxx: David Fofi, Tadeusz Sliwa, Yvon Voisin, A comparative survey on invisible structured light, SPIE Electronic Imaging - Machine Vision Applications in Industrial Inspection XII, San Jose, USA, pp. 90–97, January, 2004.

4.3 Structured light stereo systems

Like structured light systems, structured light stereo systems also use active light sources to shine patterns on the object. But structured light stereo systems require at least two cameras, and the 3D reconstruction is obtained from the pixel correspondences between the two images captured by the cameras. A conventional stereovision technique such as the technique presented in Section 5.2 can be used for the 3D reconstruction. The projected patterns by the active light sources are used to improve the accuracy of the disparity map. Zhang et al. [257] developed such a system. It consists of six video cameras and two projectors. The projectors are used as active light sources. One projector and three video cameras are dedicated to each side of the face. Two of the three video cameras are used for stereo reconstruction while the third video camera is used to capture the color image, which is useful for facial animation. Their system is capable of capturing dense depth maps of continuous facial expressions.

5

Shape modeling from images

Image-based face modeling techniques can be divided into two categories depending on whether they model the illumination effects or not. The techniques in the first category do not model illumination, and they have origins from structure from motion or stereovision. The techniques that belong to the second category model the illumination effects, and their origins can be traced to shape from shading. In this chapter, we describe techniques that belong to the first category. The techniques the belong to the second category will be introduced in Chapter 7.

The techniques that belong to the first category in general require two or more views. If the corresponding camera motions are not known, that is, the cameras are not calibrated, it becomes a structure from motion problem. If the camera motions are known, it becomes a stereovision problem. We will describe structure from motion approaches in Section 5.1, and stereovision approaches in Section 5.2. After that, we will discuss two special situations: face modeling from two orthogonal views and face modeling from a single view.

5.1 Structure from motion approach

Given two or more views of a face and assuming that the camera motions (or head poses) corresponding to the views are not known, we would like to estimate the face geometry. The general idea is to find corner matchings across different views and then estimate the camera motion and face geometry. But because faces are in general smooth, the results of corner matchings are usually very noisy. Thus, people have proposed various techniques to improve the robustness by leveraging prior knowledge on human face structure. These techniques differ mainly in two aspects: (1) the representation of the face model and (2) the motion estimation and model-fitting method.

Some work such as [183] directly used a 3D mesh to represent the face model. Due to a large number of degrees of freedom in this representation, the model-fitting process may be quite brittle. One way to reduce the number of degrees of freedom is to introduce control points [66, 67], which is similar to the B-spline surface representation (Section 2.2). Another method, which significantly reduces the number of degrees of freedom, is to use a linear space representation [135] as introduced in Section 2.3.

Both [183] and [66] used a generic face mesh to regulate the bundle adjustment process for structure and motion estimation. The vertex coordinates of the reconstructed 3D points are constrained in such a way that the vertices are not too far from the generic mesh. In [66], the model fitting is in a separate phase from the motion estimation. The 3D structure recovered in the bundle adjustment phase are thrown away. The recovered motions are used in the second phase to compute stereo data for model fitting.

In [193], no regulation terms were needed because the linear space representation itself provided enough constraints on the parameter space, and the model-fitting process directly solves for the coefficients of the linear space representation. Dimitrijevic et al. [47] developed a system to reconstruct 3D face models from uncalibrated image sequences. Their bundle adjustment technique is similar to [193] in that they also used a linear space representation to parameterize the face geometry. But they used the laser scanned data (USF dataset) to construct their basis. Amberg et al. [3] developed a model-based stereo system to recover the 3D face geometry as well as the head poses from two or more images taken simultaneously. Similar to [193] and [47], they also used linear space geometry representation. But they did not use feature point correspondences. Instead, they used the image intensity difference as the objective function. Note that using image intensity difference would not work well if the head is turning (i.e., using a single camera) due to the illumination changes caused by the head rotation.

In the rest of the section, we will describe in detail the face modeling system reported in [135, 193, 268].

5.1.1 System overview

Figure 5.1 is an overview of the face-modeling system in [268]. The interface is designed in such a way that an average user with a video camera connected to a computer can use it to easily construct his/her 3D face models. It is assumed that the camera's intrinsic parameters have been calibrated. This can be easily done by using the simple calibration procedure described in [265]. The system

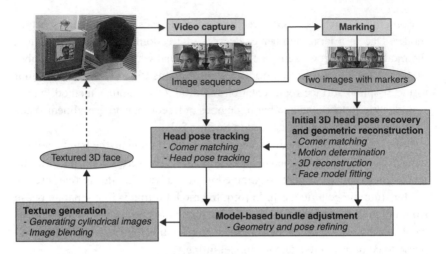

Figure 5.1. Overview of the face-modeling system in [268].

uses a linear space of deformation vectors to represent their face geometries where the basis vectors are designed manually as described in Section 2.3.2.

The first stage is video capture. The user simply sits in front of the camera and turns his/her head from one side all the way to the other side in about 5 seconds. The user then selects an approximately frontal view. This step can be done automatically by using a 3D head pose tracking algorithm as described in Chapter 10.

The video is then split into two subsequences referred to as the *left* and *right* sequences, and the selected frontal image and its successive image are called the *base images*. The second stage is feature-point marking. The user locates five markers in each of the two base images. The five markers correspond to the two inner eye corners, nose tip, and two mouth corners. This step can be done automatically by using a face feature detection system [243].

As an optional step, the user can put three markers below the chin on the frontal view. This additional information usually improves the final face model quality. Note that this manual stage can be replaced by an automatic facial feature detection (or face alignment) algorithm such as the algorithm reported in [243].

The third stage is the recovery of initial face models. The system computes the face mesh geometry and the head pose with respect to the camera frame using the two base images and markers as input. This stage of the system involves corner detection, matching, motion estimation, 3D reconstruction, and model fitting.

The fourth stage tracks the head pose in the image sequences. This is based on the same matching technique used in the previous stage, but the initial face model is also used for increasing accuracy and robustness.

The fifth stage refines the head pose and the face geometry using a technique called *model-based bundle adjustment*. The adjustment is performed by considering all the point matches in the image sequences. Note that this stage is optional. Because it is more time consuming, this step is usually skipped in live demos.

The final stage blends all the images to generate a facial texture map. This is now possible because the face regions are registered by the head motion estimated in the previous stages. At this point, a textured 3D face model is available for immediate animation or other purposes.

5.1.2 A tour of the system

In this section, we will guide the reader through each step of the system using a real video sequence as an example. The video was captured in a normal room by a static camera while the head was moving in front. There is no control on the head motion, and the motion is unknown, of course. The video sequence can be found at `http://research.microsoft.com/~zhang/Face/duane.avi`.

Note that this section intends for the reader to quickly gain knowledge of how the system works. More in-depth discussions of the technical details are provided in subsequent sections.

5.1.2.1 Marking and masking

The base images are shown in Figure 5.2, together with the five manually picked markers. We have to determine first the motion of the head and match some pixels across the two views before we can fit an animated face model to the images. However, some processing of the images is necessary because there are at least three major groups of objects undergoing different motions between the two views: background, head, and other parts of the body such as the shoulder. If we do not separate them, there is no way to determine a meaningful head motion. The technique, to be described in Section 5.1.3, allows us to mask off most irrelevant pixels automatically. Figure 5.3 shows the masked base images to be used for initial face geometry recovery.

Optionally, the user can also mark three points on the chin in one base image, as shown with three large yellow dots in Figure 5.4. Starting from these dots, the system first tries to trace strong edges, which gives the red, green, and blue curves in Figure 5.4. Finally, a spline curve is fit to the three detected curves

Figure 5.2. An example of two base images used for face modeling. Also shown are five manually picked markers indicated by yellow dots.

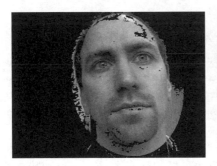

Figure 5.3. Masked images to be used in two-view image matching. See Section 5.1.3 for the technique used in obtaining the masked images.

Figure 5.4. Marking the lower part of the face with three points, which are shown in large yellow dots. This is an optional step. See text for explanation. (See plate section for color version.)

with an M-estimator. The small yellow dots in Figure 5.4 are sample points of that curve. Depending on the face shape and lighting condition, the three original curves do not necessarily represent the chin accurately, but the final spline represents the chin reasonably well. The chin curve will be used in face model fitting to be described in Section 5.1.2.5.

5.1.2.2 Matching between the two base images

One popular technique of image registration is optical flow [6, 94], which is based on the assumption that the intensity/color is conserved. This is not the case in our situation: The color of the same physical point appears to be different in images because the illumination changes when the head is moving. Therefore, a feature-based approach was used in [268], which is more robust to intensity/color variations. It consists of the following steps: (i) detecting corners in each image; (ii) matching corners between the two images; (iii) detecting false matches based on a robust estimation technique;(iv) determining the head motion; (v) reconstructing matched points in 3D space.

Corner detection. Plessey corner detector [87] was used in [268]. It locates corners corresponding to high curvature points in the intensity surface if we view an image as a 3D surface with the third dimension being the intensity. Only corners whose pixels are white in the mask image are considered. See the top row of Figure 5.5 for the detected corners of the images shown in Figure 5.2. There are 807 and 947 corners detected in the two images, respectively.

Corner matching. For each corner in the first image, an 11×11 window that is centered at the corner is selected. The selected window is compared with all the windows that have the same size and are centered at the corners in the second image. A zero-mean normalized cross correlation between two windows is computed [55]. If we rearrange the pixels in each window as a vector, the correlation score is equivalent to the cosine angle between two intensity vectors. It ranges from -1, for two windows which are not similar at all, to 1, for two windows which are identical. If the largest correlation score exceeds a prefixed threshold (0.866 was used in [268]), then that corner in the second image is considered to be the *match candidate* of the corner in the first image. The match candidate is retained as a *match* if and only if its match candidate in the first image happens to be *the corner being considered*. This symmetric test reduces many potential matching errors.

For the example shown in Figure 5.2, the set of matches established by this correlation technique is shown at the top row of Figure 5.5. There are 237 matches in total.

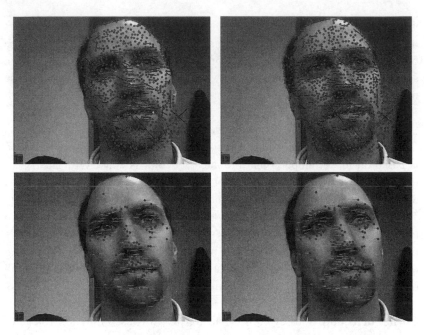

Figure 5.5. Top row: The set of matches established by correlation for the pair of images shown in Figure 5.2. Red dots are the detected corners. Blue lines are the motion vectors of the matches, with one endpoint (indicated by a red dot) being the matched corner in the current image and the other endpoint being the matched corner in the other image. Bottom row: The final set of matches after discarding automatically false matches for the pair of images shown in Figure 5.2. Green lines are the motion vectors of the matches, with one endpoint (indicated by a red dot) being the matched corner in the current image and the other endpoint being the matched corner in the other image. (See plate section for color version.)

False match detection. The set of matches established so far usually contains false matches because correlation is only a heuristic. The only geometric constraint between two images is the epipolar constraint (1.3). If two points are correctly matched, they must satisfy this constraint, which is unknown in our case. Inaccurate location of corners because of intensity variation or lack of strong texture features is another source of error. The technique described in [263] is used to detect both false matches and poorly located corners and simultaneously estimate the epipolar geometry (in terms of the essential matrix $\mathbf{E}$). That technique is based on a robust estimation technique known as the *least median squares* [182], which searches in the parameter space to find the parameters yielding the smallest value for the *median* of squared residuals computed for the entire data set. Consequently, it is able to detect false matches in as many as 49.9% of the whole set of matches.

For the example shown in Figure 5.2, the final set of matches is shown at the bottom row of Figure 5.5. There are 148 remaining matches. Compared with those shown at the top row of Figure 5.5, 89 matches have been discarded.

5.1.2.3 Robust head motion estimation

An algorithm was developed in [133] to compute the head motion between two views from the correspondences of five feature points (including eye corners, mouth corners, and nose top) and zero or more other image point matches.

If the image locations of these feature points are precise, one could use a five-point algorithm to compute camera motion. However, this is usually not the case in practice. Regardless of whether the five feature points are marked by humans or detected automatically, the positions of the feature points are typically not accurate. When there are errors in the positions, a five-point algorithm is not robust even when refined with a bundle adjustment technique. The main idea of the algorithm in [133] is to use the physical properties of the feature points to improve the robustness. In particular, they use the property of symmetry to reduce the number of unknowns. In addition, they impose reasonable lower and upper bounds on the nose height and represent the bounds as inequality constraints. As a result, the algorithm becomes significantly more robust. The algorithm will be described in more detail in Section 5.1.4.

5.1.2.4 3D reconstruction

Once the motion is estimated, matched points can be reconstructed in 3D space with respect to the camera frame at the time when the first base image was taken. Let $(\mathbf{p}, \mathbf{p}')$ be a pair of matched points, and P be their corresponding point in 3D space. 3D point P is estimated such that $\|\mathbf{p} - \hat{\mathbf{p}}\|^2 + \|\mathbf{p}' - \hat{\mathbf{p}}'\|^2$ is minimized, where $\hat{\mathbf{p}}$ and $\hat{\mathbf{p}}'$ are projections of P in both images according to (1.1).

Two views of the 3D reconstructed points for the example shown in Figure 5.2 are shown in Figure 5.6. The wireframes shown on the right are obtained by performing Delaunay triangulation on the matched points. The pictures shown on the left are obtained by using the first base image as the texture map.

5.1.2.5 Face model fitting from two views

We now only have a set of unorganized noisy 3D points from matched corners and markers. The face-model-fitting process consists of two steps: fitting to the 3D reconstructed points and fine adjustment using image information. The first consists in estimating both the *pose* of the head and the model coefficients (in the

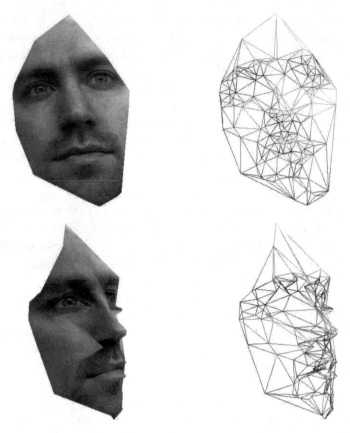

Figure 5.6. Reconstructed corner points. This coarse mesh is used later to fit a face model.

linear space representation) that minimize the distances from the reconstructed 3D points to the face mesh. The estimated head pose is defined to be the pose with respect to the camera coordinate system when the first base image was taken, and is denoted by T_0. In the second step, we search for silhouettes and other face features in the images and use them; we also use the chin curve if available from the marking step (Section 5.1.2.1), to refine the face geometry. Details of face model fitting are provided in Section 5.1.5.

Figure 5.7 shows the reconstructed 3D face mesh from the two example images (see Figure 5.2). The mesh is projected back to the two images. Figure 5.8 shows two novel views using the first image as the texture map. The texture corresponding to the right side of the face is still missing.

Figure 5.7. The constructed 3D face mesh is projected back to the two base images.

Figure 5.8. Two novel views of the reconstructed 3D face mesh with the the first base image as texture.

5.1.2.6 Determining head motions in video sequences

Now we have the geometry of the face from only two views that are close to the frontal position. As can be seen in Figure 5.8, for the sides of the face, the texture from the two images is therefore quite poor or even not available at all. Since each image only covers a portion of the face, we need to combine all the images in the video sequence to obtain a complete texture map. This is done by first determining the head pose for the images in the video sequence and then blending them to create a complete texture map.

Successive images are first matched using the same technique as described in Section 5.1.2.2. We could combine the resulting motions incrementally to determine the head pose. However, this estimation is quite noisy because it is computed only from 2D points. As we already have the 3D face geometry, a more reliable pose estimation can be obtained by combining both 3D and 2D information, as follows.

Let us denote the first base image by I_0, the images on the video sequences by $I_1,\ldots,I_v$, the relative head motion from I_{i-1} to I_i by $\mathcal{R}_i = \begin{pmatrix} \mathbf{R}_{ri} & \mathbf{t}_{ri} \\ \mathbf{0}^T & 1 \end{pmatrix}$, and the head pose corresponding to image I_i with respect to the camera frame by $\mathbf{T}_i$. Thus,

$$\mathbf{T}_i = \mathcal{R}_i \mathbf{T}_{i-1}. \tag{5.1}$$

The algorithm works incrementally, starting with I_0 and I_1. For each pair of images (I_{i-1}, I_i), we first use the corner-matching algorithm described in Section 5.1.2.2 to find a set of matched corner pairs $\{(\mathbf{p}_j,\mathbf{p}'_j)|j=1,\ldots,l\}$. For each $\mathbf{p}_j$ in I_{i-1}, we cast a ray from the camera center through $\mathbf{p}_j$ and compute the intersection P_j of that ray with the face mesh corresponding to image I_{i-1}. According to (1.1), $\mathcal{R}_i$ is subject to the following equations

$$\mathbf{A}\mathbf{P}\mathcal{R}_i\tilde{\mathrm{P}}_j = \lambda_j\tilde{\mathbf{p}}'_j \quad \text{for } j=1,\ldots,l, \tag{5.2}$$

where $\mathbf{A}$, $\mathbf{P}$, P_j, and $\mathbf{p}'_j$ are known. Each of the above equations gives two constraints on $\mathcal{R}_i$. We compute $\mathcal{R}_i$ with the technique described in Section 10.1.2. After $\mathcal{R}_i$ is computed, the head pose for image I_i in the camera frame is given by (5.1). The head pose $\mathbf{T}_0$ is known from Section 5.1.2.5.

In general, it is inefficient to use all the images in the video sequence for texture blending because head motion between two consecutive frames is usually small. To avoid unnecessary computation, the following process is used to automatically select images from the video sequence. Let us call the amount of rotation of the head between two consecutive frames the *rotation speed*. If s is the current rotation speed and α is the desired angle between each pair of selected images, the next image is selected $\lfloor(\alpha/s)\rfloor$ frames away. In [268], the initial guess of the rotation speed was set to 1 degree/frame, and the desired separation angle was equal to 5 degrees.

Figures 5.9 and 5.10 show the tracking results of the two example video sequences (The two base images are shown in Figure 5.2.) The images from each video sequence are automatically selected using the preceding algorithm.

5.1.2.7 Model-based bundle adjustment

We now have an initial face model from two base images, a set of pairwise point matches over the whole video sequence, and an initial estimate of the head poses in the video sequence which is obtained incrementally based on the initial face model. Naturally, we want to refine the face model and head pose

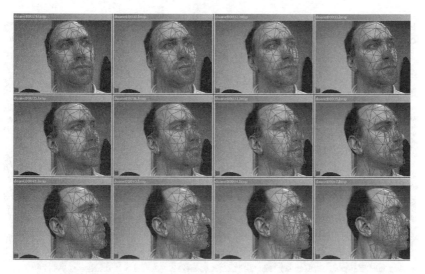

Figure 5.9. The face mesh is projected back to the automatically selected images from the video sequence where the head turns to the left.

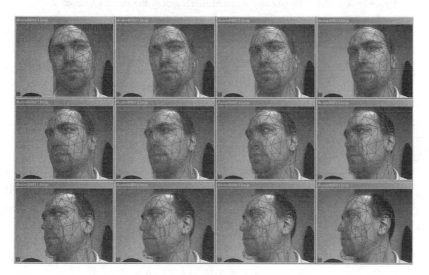

Figure 5.10. The face mesh is projected back to the automatically selected images from the video sequence where the head turns to the right. (See plate section for color version.)

estimates by taking into account all available information simultaneously. A classical approach is to perform bundle adjustment to determine the head motion and 3D coordinates of isolated points corresponding to matched image points, followed by fitting the parametric face model to the reconstructed isolated

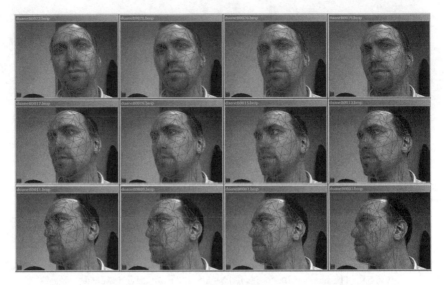

Figure 5.11. After model-based bundle adjustment, the refined face mesh is projected back to the automatically selected images from the video sequence where the head turns to the right. (See plate section for color version.)

points. Shan et al. [193] developed a technique called *model-based bundle adjustment*, which directly searches in the face model space to minimize the same objective function as that used in the classical bundle adjustment. This results in a more elegant formulation with fewer unknowns, fewer equations, a smaller search space, and hence a better posed system. More details are provided in Section 5.1.6.

Figure 5.11 shows the refined result on the right sequence, which should be compared with that shown in Figure 5.10. The projected face mesh is overlaid on the original images. We can observe clear improvement in the silhouette and chin regions.

5.1.2.8 Texture blending

After the head pose of an image is computed, an approach similar to Pighin et al.'s method [168] can be used to generate a view-independent texture map. In addition, one can construct the texture map on a virtual cylinder enclosing the face model [268]. Instead of casting a ray from each pixel to the face mesh and computing the texture blending weights on a pixel by pixel basis, a more efficient approach can be used to take advantage of the graphics acceleration hardware. This approach is described later.

For each vertex on the face mesh, we can compute the blending weight for each image based on the angle between the surface normal and the camera direction [168]. If the vertex is invisible, its weight is set to 0.0. The weights are then normalized so that for each vertex the sum of the weights over all the images is equal to 1.0.

For each image, the weights for all of the pixels are obtained by interpolating the vertex weights as follows. First, the vertex colors of the face mesh are set to be equal to their weights. Second, the cylindrical mapped mesh is rendered, and the rendered image is the weight map.

For each image, its corresponding cylindrical texture map can be generated by rendering the cylindrical mapped mesh with the image as texture map. Let C_i and W_i ($i = 1, \ldots, k$) denote the cylindrical texture maps and the weight maps. Let C denote the final blended texture map. For each pixel (u, v), its color on the final blended texture map is

$$C(u,v) = \sum_{i=1}^{k} W_i(u,v)C_i(u,v). \tag{5.3}$$

Since the rendering operations can be done using graphics hardware, this approach is very fast.

Figure 5.12 shows the blended texture map from the example video sequences in Figure 5.9 and 5.10. Figure 5.13 shows two novel views of the final 3D face model. Compared with those shown in Figure 5.8, we now have a much better texture on the side.

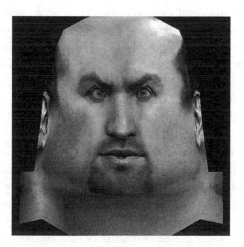

Figure 5.12. The blended texture image.

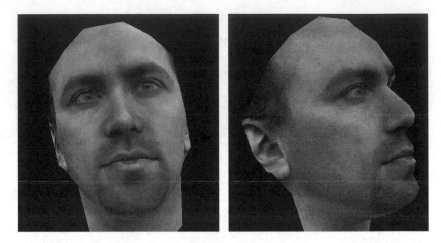

Figure 5.13. Two novel views of the final 3D face model.

5.1.3 Image masking

This section provides details left out in Section 5.1.2.1. As mentioned earlier, there are at least three major groups of objects undergoing different motions between the two views: background, head, and other parts of the body such as the shoulder. If we do not separate them, there is no way to determine a meaningful head motion. Since the camera is static, we can expect to remove the background by subtracting one image from the other. However, as the face color changes smoothly, a portion of the face may be marked as background, as shown in Figure 5.14a. Another problem with this image subtraction technique is that the moving body and the head cannot be distinguished.

As there are five feature points on the face, one can actually build a color model of the face skin. We select pixels below the eyes and above the mouth, and compute a Gaussian distribution of their colors in the RGB space. If the color of a pixel matches this face skin color model, the pixel is marked as a part of the face. An example is shown in Figure 5.14b. As we can notice, some background pixels are marked as face skin.

Either union or intersection of the two mask images is not enough to locate the face because it will include either too many (e.g., including undesired moving body) or too few (e.g., missing desired eyes and mouth) pixels. As we already have information about the position of eye corners and mouth corners, we define two ellipses as shown in Figure 5.15a. The inner ellipse covers most of the face, while the outer ellipse is usually large enough to enclose the whole head. Let d_e be the image distance between the two inner eye corners, and d_{em},

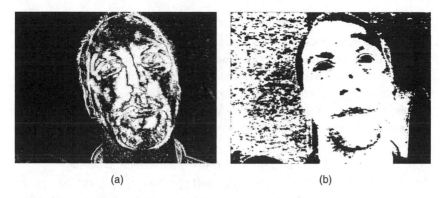

Figure 5.14. (a) Mask obtained by subtracting images (black pixels are considered as background); (b) Mask obtained by using a face skin color model (white pixels are considered as face skin).

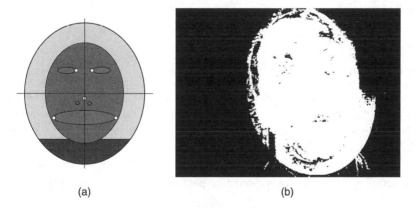

Figure 5.15. (a) Definition of face ellipses; (b) final mask obtained with the preprocessing technique.

the vertical distance between the eyes and the mouth. The width and height of the inner ellipse are set to $5d_e$ and $3d_{em}$. The outer ellipse is 25% larger than the inner one. Within the inner ellipse, the "union" operation is used. Between the inner and outer ellipses, only the image subtraction is used, except for the lower part where the "intersection" operation is used. The lower part aims at removing the moving body and is defined to be $0.6d_{em}$ below the mouth, as illustrated by the red area in Figure 5.15a. An example of the final mask is shown in Figure 5.15b.

5.1.4 Robust head motion determination from two views

This section provides details left out in Section 5.1.2.3. The system relies on an initial face modeling from two base images, and therefore a robust head motion determination is key to extract 3D information from images. This section describes an algorithm to compute the head motion between two views from the correspondences of five feature points (including eye corners, mouth corners, and nose top), and zero or more other image point matches.

5.1.4.1 Head motion estimation from five feature points

Let E_1, E_2, M_1, M_2, and N denote the left eye corner, right eye corner, left mouth corner, right mouth corner, and nose top, respectively (see Figure 5.16). Denote E as the midpoint of E_1E_2 and M the midpoint of M_1M_2. Notice that human faces exhibit some strong structural properties. For example, left and right sides are very close to being symmetric about the nose; eye corners and mouth corners are almost coplanar. Therefore it is reasonable to make the following assumptions:

- NM is perpendicular to M_1M_2,
- NE is perpendicular to E_1E_2, and
- E_1E_2 is parallel to M_1M_2.

Let π be the plane defined by E_1, E_2, M_1, and M_2. Let O denote the projection of point N on plan π. Let Ω_0 denote the coordinate system with O as the origin, ON as the Z-axis, OE as the Y-axis. In this coordinate system, based on the assumptions mentioned earlier, we can define the coordinates of E_1, E_2, M_1, M_2, N as $(-a,b,0)^T$, $(a,b,0)^T$, $(-d,-c,0)^T$, $(d,-c,0)^T$, $(0,0,e)^T$, respectively. Thus, we only need five parameters to define these five points

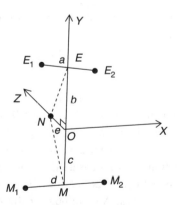

Figure 5.16. The new coordinate system Ω_0.

in this local coordinate system, instead of nine parameters for generic five points.

Let $\mathbf{t}$ denote the coordinates of O in the camera coordinate system and $\mathbf{R}$ the rotation matrix whose three columns correspond to the three coordinate axes of Ω_0. We call $\mathbf{T} = \left(\begin{smallmatrix} \mathbf{R} & \mathbf{t} \\ \mathbf{0}^T & 1 \end{smallmatrix}\right)$ the *head pose transform*. For each point $P \in \{E_1, E_2, M_1, M_2, N\}$, its coordinates in the camera coordinate system are $\mathbf{R}P + \mathbf{t}$.

Given two images of the head under two different poses (assuming the camera is static), let $\mathbf{T} = \left(\begin{smallmatrix} \mathbf{R} & \mathbf{t} \\ \mathbf{0}^T & 1 \end{smallmatrix}\right)$ and $\mathbf{T}' = \left(\begin{smallmatrix} \mathbf{R}' & \mathbf{t}' \\ \mathbf{0}^T & 1 \end{smallmatrix}\right)$ be the corresponding head pose transforms. For each point $P_i \in \{E_1, E_2, M_1, M_2, N\}$, if we denote its image point in the first view by $\mathbf{p}_i$ and that in the second view by $\mathbf{p}'_i$, according to (1.2), we have

$$\mathbf{p}_i = \boldsymbol{\phi}(\mathbf{T}, P_i) \quad \text{and} \quad \mathbf{p}'_i = \boldsymbol{\phi}(\mathbf{T}', P_i). \tag{5.4}$$

Notice that we can fix one of the a, b, c, d, e since the scale of the head size cannot be determined from the images. As is well known, each pose has 6 degrees of freedom. Therefore the total number of unknowns is $6 + 6 + 4 = 16$, and the total number of equations is 20. If we instead use their 3D coordinates as unknowns as in any typical bundle adjustment algorithms, we would end up with 20 unknowns, the same number of the available equations. By using the generic properties of the face structure, the system becomes overconstrained, making the pose determination more robust.

To make the system even more robust, one can add an inequality constraint on e. The idea is to force e to be positive and not too large compared to a, b, c, d. This is obvious since the nose is always out of plane π. In particular, the following inequality was used in [133]:

$$0 \le e \le 3a, \tag{5.5}$$

where 3 was used as the upper bound of e/a based on empirical observation. The inequality constraint is finally converted to equality constraint by using a penalty function:

$$P_{\text{nose}} = \begin{cases} e^2 & \text{if } e < 0; \\ 0 & \text{if } 0 \le e \le 3a; \\ (e - 3a)^2 & \text{if } e > 3a. \end{cases} \tag{5.6}$$

In summary, based on Equations (5.4) and (5.6), we can estimate a, b, c, d, e, $(\mathbf{R}, \mathbf{t})$, and $(\mathbf{R}', \mathbf{t}')$ by minimizing

$$\mathcal{F}_{5\text{pts}} = \sum_{i=1}^{5} w_i (\|\mathbf{p}_i - \boldsymbol{\phi}(\mathbf{T}, \mathrm{P}_i)\|^2 + \|\mathbf{p}_i' - \boldsymbol{\phi}(\mathbf{T}', \mathrm{P}_i))\|^2) + w_n P_{\text{nose}}, \qquad (5.7)$$

where w_i's and w_n are the weighting factors, reflecting the contribution of each term. In [133], w_i was set to 1 except for the nose term, which has a weight of 0.5 because it is usually more difficult to locate the nose tip accurately than other feature points. The weight for penalty, w_n, was set to 10. The objective function (5.7) can be minimized by using a Levenberg–Marquardt method [150]. As mentioned earlier, a was set to a constant during minimization since the global head size cannot be determined from images.

5.1.4.2 Incorporating image point matches

If we estimate camera motion using only the five user marked points, the result is sometimes not very accurate because the feature points contain errors. In this section, we describe how to incorporate the image point matches (obtained as described in Section 5.1.2.2) to improve precision.

Let $(\mathbf{p}_j, \mathbf{p}_j')$ $(j = 1, \ldots, K)$ be the K point matches, each corresponding to the projection of a 3D point P_j according to the perspective projection (5.4). Obviously, we have to estimate P_j's that are unknown. Assuming that each image point is extracted with the same accuracy, we can estimate a, b, c, d, e, $(\mathbf{R}, \mathbf{t})$, $(\mathbf{R}', \mathbf{t}')$, and $\{\mathrm{P}_j\}$ $(j = 1, \ldots, K)$ by minimizing

$$\mathcal{F} = \mathcal{F}_{5\text{pts}} + w_p \sum_{j=1}^{K} (\|\mathbf{p}_j - \boldsymbol{\phi}(\mathbf{T}, \mathrm{P}_i)\|^2 + \|\mathbf{p}_j' - \boldsymbol{\phi}(\mathbf{T}', \mathrm{P}_i)\|^2), \qquad (5.8)$$

where $\mathcal{F}_{5\text{pts}}$ is given by (5.7), and w_p is the weighting factor. w_p can be set to 1 by assuming that the extracted points have the same accuracy as those of eye corners and mouth corners. The minimization can again be performed by using a Levenberg–Marquardt method.

This is quite a large minimization problem since we need to estimate $16 + 3K$ unknowns, and therefore it is computationally expensive especially for large K (usually $K > 100$). Fortunately, as shown in [264], we can eliminate the 3D points using a first-order approximation. More precisely, it can be shown that if $\mathbf{p}_j$ and $\mathbf{p}_j'$ are in normalized image coordinates, we have

$$\|\mathbf{p}_j - \boldsymbol{\phi}(\mathbf{T}, \mathrm{P}_i)\|^2 + \|\mathbf{p}_j' - \boldsymbol{\phi}(\mathbf{T}', \mathrm{P}_i)\|^2 \approx \frac{(\tilde{\mathbf{p}}_j'^T \mathbf{E} \tilde{\mathbf{p}}_j)^2}{\tilde{\mathbf{p}}_j^T \mathbf{E}^T \mathbf{Z} \mathbf{Z}^T \mathbf{E} \tilde{\mathbf{p}}_j + \tilde{\mathbf{p}}_j'^T \mathbf{E} \mathbf{Z} \mathbf{Z}^T \mathbf{E}^T \tilde{\mathbf{p}}_j'},$$

where $\mathbf{Z} = \begin{pmatrix} 1 & 0 \\ 0 & 1 \\ 0 & 0 \end{pmatrix}$, and $\mathbf{E}$ is the essential matrix between the two images (i.e., $\mathbf{E} = [\mathbf{t}_r]_\times \mathbf{R}_r$). Here, $(\mathbf{R}_r, \mathbf{t}_r)$ is the relative motion between two views, that is,

$$\begin{pmatrix} \mathbf{R}' & \mathbf{t}' \\ \mathbf{0}^T & 1 \end{pmatrix} = \begin{pmatrix} \mathbf{R}_r & \mathbf{t}_r \\ \mathbf{0}^T & 1 \end{pmatrix} \begin{pmatrix} \mathbf{R} & \mathbf{t} \\ \mathbf{0}^T & 1 \end{pmatrix}. \tag{5.9}$$

Thus,

$$\mathbf{R}_r = \mathbf{R}' \mathbf{R}^T,$$

$$\mathbf{t}_r = \mathbf{t}' - \mathbf{R}' \mathbf{R}^T \mathbf{t}.$$

In summary, the objective function (5.8) becomes

$$\mathcal{F} = \mathcal{F}_{5\text{pts}} + w_p \sum_{j=1}^{K} \frac{(\tilde{\mathbf{p}}_j'^T \mathbf{E} \tilde{\mathbf{p}}_j)^2}{\tilde{\mathbf{p}}_j^T \mathbf{E}^T \mathbf{Z} \mathbf{Z}^T \mathbf{E} \tilde{\mathbf{p}}_j + \tilde{\mathbf{p}}_j'^T \mathbf{E} \mathbf{Z} \mathbf{Z}^T \mathbf{E}^T \tilde{\mathbf{p}}_j'}. \tag{5.10}$$

Notice that this is a much smaller minimization problem. We only need to estimate 16 parameters as in the five-point problem (5.7), instead of $16 + 3K$ unknowns.

To obtain a good initial estimate, we first use only the five feature points to estimate the head motion by using the algorithm described in Section 5.1.4.1. Thus we have the following two step algorithm:

Step 1. Set $w_p = 0$. Solve minimization problem (5.10).
Step 2. Set $w_p = 1$. Solve minimization problem (5.10) using the result of step 1 as the initial estimates.

Notice that this idea can be applied to the more general cases where the number of feature points is not five. For example, if there are only two eye corners and mouth corners, we'll end up with 14 unknowns and $16 + 3K$ equations. Other symmetric feature points (outside eye corners, nostrils, etc.) can be added to (5.10) in a similar way by using the local coordinate system Ω_0.

5.1.4.3 Experimental results

In this section, we show some test results to compare the algorithm of the previous section with traditional algorithms which do not take advantage of the physical properties. Since there are multiple traditional algorithms, Liu and Zhang [133] implemented the algorithm as described in [262] for comparison. It works by first computing an initial estimate of the head motion from the essential matrix [55] and then reestimate the motion with a nonlinear least-squares technique.

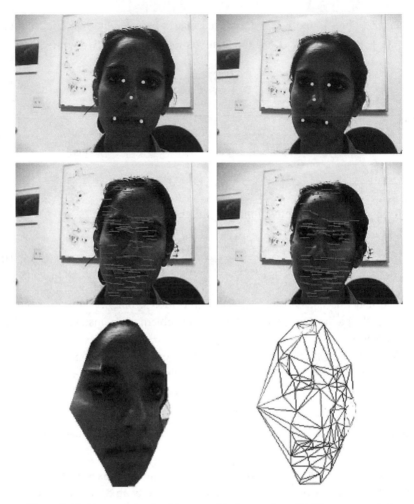

Figure 5.17. Top row: a pair of images with five markers. Middle row: matched image points. Bottom row: a novel view of the 3D reconstruction of the image matching points with the head motion computed by the new algorithm that takes advantage of the physical properties. Note that the traditional motion estimation failed in this example.

The traditional algorithm and the new algorithm were run on many real-world examples. It was found that in many cases the traditional algorithm fails while the new algorithm successfully produces reasonable motion estimates. Figure 5.17 is such an example. The motion computed by the traditional algorithm is completely bogus, and the 3D reconstruction gives meaningless results, but the new algorithm gives a reasonable result.

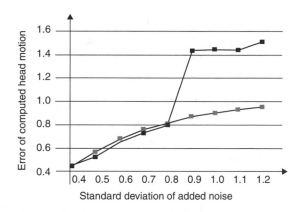

Figure 5.18. Comparison of the new algorithm with the traditional algorithm. The blue curve shows the results of the traditional algorithm and the red curve shows the results of the new algorithm.

In order to obtain the ground truth, Liu and Zhang [133] also performed experiments on artificially generated data. They arbitrarily selected 80 vertices from a 3D face model (Figure 2.1) and projected them on two views (the head motion is 8 degrees apart). The image size is 640 by 480 pixels. The five 3D feature points (eye corners, nose tip, and mouth corners) are also projected to generate their image coordinates. Gaussian noise is then added to the coordinates (u, v) of the image points. The Gaussian noise has mean zero and standard deviation ranging from 0.4 to 1.2 pixels. Notice that the noise is added to the feature points' coordinates as well. The results are plotted in Figure 5.18. The blue curve shows the results of the traditional algorithm and the red curve shows the results of the new algorithm. The horizontal axis is the standard deviation of the noise distribution. The vertical axis is the difference between the estimated motion and the actual motion. The translation vector of the estimated motion is scaled so that its magnitude is the same as the actual motion. The difference between two rotations is measured as the Euclidean distance between the two rotational matrices. The average of the combined motion errors from 20 random trials is computed for each noise level. We can see that as the noise increases, the error of the traditional algorithm has a sudden jump at certain noise level, indicating failures in several trials; the errors of the new algorithm increase much more slowly.

5.1.5 Face model fitting from two views

This section describes the details left out in Section 5.1.2.5. The face-model-fitting process consists of two steps: fitting to 3D reconstructed points and fine adjustment using image information.

5.1.5.1 3D fitting

Given a set of reconstructed 3D points from matched corners and markers, the fitting process searches for both the *pose* of the face and the model coefficients to minimize the distances from the reconstructed 3D points to the face mesh. The pose of the face is the transformation $\mathbf{T} = \begin{pmatrix} s\mathbf{R} & \mathbf{t} \\ \mathbf{0}^T & 1 \end{pmatrix}$ from the coordinate frame of the neutral face mesh to the camera frame, where $\mathbf{R}$ is a 3×3 rotation matrix, $\mathbf{t}$ is a translation, and s is a global scale. For any 3D vector P, we use notation $\mathbf{T}(\mathrm{P}) = s\mathbf{R}\mathrm{P} + \mathbf{t}$.

The vertex coordinates of the face mesh in the camera frame is a function of both the model coefficients and the pose of the face. Given model coefficients $C = (c_1, \ldots, c_m)$ and pose $\mathbf{T}$, the face geometry in the camera frame is given by

$$S = \mathbf{T}\left(S^0 + \sum_{j=1}^{m} c_j \mathcal{M}^j\right). \tag{5.11}$$

Since the face mesh is a triangular mesh, any point on a triangle is a linear combination of the three triangle vertexes in terms of barycentric coordinates. So any point on a triangle is also a function of $\mathbf{T}$ and model coefficients. Furthermore, when $\mathbf{T}$ is fixed, it is simply a linear function of the model coefficients C. This concept is described in (2.13) of Section 2.3.3 where S on the right-hand side is a function of C while $\mathbf{B}$, the semantic coordinate of P, is independent of C.

Let $(\mathrm{P}_1, \mathrm{P}_2, \ldots, \mathrm{P}_n)$ be the reconstructed corner points and $(\mathrm{Q}_1, \mathrm{Q}_2, \ldots, \mathrm{Q}_5)$ be the reconstructed face feature points. Denote the distance from P_i to the face mesh S by $d(\mathrm{P}_i, S)$. Assume feature point Q_j corresponds to vertex V_{m_j} of the face mesh, and denote the distance between Q_j and V_{m_j} by $d(\mathrm{Q}_j, \mathrm{V}_{m_j})$. The fitting process consists in finding pose $\mathbf{T}$ and model coefficients $\{c_1, \ldots, c_n\}$ by minimizing

$$\sum_{i=1}^{n} w_i d^2(\mathrm{P}_i, S) + \sum_{j=1}^{5} d^2(\mathrm{Q}_j, \mathrm{V}_{m_j}), \tag{5.12}$$

where w_i is a weighting factor.

To solve this problem, we use the deformable iterative closest point approach described in Section 4.1.1 (Algorithm 1). Each iteration consists of two phases. At the first phase (Step (3) and (4) in Algorithm 1), we fix $\mathbf{T}$ while solving for the model coefficients C. For each P_i, we find the closest point G_i on the current face mesh S. Let $\mathbf{B}_i$ denote the semantic coordinate of G_i, and $\mathbf{D}_j$ denote the semantic coordinate of V_{m_j}. That is, $\mathrm{G}_i = \mathbf{B}_i S$ and $\mathrm{V}_{m_j} = \mathbf{D}_j S$.

We find C to minimize

$$\sum_{i=1}^{n} w_i ||\mathrm{P}_i - \mathbf{B}_i \mathcal{S}||^2 + \sum_{j=1}^{5} ||\mathrm{Q}_j - \mathbf{D}_j \mathcal{S}||^2. \qquad (5.13)$$

We set w_i to be 1 at the first iteration and $1.0/(1 + d^2(\mathrm{P}_i, \mathrm{G}_i))$ in the subsequent iterations. The reason for using weights is that the reconstruction from images is noisy and such a weight scheme is an effective way to avoid overfitting to the noisy data [68]. Since both G_i and V_{m_j} are linear functions of the model coefficients C for fixed $\mathbf{T}$, the above problem is a linear least-square problem.

At the second phase (step (1) and (2) in Algorithm 1), we fix the model coefficients C and solve for the pose $\mathbf{T}$. To do that, we recompute G_i using the new model coefficients. Given a set of 3D corresponding points $(\mathrm{P}_i, \mathrm{G}_i)$ and $(\mathrm{Q}_j, \mathrm{V}_{m_j})$, there are well-known algorithms to solve for the pose. For example, one can use the quaternion-based technique described in [91].

To initialize this iterative process, the five feature points can be used to compute an initial estimate of the pose. In addition, to obtain a reasonable estimate of the head size, we solve for the head-size-related model coefficients such that the resulting face mesh matches the bounding box of the reconstructed 3D points. Occasionally the corner-matching algorithm may produce points not on the face. In that case, the model coefficients will be out of the valid ranges, and we throw away the point that is the most distant from the center of the face. This process can be repeated until the model coefficients become valid.

5.1.5.2 Fine adjustment using image information

After the geometric fitting process, we obtain a face mesh that is a close approximation to the real face. To further improve the result, we can search for silhouettes and other additional face features in the images and use them, together with the chin curve if available from the marking step (Section 5.1.2.1), to refine the face geometry. The general problem of locating silhouettes and face features in images is a challenging problem and is still a very active research area in computer vision. However, the face mesh that we have obtained provides a good estimate of the locations of the face features, so we only need to perform search in a small region.

We can use the snake approach [108] to compute the silhouettes of the face. The silhouette of the current face mesh is used as the initial estimate. For each point on this piecewise linear curve, we find the maximum gradient location along the normal direction within a small range (e.g., 10 pixels on each side was used in [268]). Then we can solve for the vertices, which acted as the control points of the snake, to minimize the total distance between all the points and their corresponding maximum gradient locations. In the case where the user chooses to put three markers below the chin, the system treats these three markers as the silhouette points.

A similar approach can be used to find the upper lips.

If the outer eye corners are not marked manually or detected automatically, we can find the outer eye corners as follows. First, we rotate the current estimate of the outer eye corner, which is given by the face mesh, around the inner eye corner by a small angle, and look for the eye boundary using image gradient information. This is repeated for several angles, and the boundary point that is the most distant to the inner corner is chosen as the outer eye corner.

We could also use the snake approach to search for eyebrows. However, a slightly different approach was used in [268]. Instead of maximizing image gradients across contours, they minimized the average intensity of the image area that is covered by the eyebrow triangles. Again, the vertices of the eyebrows are only allowed to move in a small region bounded by their neighboring vertices.

We can then use the face features and the image silhouettes including the chin curve as constraints in the system to further improve the mesh. Notice that each vertex on the mesh silhouette corresponds to a vertex on the image silhouette. The correspondence is a byproduct of the snake-fitting procedure described earlier where the image silhouette (i.e., snake) is parameterized in the same way as the face mesh silhouette. We cast a ray from the camera center through the vertex on the image silhouette. The projection of the corresponding mesh vertex on this ray acts as the target position of the mesh vertex. Let V denote the mesh vertex, which is a function of the pose $\mathbf{T}$ and model coefficients C. Let H denote the projection point on the ray. We have equation $V = H$. For each additional face feature such as an outer eye corner, we can obtain an equation in a similar way. These equations are added to Equation 5.12. The total set of equations is solved as before, that is, we first fix the pose $\mathbf{T}$ and use a linear least-square approach to solve the model coefficients, and then fix the model coefficients while solving for the pose.

5.1.6 *Model-based bundle adjustment*

As mentioned in Section 5.1.2.7, we are interested in refining the initial face model as well as the head pose estimates by taking into account all available information from multiple images simultaneously. In this section, we briefly outline the model-based bundle adjustment. The interested reader is encouraged to read [193] for details.

5.1.6.1 Problem formulation

As described in Section 2.3, a face mesh $\mathcal{S}$ is defined by m model coefficients $\{c_j | j = 1, \ldots, m\}$ according to (2.4). To completely define the face geometry in the camera coordinate system, we still need to know the head pose $\mathbf{T}$, for example, in the first base image. Thus, the face geometry given by (5.11), that is, $\mathcal{S} = \mathbf{T}(\mathcal{S}^0 + \sum_{j=1}^{m} c_j \mathcal{M}^j)$, is the face mesh in the camera coordinate system. Therefore, including the six parameters for $\mathbf{T}$, the total number of model parameters is $M = m + 6$, and they are collectively designated by vector $\hat{C}$. Let us denote the surface by $\mathcal{S}(\hat{C})$.

Furthermore, we assume there are Q semantically meaningful points (*semantic points* for short) $\{Q_j | j = 1, \ldots, Q\}$ on the face. If there are no semantic points available, then $Q = 0$. In the system of [268], $Q = 5$ since they used five semantic points: two inner eye corners, two mouth corners, and the nose tip. The relationship between the jth semantic point Q_j and the face parameters $\hat{C}$ is described by (See Equation (2.13) in Section 2.3.3)

$$Q_j = \mathcal{Q}(\hat{C}, j). \tag{5.14}$$

Obviously, point $Q_j \in \mathcal{S}(\hat{C})$.

We are given a set of N image frames, and a number of points of interest across images have been established as described earlier. Image i is taken by a camera with unknown pose parameters $\mathbf{M}_i$, which describes the position and orientation of the camera with respect to the world coordinate system in which the face mesh is described. A 3D point P_k and its image point $\mathbf{p}_{i,k}$ are related by (1.2), that is, $\mathbf{p}_{i,k} = \boldsymbol{\phi}(\mathbf{M}_i, P_k)$.

Because of occlusion, feature detection failure, and other reasons, a point on the face may be observed and detected in a subset of images. Let us call the set of image points corresponding to a single point on the face a *feature track*. Let P be the total number of feature tracks, Θ_k be the set of frame numbers of the kth feature track, $\mathbf{p}_{i,k}$ ($i \in \Theta_k$) be the feature point in the ith frame that belongs to the kth feature track, and P_k be the corresponding 3D point, which is unknown, on the face surface. Furthermore, we assume that the jth semantic point Q_j is observed and detected in zero or more images. Let Ω_j be the, possibly empty, set of frame numbers in which Q_j are detected, and $\mathbf{q}_{l,j}$ ($l \in \Omega_j$) be the detected semantic point in the lth frame.

We can now state the problem as follows:

Problem 1: Given P tracks of feature points $\{\mathbf{p}_{i,k} | k = 1, \ldots, P; i \in \Theta_k\}$ and Q tracks of semantic points $\{\mathbf{q}_{l,j} | j = 1, \ldots, Q; l \in \Omega_j\}$, determine the face model parameters $\hat{C}$ and the camera pose parameters $\mathbf{M} = [\mathbf{M}_1^T, \ldots, \mathbf{M}_N^T]^T$.

The objective is to solve this problem in an optimal way. By *optimal* we mean to find simultaneously the face model parameters and camera parameters by minimizing some statistically and/or physically meaningful cost function. As in the classical point-based bundle adjustment, it is reasonable to assume that the image points are corrupted by independent and identically distributed Gaussian noise because points are extracted independently from images by the same algorithm. In that case, the maximum likelihood estimation is obtained by minimizing the sum of squared errors between the observed image points and the predicted feature points. More formally, the problem becomes

$$\min_{\mathbf{M},\hat{C},\{\mathrm{P}_k\}} \left(\sum_{k=1}^{P} \sum_{i\in\Theta_k} \|\mathbf{p}_{i,k} - \boldsymbol{\phi}(\mathbf{M}_i,\mathrm{P}_k)\|^2 + \sum_{j=1}^{Q} \sum_{l\in\Omega_j} \|\mathbf{q}_{l,j} - \boldsymbol{\phi}(\mathbf{M}_l,\mathrm{Q}_j)\|^2 \right),$$
(5.15)

subject to $\mathrm{P}_k \in \mathcal{S}(\hat{C})$, where $\mathrm{Q}_j = \mathcal{Q}(\hat{C},j)$ as defined in (5.14). Note that although the part for the general feature points (the first term) and the part for the semantic points (the second term) have the same form, we should treat them differently. Indeed, the latter provides stronger constraint in bundle adjustment than the former. We can simply substitute Q_j in the second part by $\mathcal{Q}(\hat{C},j)$, whereas P_k must be searched on the surface $\mathcal{S}(\hat{C})$.

We observe that in (5.15), unknown 3D points $\{\mathrm{P}_k\}$, which correspond to feature tracks, are not involved at all in the second term. Furthermore, in the first term, the second summation only depends on each individual P_k. We can therefore rewrite (5.15) as

$$\min_{\mathbf{M},\hat{C}} \left(\sum_{k=1}^{P} \left(\min_{\mathrm{P}_k} \sum_{i\in\Theta_k} \|\mathbf{p}_{i,k} - \boldsymbol{\phi}(\mathbf{M}_i,\mathrm{P}_k)\|^2 \right) + \sum_{j=1}^{Q} \sum_{l\in\Omega_j} \|\mathbf{q}_{l,j} - \boldsymbol{\phi}(\mathbf{M}_l,\mathrm{Q}_j)\|^2 \right),$$
(5.16)

subject to $\mathrm{P}_k \in \mathcal{S}(\hat{C})$. This property is reflected in the sparse structure of the Jacobian and Hessian of the objective function. As in the classical bundle adjustment, exploiting the sparse structure leads a much more efficient implementation. In [193], a first-order approximation was used to eliminate the structure parameters $\{\mathrm{P}_k\}$, thus resulting in a much smaller minimization problem.

In most practical problems, not all possible values of parameters $\hat{C}$ are acceptable, and it is often necessary or desirable to impose constraints. There are many forms of constraints: linear or nonlinear, equality or inequality. The reader is referred to [57] for various techniques to deal with constrained optimization problems. One useful case is when a parameter c_m is subject to bounds: $l_m \leq c_m \leq u_m$. This case arises when one uses the linear space of deformation vectors where there are natural lower and upper bounds on each model coefficient (Section 2.3.2).

For each such constraint, we can add to (5.15) two penalty terms for the lower and upper bound. For the lower bound, the penalty term is defined by

$$p_m = \begin{cases} 0 & \text{if } c_m \geq l_m; \\ \rho(l_m - c_m)^2 & \text{otherwise,} \end{cases}$$

where the nonnegative value ρ is the penalty parameter.

If we use a statistic model constructed from a set of face meshes (Section 2.3.1), we can use the prior to impose the constraints on the model coefficients as indicated in (2.5). That is, we add the term $-\log(\Pr(c_1, \ldots, c_m))$ to (5.15).

5.1.6.2 Comparison between CBA and MBA

Compared with the classical point-based bundle adjustment (CBA), the model-based bundle adjustment (5.15) (MBA) has a similar form except that it contains model parameters $\hat{C}$, and points P_k are constrained on $\mathcal{S}(\hat{C})$. In CBA, there are no model parameters but points P_k are free. Although it appears that MBA has more parameters to estimate, the actual number of free parameters is usually smaller because of the constraint on points P_k. Indeed, the total number of free parameters in CBA is equal to $6(N-1) - 1 + 3P$ ("-1" is due to the fact that the global scale cannot be determined), while the total number of free parameters in MBA is equal to $6(N-1) - 1 + M + 2P$ because each point on a surface has 2 degrees of freedom. As long as $P > M$ (the number of feature tracks is larger than that of model parameters), the parameter space for MBA is smaller than for CBA. In a typical setup, $P > 1500$ while $M = 71$.

5.1.6.3 Experimental results

The reader is referred to [193] for a comparison between the MBA algorithm and the classical bundle adjustment. In this section, we only show how the MBA improves the initial face models.

A typical sequence contains 23 to 26 images of resolution 640×480. The number of feature tracks ranges from 1,500 to 2,400. There are 50 to 150 image matches between each pair of neighboring views. For each sequence, the total running time of the MBA algorithm is about 6 to 8 minutes on a 850-MHz Pentium III machine. We have already seen an example in Section 5.1.2. Two more examples are shown later. For each example, we show both the initial

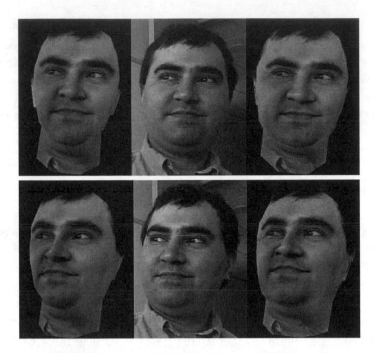

Figure 5.19. First textured face model. Left: initial guess; Middle: original images; Right: MBA.

guesses (results from the rapid face-modeling system) and the final results from the MBA algorithm.

The first example is shown in Figure 5.19. The left column is the initial guess. The right column is the result from the MBA algorithm. The images in the middle are the acquired images. We can see that the face of the initial guess is too narrow compared to the actual face, and there is a clear improvement with the result from the MBA algorithm.

The second example is shown in Figure 5.20. We can see that the profile of the initial guess is quite different from the actual person. With MBA, the profile closely matches the profile of the actual person.

5.1.7 *More experimental results*

It was reported in [268] that they have constructed 3D face models for well over two hundred people. They did live demonstrations at ACM Multimedia 2000, ACM1, CHI2001, ICCV2001 and other events such as the 20th anniversary of the PC, where they set up a booth to construct face models for visitors. At each of these events, the success rate was 90% or higher. In ACM1, most of the

Figure 5.20. Second textured face model. Left: initial guess; Middle: original images; Right: MBA.

visitors are kids or teenagers. The kids are usually more difficult to model since they have smooth skins, but their system worked very well. They observed that the main factor for the occasional failure is the head turning too fast.

In their live demonstrations, the optional model-based bundle adjustment was not conducted because it was quite time consuming (about 6 to 8 minutes on a 850-MHz Pentium III machine). Without that step, their system took approximately one minute after data-capture and manual marking to generate a textured face model. Most of this time is spent on head tracking in the video sequences. All the results shown in this section were produced in this way.

Figure 5.21 shows side-by-side comparisons of eight reconstructed models with the real images. Figure 5.22 shows the reconstructed face models of their group members immersed in a virtualized environment. In these examples, the video sequences were taken using ordinary video camera in people's offices or in live demonstrations. No special lighting equipment or background was used.

Note that in Figure 5.22, the eyes on the face mesh were cropped out, and textured eyeball models were automatically placed behind the eye regions of the face mesh so that the eyeballs can rotate thus generating eye gaze animation. A generic eyeball mesh and generic eye texture image were predesigned. After a face model is reconstructed, the system scales the generic eyeball mesh based on the size of the eye region in the reconstructed face mesh. A color transformation is applied to the generic eye texture to match the person's eye color. As one can see from Figure 5.22, it is a challenging problem to make the synthesized eyeballs look natural and consistent with the person's eye color.

5.2 Stereovision approach

Face-modeling systems that use stereovision approaches usually have two or more cameras. We will limit our discussions to the two camera case. It is

Figure 5.21. Side-by-side comparison of the original images with the reconstructed models of various people in various environment settings.

assumed that either the transformation matrices between the two cameras are known or the fundamental matrix is known. If the transformation matrices are known, one can obtain the fundamental matrix as follows. Let $\mathbf{A}$ and $\mathbf{A}'$ denote the internal parameter matrices of the two cameras, respectively. Let $\mathbf{R}$ and $\mathbf{t}$ denote the rotation matrix and translation vector of the second camera with respect to the first camera. Denote $\mathbf{P} = A(I_{3 \times 3} \quad \mathbf{0})$ and $\mathbf{P}' = A'(\mathbf{R} \quad \mathbf{t})$. The pseudo-inverse of $\mathbf{P}$ is $\mathbf{P}^{+} = \begin{pmatrix} A^{-1} \\ \mathbf{0}^{T} \end{pmatrix}$. Denote $\widetilde{\mathsf{C}} = \begin{pmatrix} \mathbf{0} \\ 1 \end{pmatrix}$. The fundamental matrix is

$$F = [\mathbf{P}'\widetilde{\mathsf{C}}]_{\times} \mathbf{P}'\mathbf{P}^{+}. \tag{5.17}$$

Alternatively, one could obtain the fundamental matrix from a set of point correspondences on the two images. The simplest method is the normalized eight-point algorithm. The readers are referred to [88] for details.

Figure 5.22. Face models of computer vision group members at Microsoft Research in a virtualized environment. The eye regions of the face mesh were cropped out, and textured eyeball models were automatically placed behind the eye regions of the face mesh so that the eyeballs can rotate.

Given a fundamental matrix, the next step is to rectify the two images so that (1) the epipolar lines on the rectified images are parallel to the x-axis, and (2) each pair of epipolar lines corresponding to the same y-coordinate on the two rectified images match each other. As a result, the disparities are along the x-direction only.

To perform rectification, one needs to find two 2D projective transformations (3×3 matrices) and apply them to the two images, respectively. The projective transformations can be computed from the fundamental matrix [88, 136].

After rectification, we need to compute the disparity map. For every pixel location (u, v) on the first image (after rectification), the goal is to compute a disparity value $d = d(u, v)$ so that the pixel (u, v) on the first image matches the pixel $(u + d(u, v), v)$ on the second image. Chen and Medioni [32] developed a stereovision-based face-modeling system where the disparity map $d(u, v)$ is computed by the following procedure. First, a similarity field $\Phi(u, v, d)$ is computed over a 3D volume in (u, v, d) space, where $\Phi(u, v, d)$ is defined as the cross-correlation between the subwindow centered at (u, v) on the first image and the subwindow centered at $(u + d(u, v), v)$ on the second image. Second, the disparity map $d(u, v)$ is extracted out by starting with a set of seed voxels (e.g., provided semiautomatically) and tracing locally maximal voxels to gradually expand the surface. Finally, a quadratic fitting is performed at each voxel to obtain subpixel resolution.

From the disparity map, we obtain a 3D point cloud. The points are usually noisy, and there might be holes and spikes. In addition, many applications require registration of the point clouds with a face model. Therefore a post-processing step is needed to clean up the point cloud and register with a face model. This can be done by using techniques presented in [121, 122].

Note that the stereo reconstruction method does not use any prior knowledge on faces. One could inject a face model representation into the stereo reconstruction process to improve the robustness. In fact, this is a special case of the model-based bundle adjustment formulation of (5.16) in Section 5.1.6. Since camera motions are known, we only need to solve for the face model coefficients C in (5.16).

5.3 Two orthogonal views

A number of researchers have proposed to create face models from two orthogonal views [2, 40, 96]: one frontal view and one side view. The frontal view provides the information relative to the horizontal and vertical axis, whereas the side view provides depth information. A number of feature points are needed on both views. The feature points are typically the points around face features including eyebrows, eyes, nose, and mouth. The feature points on the front view could be obtained automatically by using face alignment techniques such as those presented in [126, 243]. But it is more challenging to automatically detect face feature points for the side views. Some systems provide a semiautomatic interface for marking the feature points to reduce the amount of manual work.

Due to occlusions, some feature points on the front view may not be visible on the side view, and vice versa. If a feature point appears on the front view but not on the side view, only its x- and y-coordinates can be obtained directly while its z-coordinate needs to be inferred. Furthermore, the number of feature points (obtained automatically or manually) is usually quite small. Therefore, it is necessary to infer the rest of the points on the face mesh. A parametric face geometry representation with small number of parameters is useful for both tasks.

Suppose we use a linear space representation as in Equation (2.4). Let $\mathbf{p}_i = (x_{1,i}, y_{1,i})$ denote the feature points on the front view, and let P_i denote the 3D point on the face model that corresponds to $\mathbf{p}_i$. Let $\mathbf{q}_j = (y_{2,j}, z_{2,j})$ denote the feature points on the side view, and let Q_j denote the 3D point on the face model that corresponds to $\mathbf{q}_j$. Note that P_i and Q_j are linear functions of the coefficients $C = (c_1, \ldots, c_m)^T$. Denote $P_i = f_i(C)$ and $Q_j = g_j(C)$ where f_i and g_j are linear functions of C. We have the following equations:

$$\begin{pmatrix} 1 & 0 & 0 \\ 0 & 1 & 0 \end{pmatrix} f_i(C) = a_1 \begin{pmatrix} x_{1,i} \\ y_{1,i} \end{pmatrix} + \begin{pmatrix} t_{x_1} \\ t_{y_1} \end{pmatrix}, \qquad (5.18)$$

$$\begin{pmatrix} 0 & 1 & 0 \\ 0 & 0 & 1 \end{pmatrix} g_j(C) = a_2 \begin{pmatrix} y_{2,j} \\ z_{2,j} \end{pmatrix} + \begin{pmatrix} t_{x_2} \\ t_{y_2} \end{pmatrix}, \qquad (5.19)$$

where a_1 and a_2 are the unknown scaling factors of the two image coordinates and $\begin{pmatrix} t_{x_1} \\ t_{y_1} \end{pmatrix}$ and $\begin{pmatrix} t_{x_2} \\ t_{y_2} \end{pmatrix}$ are the unknown translations.

Given enough feature points, Equations (5.18) and (5.19) can be solved by a linear system solver. But if the number of feature points is small, a more stable solution is to use an iterative approach. First, we set C to be zero and solve for $a_1, a_2, \begin{pmatrix} t_{x_1} \\ t_{y_1} \end{pmatrix}$, and $\begin{pmatrix} t_{x_2} \\ t_{y_2} \end{pmatrix}$. That is, we use the average face model to estimate the translations and scalings. Second, we fix $a_1, a_2, \begin{pmatrix} t_{x_1} \\ t_{y_1} \end{pmatrix}$, and $\begin{pmatrix} t_{x_2} \\ t_{y_2} \end{pmatrix}$, and solve for C. Let r denote the rank of the linear system. If $m > r$, we can set $c_{r+1}, \ldots, c_m$ to be zeros and solve for $c_1, \ldots, c_r$. We can then fix C and refine $a_1, a_2, \begin{pmatrix} t_{x_1} \\ t_{y_1} \end{pmatrix}$ and $\begin{pmatrix} t_{x_2} \\ t_{y_2} \end{pmatrix}$, and so on. Usually two to three iterations is sufficient.

Figure 5.23 shows two orthogonal views. The feature points on the front view are computed automatically. The feature points on the side view are provided manually. Figure 5.24 shows the reconstructed 3D face model by using a linear

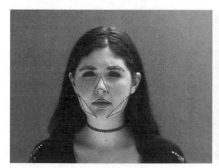

Figure 5.23. Example of shape modeling from two orthogonal views. Left: front view where the markers are detected automatically. Right: side view where the markers are provided manually.

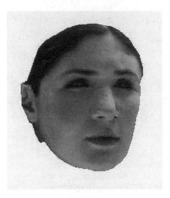

Figure 5.24. The resulting 3D face model constructed from the two images in Figure 5.23.

space representation where the basis vectors are manually designed as described in Section 2.3.2.

5.4 A single view

In this section, we consider the situation where there is only a single view available and the pose of the face is unknown. We assume there is a set of face feature points available. As mentioned earlier, face feature points can be obtained either automatically by using face alignment techniques or manually. Let $Q_j, j = 1, \ldots, Q$ denote the face feature points on the 3D face model. Let $\mathbf{q}_j$ denote the 2D coordinates of the feature points on the image. Let $\widetilde{Q}_j$ and $\widetilde{\mathbf{q}}_j$ denote the homogeneous coordinates of Q_j and $\mathbf{q}_j$, respectively. The projection equation (1.1) yields

$$\lambda \widetilde{\mathbf{q}}_j = \mathbf{APM}\widetilde{Q}_j, \tag{5.20}$$

where $\mathbf{A}$ is the camera intrinsic parameter matrix, $\mathbf{P}$ is the perspective projection matrix, and $\mathbf{M}$ is the 3D rigid transformation matrix (rotation and translation). We assume the intrinsic parameter matrix is known. In case the intrinsic parameters are not available, one can generate an intrinsic parameter matrix by using a reasonable focal length value and assuming the image center to be the principal point.

As in (1.2), we use $\boldsymbol{\phi}$ to denote the nonlinear 3D-2D projection function defined in (5.20). That is,

$$\mathbf{q}_j = \boldsymbol{\phi}(\mathbf{M}, Q_j). \tag{5.21}$$

Let $\mathbf{D}_j$ denote the semantic coordinate of the point on the face model that corresponds to face feature point Q_j. From (2.13), we have

$$Q_j = \mathbf{D}_j \mathcal{S}, \tag{5.22}$$

where $\mathcal{S}$ is a linear function of the geometric model coefficients C.
Combining (5.21) and (5.22), we obtain

$$\mathbf{q}_j = \boldsymbol{\phi}(\mathbf{M}, \mathbf{D}_j \mathcal{S}). \tag{5.23}$$

We can then solve (5.23) using an iterative procedure.

First, we set C to zero and evaluate $\mathcal{S}$ and subsequently Q_j from (5.22). Pose matrix $\mathbf{M}$ can be obtained from the 3D-2D correspondence of (5.20) by using a method described in Section 10.1.2.

Second, we fix $\mathbf{M}$ in (5.23) and solve for C. Without loss of generality, we assume A to be an identity matrix. Denote

$$\mathbf{M} = \begin{pmatrix} \mathbf{R} & \mathbf{t} \\ \mathbf{0}^T & 1 \end{pmatrix},$$

where $\mathbf{R} = (R_1, R_2, R_3)^T$ and $\mathbf{t} = (t_x, t_y, t_z)$. Denote $\mathbf{q}_j = (u_j, v_j)^T$. (5.23) can be written as

$$\frac{R_1^T (\mathbf{D}_j \mathcal{S}^0 + \sum_{i=1}^m c_i \mathbf{D}_j \mathcal{M}^i) + t_x}{R_3^T (\mathbf{D}_j \mathcal{S}^0 + \sum_{i=1}^m c_i \mathbf{D}_j \mathcal{M}^i) + t_z} = u_j, \tag{5.24}$$

$$\frac{R_2^T (\mathbf{D}_j \mathcal{S}^0 + \sum_{i=1}^m c_i \mathbf{D}_j \mathcal{M}^i) + t_y}{R_3^T (\mathbf{D}_j \mathcal{S}^0 + \sum_{i=1}^m c_i \mathbf{D}_j \mathcal{M}^i) + t_z} = v_j. \tag{5.25}$$

By multiplying the denominator on both sides of the equations, we obtain their linear forms

$$R_1^T \left(\mathbf{D}_j \mathcal{S}^0 + \sum_{i=1}^m c_i \mathbf{D}_j \mathcal{M}^i \right) + t_x = u_j \left(R_3^T (\mathbf{D}_j \mathcal{S}^0 + \sum_{i=1}^m c_i \mathbf{D}_j \mathcal{M}^i) + t_z \right),$$

$$\tag{5.26}$$

$$R_2^T \left(\mathbf{D}_j \mathcal{S}^0 + \sum_{i=1}^{m} c_i \mathbf{D}_j \mathcal{M}^i \right) + t_y = v_j \left(R_3^T (\mathbf{D}_j \mathcal{S}^0 + \sum_{i=1}^{m} c_i \mathbf{D}_j \mathcal{M}^i) + t_z \right).$$

$$(5.27)$$

With simple algebraic manipulations, we obtain

$$\sum_{i=1}^{m} c_i (R_1^T - u_j R_3^T) \mathbf{D}_j \mathcal{M}^i = (u_j R_3^T - R_1^T) \mathbf{D}_j \mathcal{S}^0 + u_j t_z - t_x, \qquad (5.28)$$

$$\sum_{i=1}^{m} c_i (R_2^T - v_j R_3^T) \mathbf{D}_j \mathcal{M}^i = (v_j R_3^T - R_2^T) \mathbf{D}_j \mathcal{S}^0 + v_j t_z - t_y. \qquad (5.29)$$

Thus, C can be obtained by solving this linear system of equations.

Figure 5.25. Example of shape modeling from a single image. Left: input image. Right: result of image alignment.

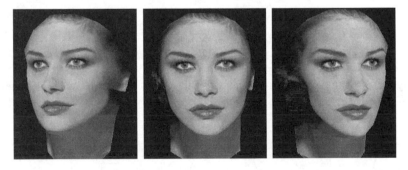

Figure 5.26. Different views of the 3D model reconstructed from the input image in Figure 5.25.

After we obtain C, we fix it and reestimate **M** as described in the first step, and the iteration continues.

Since there is only a single view, the depth of the reconstructed model is in general not accurate. In Chapter 7, we will describe techniques that use shading information to refine the geometry.

Figure 5.25 shows an example. The left is the input image, and the right is the feature alignment result. Figure 5.26 shows different views of the reconstructed 3D model.

6

Appearance modeling

In addition to its shape, the image of an object also depends on its surface reflectance properties and the lighting environment. In this chapter, we describe techniques to recover the reflectance properties and lighting environment. These techniques usually assume that the geometry of the object is known.

6.1 Reflectometry

Refectometry is the measurement of a material's reflectance property which can be represented as a four-dimensional Bidirectional Reflectance Distribution function, or BRDF. A device for measuring BRDFs is called a *gonioreflectometer*. One such device was designed by Murray-Coleman and Smith [154]. It consists of a photometer that moves relative to the material to be measured. The material moves relative to a light source. All the motions are controlled by a computer.

A simpler device, called imaging gonioreflectometer, was developed at Lawrence Berkeley Laboratory [229]. It uses a fish-eye lens camera and a half-silvered hemisphere to replace the mechanically controlled photometer. In this way, it only needs one mechanical driver that pivots the light source. This device is much easier to build, and the capturing is much faster than the one built by Murray-Coleman and Smith [154]. Since the captured data are usually noisy and incomplete, Ward [229] proposed a parametric function, called an anisotropic Gaussian model, to represent the BRDF. The parametric function consists of four parameters, which are determined by fitting the parametric function to the data captured by the imaging gonioreflectometer.

6.1.1 Uniform BRDF

Marschner et al. [144] proposed an image-based BRDF measurement system as shown in Figure 6.1. The setup is much simpler than the imaging

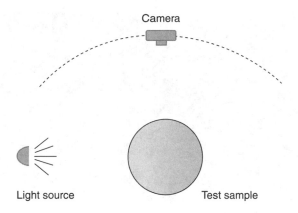

Figure 6.1. The BRDF measurement setup proposed by Marschner et al. [144].

gonioreflectometer developed by Lawrence Berkeley Laboratory in that it does not require a half-silvered hemisphere and a wide-angle lens. The geometry of the measured object is assumed to be known (e.g., obtained by using a laser scanner). In addition, they assume that the surface of the object is curved and all the points on the measured object have the same BRDF (i.e., uniform BRDF). For a fixed position of the light source and the camera, each pixel in the image captures the reflectance measurement corresponding to a different surface normal. Therefore, if we focus on a single point on the surface, a single image provides all the reflectance measurements of this point after going through arbitrary rotations with respect to the light source. Therefore, there is no need to move the light source. In order to obtain a full four-dimensional BRDF, they would need to take images for all the camera positions on a two-dimensional grid. To reduce the amount of images that need to be taken, they further assume an isotropic BRDF. That is, the reflectance is independent of rotating the incident and view directions about the surface normal. In order words (see Figure 3.1 in Section 3.1.1),

$$\rho(\theta_i, \phi_i, \theta_r, \phi_r) = \rho(\theta_i, 0, \theta_r, \phi_r - \phi_i). \tag{6.1}$$

This reduces one degree of freedom. Therefore, they only need to move the camera along one degree of freedom, which significantly simplifies the hardware setup and reduces the capturing time.

To obtain the BRDF measurement from the captured data, a calibration procedure is required. It consists of geometric calibration and radiometric calibration. The geometric calibration determines the relative geometric positions of the light source, the measured object, and the camera. It also needs to track the camera positions as it moves. In their implementation, Marschner et al. [144]

Figure 6.2. A snapshot of the BRDF measurement. Courtesy of Marschner et al. [144].

used predefined 3D patterns to simplify the geometric calibration task. The radiometric calibration determines the radiance reflected to the camera and the irradiance due to the light source. For the details of geometric and radiometric calibration procedures, the readers are referred to [144].

Figure 6.2 is a snapshot of a BRDF measurement session [144] where the BRDF of the child's forehead skin is measured. The child wears a pattern which is used to track the child's head pose. From their measured BRDF data on multiple people's skin, Marschner et al. [144] observed that human skin's BRDF is almost Lambertian for small incident angles θ_i. But for larger incident angles, the reflectance is neither Lambertian nor specular. Furthermore, it cannot be explained by the Torrance-Sparrow reflectance model either.

6.1.2 *Spatially varying BRDF*

Debevec et al. [43] developed a system to capture spatially varying reflectance properties of a human face's skin area. Instead of assuming a uniform BRDF as in [144], Debevec et al. allows the reflectance properties to vary from point to point on the face. The tradeoff is that they do not obtain a full BRDF for each point on the face.

For each point on the surface, its BRDF is a four-dimensional function. Let (u, v) denote the parametric coordinates of the points on the surface. Then the spatially varying BRDF can be written as a six-dimensional function

$$\rho_{(u,v)}(\theta_i, \phi_i, \theta_r, \phi_r) = f(u, v, \theta_i, \phi_i, \theta_r, \phi_r). \tag{6.2}$$

Figure 6.3. A snapshot of the reflectance field acquisition system developed by Debevec et al.Courtesy of Debevec et al. [43] by permission of Mitsubishi Electric Research Laboratories, Inc.

To capture a full BRDF for each point, one would need a two-dimensional array of light sources, and a two-dimensional array of cameras.

Figure 6.3 is a snapshot of the system built by Debevec et al. [43]. It consists of a two-axis rotation system that controls the motion of a directional light source. This accounts for the two-dimensional array of light sources. But the system consists of only a sparse set of cameras. As a result, they do not obtain a full BRDF. They instead model a reflectance function as a Lambertian component plus a specular component as shown in (3.6) where the specular component was represented by the Torrance-Sparrow model. The parameters of the reflectance functions are estimated through data fitting. The details are referred to [43].

6.1.3 Subsurface scattering

The BRDF model is in fact a simplification of a more general bidirectional surface scattering distribution function (BSSRDF). BRDF model assumes that a light ray that enters a surface at a point will leave the surface at the same point. This is valid for metals, but not for materials that exhibit translucent appearance such as human skin. For translucent materials, the light, after entering a material, may scatter multiple times inside the material before leaves the material. While a spatially varying BRDF is a six-dimensional function (Equation (6.2)), a spatially varying BSSRDF is a eight-dimensional function: $f(u_i, v_i, \theta_i, \phi_i, u_r, v_r, \theta_r, \phi_r)$ where (u_i, v_i) specifies the position where the incident light ray enters the surface, and (u_r, v_r) specified the position where the light ray leaves the surface. A simplified BSSRDF model was proposed by Jensen et al. [103].

As pointed out in [43, 83, 238], human skins consist of three layers: oil layer, epidermis layer, and dermis layer. The oil layer is responsible for the specular reflectance. The epidermis layer and dermis layer are responsible for the diffuse reflectance due to subsurface scattering. Hanrahan and Krueger [83] developed a reflectance model for such layered surfaces that take into account of surface scattering. Based on the BSSRDF model developed by Jensen et al. [102, 103], Weyrich et al. [237, 238] represented the skin reflectance as three components: specular component due to the oil layer, an diffuse albedo component due to the epidermis layer, and a translucent component due to the dermis layer. The specular component is represented as a BRDF. The diffuse component is represented by an albedo map, while the translucent component is represented by a translucent map. They developed a system to measure the reflectance parameters. Figure 6.4 shows the light dome they built for image capturing (courtesy of Weyrich et al. [238]). It consists of 150 LED light sources, and

Figure 6.4. A snapshot of the face-scanning dome developed by Weyrich et al. for measuring skin reflectance. Courtesy of Weyrich et al. [238].

16 digital cameras. A 3D face-scanning system was used to obtain the 3D geometry of the subject. The parameters of the specular reflectance and the diffuse albedo map are estimated from the captured images. The parameters for the translucent map are obtained by using a dedicated subsurface measurement device.

6.2 Reconstruction of irradiance environment maps

The techniques that are discussed in the previous section recover the surface reflectance properties while assuming that both the geometry and lighting are known. Those techniques typically require hardware setup. In this section, we describe a technique, developed by Wen et al. [236], that estimates the lighting from a single face image under the assumption that the 3D face geometry is known and the skin reflectance is Lambertian.

By following the notation of Section 3.2, for any given point P on the face, let N denote its normal and ρ denote its albedo. From Equation (3.11), the reflected radiance at P is

$$I = \rho E(N). \tag{6.3}$$

Note that $E(N)$ is a function of N, but ρ is a function of P. In the following, we treat ρ as a function of N with the understanding that when there are multiple points, P_1, ..., P_n, whose normals are equal to the same normal N, then the average albedo of these points, $\frac{1}{n}\sum_{i=1}^{n}\rho(P_i)$, is used as the albedo $\rho(N)$. In this way, we treat I as a function of N as well.

From Equation (3.16), we represent the irradiance as a linear combination of the first nine spherical harmonics basis functions:

$$E(N) = \sum_{0 \le l \le 2, -l \le m \le l} L_{l,m} Y_{l,m}(N). \tag{6.4}$$

We can expand the albedo $\rho(N)$ using spherical harmonics as

$$\rho(N) = \rho_{00} + \Psi(N), \tag{6.5}$$

where ρ_{00} is the constant component, and $\Psi(N)$ contains other higher-order components. (6.5) and (6.4) yield

$$
\begin{aligned}
I(N) &= \rho(N)E(N) \\
&= [\rho_{00} + \Psi(N)]\left[\sum_{0 \le l \le 2, -l \le m \le l} L_{l,m} Y_{l,m}(N)\right] \\
&= \rho_{00}\sum_{0 \le l \le 2, -l \le m \le l} L_{l,m} Y_{l,m}(N) + \Psi(N)\sum_{0 \le l \le 2, -l \le m \le l} L_{l,m} Y_{l,m}(N).
\end{aligned} \tag{6.6}
$$

Theorem 1 *If* $\Psi(\mathrm{N})$ *does not contain any components of order less than or equal to 4, then* $\Psi(\mathrm{N}) \sum_{0 \le l \le 2, -l \le m \le l} L_{l,m} Y_{l,m}(\mathrm{N})$ *does not contain any components of order less than or equal to 2.*

Proof According to [35], the multiplication of two spherical harmonic basis functions satisfies the following relation

$$Y_{l_1,m_1}(\mathrm{N}) Y_{l_2,m_2}(\mathrm{N})$$

$$= \sum_{l=|l_1-l_2|}^{l_1+l_2} \sum_{m=-l}^{l} \{C\langle l_1,l_2 : 0,0|l,0\rangle \cdot C\langle l_1,l_2 : m_1,m_2|l,m\rangle Y_{l,m}(\mathrm{N})\}, \qquad (6.7)$$

where $C\langle l_1,l_2 : m_1,m_2 | l,m \rangle$ are the Clebsch-Gordan coefficients. Furthermore, the coefficient of $Y_{l,m}(\mathrm{N})$ on the right-hand side is nonzero if and only if $m = m_1 + m_2$, l range from $|l_1 - l_2|$ to $l_1 + l_2$ and $l_1 + l_2 - l$ is even.

In (6.6), if we expand $\Psi(\mathrm{N}) \sum_{0 \le l \le 2, -l \le m \le l} L_{l,m} Y_{l,m}(\mathrm{N})$, each term is of the form $Y_{l_1,m_1}(\mathrm{N}) Y_{l_2,m_2}(\mathrm{N})$, where $Y_{l_1,m_1}(\mathrm{N})$ comes from $\Psi(\mathrm{N})$ and $Y_{l_2,m_2}(\mathrm{N})$ comes from $\sum_{0 \le l \le 2, -l \le m \le l} L_{l,m} Y_{l,m}(\mathrm{N})$. Thus, $0 \le l_2 \le 2$. Since $\Psi(\mathrm{N})$ does not contain any components of order less than or equal to 4, we have $l_1 \ge 5$. Therefore, $|l_1 - l_2| \ge 3$. From (6.7), we can see that all the nonzero terms have $l \ge |l_1 - l_2| \ge 3$. Thus, $Y_{l_1,m_1}(\mathrm{N}) Y_{l_2,m_2}(\mathrm{N})$ does not contain any terms of order less than or equal to 2. ∥

Theorem 1 states that if the face albedo does not contain any lower-frequency components (except the constant component), then the first nine harmonic components in the expansion of $I(\mathrm{N})$ is equal to the irradiance environment map $E(\mathrm{N})$ times the average albedo ρ_{00}. We hypothesize that human face skins are approximately this type of surfaces. Intuitively, the skin color of a person's face has dominant constant component, but there are some fine details corresponding to high-frequency components in frequency domain. Therefore, the first four order components must be very small. To verify this, Wen et al. [236] used Spharmonickit [201] to compute the spherical harmonic coefficients for the function $\rho(\mathrm{N})$ of the albedo map shown in Figure 6.5, which was obtained by Marschner et al. [143]. There are normals that are not sampled by the albedo map, where they assigned $\rho(\mathbf{n})$ the mean of existing samples. They found that the coefficients of order $1,2,3,4$ components are less than 6% of the constant coefficient.

We call $I_{sphere} = \rho_{00} E(\mathrm{N})$ a *pseudo irradiance environment map*, which is an irradiance environment map scaled by a constant color (i.e., the average albedo ρ_{00}). To obtain I_{sphere}, we can decompose the image $I(\mathrm{N})$ into a linear combination of the spherical harmonic basis functions and the first nine components are the pseudo irradiance environment map. Let $h_1, h_2, ..., h_9$ denote the first nine basis functions, their coefficients can be obtained by solving the following

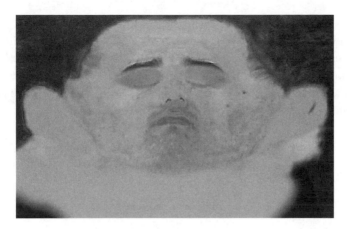

Figure 6.5. A face albedo map.

linear system

$$I(\mathrm{N}) = \sum_{0 \le l \le 2, -l \le m \le l} L_{l,m} Y_{l,m}, \tag{6.8}$$

where $L_{0,0}$, $L_{1,-1}$, $L_{1,0}$, $L_{1,1}$, $L_{2,-2}$, $L_{2,-1}$, $L_{2,0}$, $L_{2,1}$, and $L_{2,2}$ are the nine coefficients to be solved. Note that we have an equation for every pixel in the face skin region; therefore, the number of equations is usually much larger than the number of unknowns. However, if the face is frontal, the system is actually underconstrained because there are no equations corresponding to back-faced normals. To produce visually plausible results without conflicting with the information provided by the frontal image, we can make assumptions about lighting in the back to better constrain the problem. One assumption is a symmetric lighting environment, that is, the back has the same lighting distribution as the front. This assumption is equivalent to assuming $L_{l,m} = 0$, for $(l,m) = (1,0),(2,-1)$, and $(2,1)$ in (6.8). The other five coefficients can then be solved uniquely according to [176]. This assumption works well for the lighting environments where the lights mainly come from two sides of the face. A different assumption is that the back is dark. This works well if the lights mainly come from the front of the face.

6.2.1 *Face relighting with pseudo irradiance environment maps*

The pseudo irradiance environment maps can be used for face relighting. We describe two different types of face relighting applications in the section. The first is to rotate the face in the same lighting environment. The second is to transfer the lighting environment from one face image to another.

6.2.1.1 Rotating the face in the same lighting environment

When a face is rotated in the same lighting environment, the intensity of the face at each point will change due to the incident lighting changes. For any given point P on the face, let N denote its normal before rotation, and N' its normal after rotation. Let ρ denote the albedo at P. Let I and I' denote the image intensity before and after rotation, respectively. (6.3) yields

$$
\begin{aligned}
I &= \rho E(N), \\
I' &= \rho E(N').
\end{aligned}
\tag{6.9}
$$

Therefore,

$$
\frac{I'}{I} = \frac{E(N')}{E(N)}.
\tag{6.10}
$$

Multiplying the top and bottom by ρ_{00} in (6.10), we have

$$
\frac{E(N')}{E(N)} = \frac{\rho_{00} E(N')}{\rho_{00} E(N)} = \frac{I_{sphere}(N')}{I_{sphere}(N)}.
\tag{6.11}
$$

Thus,

$$
\frac{I'}{I} = \frac{I_{sphere}(N')}{I_{sphere}(N)}.
\tag{6.12}
$$

What this equation means is that for any point on the face, the ratio between its intensity after rotation and its intensity before rotation is equal to the intensity ratio of two points on the pseudo irradiance environment map. In other words, the image intensity after rotation can be obtained by multiplying the image intensity before rotation with the intensity ratio:

$$
I' = \frac{I_{sphere}(N')}{I_{sphere}(N)} \cdot I.
\tag{6.13}
$$

A generic face mesh, as shown in Figure 6.6a, is used as the geometry of the face. Figure 6.6b shows the feature points, which are used to align an image with the generic mesh. Figure 6.7 shows an example of rotating the face in the lighting environment. Since we always display the frontal face, it is better to think of it as the lighting environment is rotating. In Figure 6.7, the middle image is the input image. The pseudo irradiance environment map is shown below the input image. It is computed by assuming the back is dark since the lights mostly come from the frontal directions. The rest of the images in the sequence show the relighting results when the lighting environment rotates. Below each image, we show the corresponding rotated pseudo irradiance environment map. The environment rotates approximately 45° between each two images, a total of

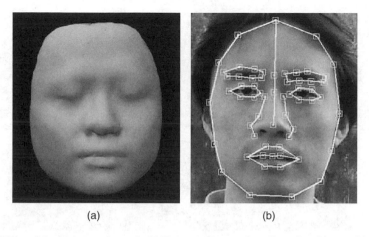

(a)   (b)

Figure 6.6. (a) A generic mesh. (b) Feature points used to align a face image with the generic mesh.

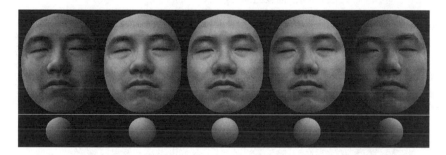

Figure 6.7. The middle image is the input. The sequence shows synthesized results of 180° rotation of the lighting environment.

180° rotation. From the middle image to the right in the image sequence, the frontal environment turns to the person's left side. On the fourth image, we can see that part of his right face gets darker. On the last image, a larger region on his right face becomes darker. This is consistent with the rotation of the lighting environment.

Figure 6.8 shows a different person in a similar lighting environment. Again, the generic mesh in Figure 6.6a is used to compute its pseudo irradiance environment map. For this example, the ground truth images are captured at various rotation angles for a side-by-side comparison. The top row images are the ground truth images, while the images at the bottom are the synthesized results with the middle image as the input. We can see that the synthesized results match very well with the ground truth images. There are some small differences mainly

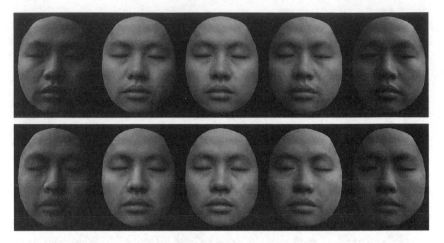

Figure 6.8. The comparison of synthesized results and ground truth. The top row is the ground truth. The bottom row is the synthesized result, where the middle image is the input. (See plate section for color version.)

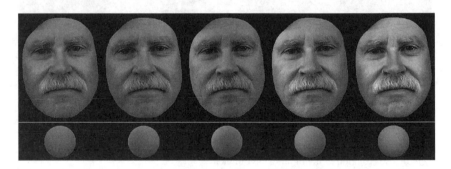

Figure 6.9. The middle image is the input. The sequence shows a 180° rotation of the lighting environment. (See plate section for color version.)

on the first and last images due to specular reflections. (According to Marschner et al. [144], human skin is almost Lambertian at small light incidence angles and has strong non-Lambertian scattering at higher angles.)

Figure 6.9 shows another example. Again, the middle image is the input and the generic face mesh is used as the 3D geometry. In this example, the lights mainly come from two sides of the face. The bright white light on the person's right face comes from sky light and the reddish light on his left face comes from the sunlight reflected by a red-brick building. The pseudo irradiance environment map is computed based on a symmetric lighting assumption. The image sequence shows a 180° rotation of the lighting environment.

6.2.1.2 Lighting transfer

Given two face images I and I' of two different people under two different lighting environment. We would like to change the lighting condition of the first image so that it matches the lighting condition of the second image. In other words, we would like to transfer the lighting environment of the second image to the first one. Let $E'(N)$ denote the irradiance environment map of the second image. Then the image that we would like to generate is

$$I'' = \rho E'. \tag{6.14}$$

Let I'_{sphere} denote the second image's pseudo irradiance environment map, and ρ'_{00} the second image's average albedo. Then

$$\frac{I''}{I} = \frac{\rho E'}{\rho E} = \frac{E'}{E} = \frac{\rho_{00} I'_{\text{sphere}}}{\rho'_{00} I_{\text{sphere}}}. \tag{6.15}$$

If we assume that the two people have similar average albedo, that is, $\rho_{00} \approx \rho'_{00}$, then Equation 6.15 yields

$$I'' \approx \frac{I'_{\text{sphere}}}{I_{\text{sphere}}} \cdot I. \tag{6.16}$$

This is the equation for lighting transfer between two face images. If the two people do not have similar average albedo, there will be a global color shift on the resulting image.

Figure 6.10 shows two examples of lighting transfer. In Figure 6.10a, we relight a female's face shown on the left to match the lighting condition of a male shown in the middle. The synthesized result is shown on the right. Notice the darker region on the right face of the middle image. The synthesized result shows similar lighting effects. Figure 6.10b shows an example of relighting a male's face to match the lighting condition of a different male's image. Again, the left and middle faces are input images. The image on the right is the synthesized result. From the middle image, we can see that the lighting on his left face is a lot stronger than the lighting on his right face. We see similar lighting effects on the synthesized result. In addition, the dark region due to attached shadow on the right face of the synthesized image closely matches the shadow region on the right face of the middle image.

6.2.1.3 Lighting editing

After obtaining the pseudo irradiance environment map for a given face image, one can edit the lighting of the image by interactively modifying the spherical harmonic coefficients. Each time when a coefficient is modified, a new pseudo

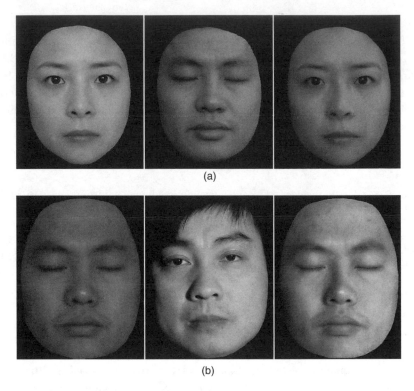

Figure 6.10. Relighting under different lighting. Left: Face to be relighted. Middle: Target face. Right: Result. (See plate section for color version.)

irradiance environment map is obtained. We can then use Equation (6.16) to compute the image under the modified lighting environment.

Figure 6.11 shows four examples of interactive lighting editing by modifying the spherical harmonics coefficients. For each example, the left image is the input image and the right image is the result after modifying the lighting. In Figure 6.11a, lighting is changed to attach shadow on the person's left face. In Figure 6.11b, the light on the person's right face is changed to be more reddish while the light on her left face becomes slightly more blueish. In c, the bright sunlight move from the person's left face to his right face. In (d), we attach shadow to the person's right face and change the light color as well. Such editing would be difficult to do with the currently existing tools such as *Photoshop*.

6.2.2 *Application to face recognition*

The face-relighting technique described in Section 6.2.1 can be used for face recognition to handle illumination variations. In face recognition, if a probe

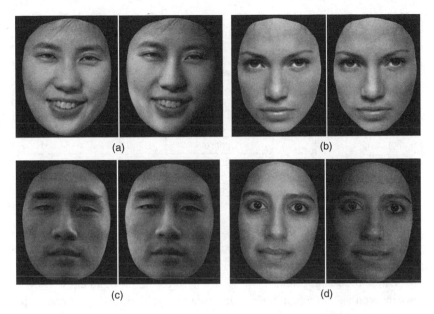

Figure 6.11. Interactive lighting editing by modifying the spherical harmonics coefficients of the pseudo irradiance environment map. (See plate section for color version.)

face image is taken under a different lighting condition from an image in the gallery (i.e., a database of registered face images), it will cause difficulties when one tries to match the probe image to a gallery image directly. One solution is to relight all the face images to a canonical lighting condition. This is an approach taken by Qing et al. [173, 174] who used the face relighting technique described in Section 6.2.1 for face recognition. We describe their face recognition experiments in the rest of the section.

Given that their main purpose was to validate the effect of face relighting, Qing et al. [173, 174] performed face recognition by simple normalized cross correlation between a probe image and a gallery image. They assumed that the images have been geometrically aligned. They did not use any geometric information for face recognition. Their experiments were conducted on two datasets: CMU-PIE face database [197] and Yale B face database [72].

The CMU-PIE dataset consists of two subsets: illumination subset and lighting subset. The images in the illumination subset were captured when the room lights were turned off and the subject did not wear glasses. The images in the lighting subset were captured when the room lights were turned on, and the subjects did not have to take off their glasses. In both subsets, there are 21 flashes to illuminate the faces, and the flash index numbers range from "02" to "21". Figure 6.12 shows their experiment results on the CMU-PIE dataset.

Gallery	Probe	Canonical illumination	Error rate (%)	
			Manual alignment	Loose alignment
Flash 11 illumination subset	Illumination subset	No relighting	47.1	47.1
		Uniform	4.0	13.7
		Frontal flash	3.4	13.5
Flash lighting subset	Lighting subset	No relighting	14.3	14.3
		Uniform	0.0	0.0
		Frontal flash	0.0	0.0

Figure 6.12. Face recognition results on CMU-PIE dataset. Courtesy of Qing et al. [174].

They chose images corresponding to flash number "11" in each subset as the gallery images. Note that only a single gallery image is used for each subset. The rest of the images in each subset are used as the probe images. The two rows marked as "no relighting" are the face recognition results without using face relighting. The rest of the rows are the results with face relighting where all the images were relit to a canonical illumination by using the method described in Section 6.2.1. They tested with two different types of canonical illumination conditions: (1) a uniform illumination (the rows marked as "uniform"), and (2) a frontal flash with the room lighting on (the rows marked as "frontal flash"). To measure the sensitivity to face alignment accuracy, they did experiments with two different face alignment methods: manual face alignment where face feature points are labeled manually, and a loose face alignment where the manually labeled eye locations are used to infer the locations of the rest of the face features. The last two columns are the face recognition error rates with manual alignment and loose alignment, respectively. From Figure 6.12, we can see that face relighting significantly improves face recognition performance.

The images in Yale B face database were divided into four subsets as in [72]. Each subset consists of images illuminated from a specific range of directions. For example, images in subset 1 are illuminated from near-frontal face directions, while images in subset 4 are illuminated from near-side directions. For each subject, the image taken with a frontal point source is used as the gallery image. Similar to their experiments on CMU-PIE dataset, Qing et al. [174] conducted experiments on Yale B dataset with two different types of canonical illumination conditions and two different alignment methods. Figure 6.13 shows the results with manual alignment. Figure 6.14 shows the results with loose alignment. Again, the results show that face relighting improves face

Canonical illumination	Error rate (%)			
	Subset 1	Subset 2	Subset 3	Subset 4
No relighting	0.0	2.5	25.0	60.0
Uniform	0.0	0.0	5.0	19.6
Frontal flash	0.0	0.0	0.0	10.0

Figure 6.13. Face recognition results on Yale B face database with manual alignment. Courtesy of Qing et al. [174].

Canonical illumination	Error rate (%)			
	Subset 1	Subset 2	Subset 3	Subset 4
No relighting	0.0	2.5	25.0	60.0
Uniform	0.0	0.0	8.3	20.0
Frontal flash	0.0	0.8	8.3	18.6

Figure 6.14. Face recognition results on Yale B face database with loose alignment. Courtesy of Qing et al. [174].

recognition performance significantly. It is also interesting to see that for faces in subset 4, the recognition performance is still not very good even after face relighting. This is because for images in this subset, the faces are illuminated from the side. As a result, half of the face is quite dark, while the other half is much brighter. In fact, some pixels in the dark region are under cast shadow, and some pixels in the bright region may be saturated. The face-relighting technique of Section 6.2.1 does not handle such harsh lighting conditions very well. In Section 7.5, we will describe a more sophisticated technique that is capable of handling harsh lighting conditions.

The results in Figure 6.13 are slightly worse than those of the illumination cone method [72], nine point light method [119], and harmonic exemplar method [255]. But these techniques typically require seven to nine gallery images per subject while the technique used in Qing et al. [174] only requires a single gallery image per subject. Compared with the illumination normalization method [224], which also uses a single gallery image, the results of Qing et al. [174] are better.

6.3 Illumination recovery from specular reflection

Section 6.2 completely ignores non-Lambertian reflections. As shown by Hanrahan and Krueger [83] and Marschner et al. [144], the reflection on human skin is in general not Lambertian when the light incident angle is large. In

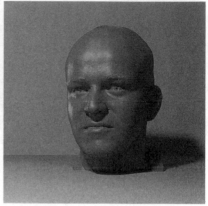

Figure 6.15.   Rendered images showing measured BRDFs of two different people. Courtesy of Marschner et al. [144].

addition, the specularity is person dependent. Figure 6.15 shows two images rendered with the measured skin BRDFs of two different people [144]. The image on the right exhibits quite strong specular reflections.

In this section, we describe a technique that recovers illumination from specular reflection [156]. It assumes the geometry is known, and the specular reflectance property is homogeneous, that is, the specular reflectance property is the same for all the points on the surface. This technique is particularly suited for glossy surfaces for which it is relatively easy to separate the specular reflection components from the diffuse reflection components on the input images.

Figure 6.16 is an overview of the algorithm. The input is a set of images taken at different view angles of the object. The first step is to separate each input image into a diffuse reflection component and a specular reflection component. The diffuse reflection components are combined into a single texture map, called *diffuse texture map*. The specular reflection component for each input image is called a *specular image*. At the second step, it obtains an initial estimation of the illumination distribution which is represented as a set of point light sources on a surface of a hemisphere. The hemisphere is called *illumination hemisphere*. The third step factors out the specular reflection parameters and refines the illumination distribution. The specular reflection is parameterized by the Torrance-Sparrow model (Equation 3.6).

6.3.1 Diffuse texture map

Since the diffuse reflection is view invariant, the diffuse reflection component at each surface point can be represented by a single color vector. Such color vectors

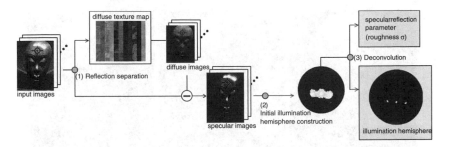

Figure 6.16. An overview of the system that recovers illumination from specular reflection. Courtesy of Nishino et al. [156].

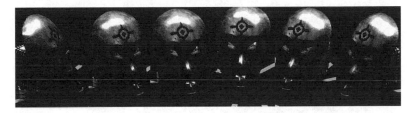

Figure 6.17. Extraction of diffuse texture map. (a) Input image. (b) Diffuse reflection component. (c) Specular image. Courtesy of Nishino et al. [156].

across all the surface points form the diffuse texture map. To extract the diffuse reflection component for each surface point, Nishino et al. [156] examined the corresponding pixels on all the input images and chose the one with the minimum color magnitude (norm of the color vector) as the diffuse reflection component for this point. An alterative strategy, which works better when the number of input images is large, is to take the pixel with the median magnitude [241].

Note that the obtained diffuse texture map is not an albedo map since it contains lighting. It can be potentially used to obtain a pseudo irradiance environment map by using the technique described in Section 6.2.

For each input image and each pixel, we subtract its color from its diffuse reflection component. The resulting image is called *specular image* which mainly consists of the specular reflection component. Figure 6.17 shows six input images of a face mask. Figure 6.18a is one of the input images. The diffuse reflection component is shown in Figure 6.18b, and the specular image is shown in Figure 6.18c.

6.3.2 Lighting hemisphere

The illumination distribution can be represented by a set of point light sources located on a sphere surrounding the object. To simplify implementation,

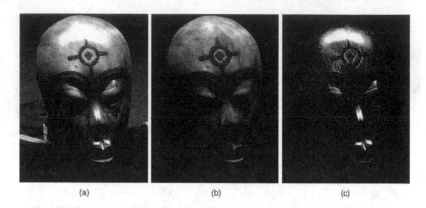

(a)   (b)   (c)

Figure 6.18. Extraction of diffuse texture map. (a) Input image. (b) Diffuse reflection component. (c) Specular image. Courtesy of Nishino et al. [156].

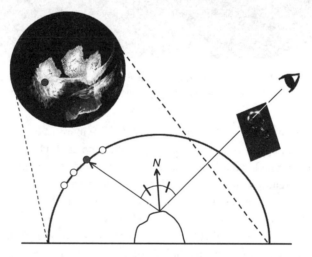

Figure 6.19. Construction of the initial lighting hemisphere. Courtesy of Nishino et al. [156].

Nishino et al. [156] used a hemisphere instead, which is called a *lighting hemisphere*.

Figure 6.19 is a diagram showing how to obtain an initial estimate of the lighting hemisphere. For each specular image and each pixel, we cast a ray from the pixel toward its corresponding surface point. We then mirror-reflect the ray with respect to the surface normal. The intersection point between the reflected ray and the hemisphere is considered as a point light source that contributes to the specular reflection component of this pixel. The color of the intersection point is set to be equal to that of the pixel value on the specular image. In this way, we obtain a partial lighting hemisphere for each specular image. The partial lighting hemispheres for all the specular images are then combined to form an overall lighting hemisphere.

6.3.3 Specular reflection parameter estimation

Let N_L denote the number of nodes on the hemisphere where each node represents a point light source. Let N_C denote the number of input images. In the following, we use l as the light source index and c as the index for input images (cameras). Based on Torrance-Sparrow model (see Equation (3.6)), the specular reflection component at surface P for camera c is modeled as

$$I_\lambda(c, P) = k_s(P) \sum_{l=1}^{N_l} \frac{F_\lambda(l, c, P) \, D(l, c, P) \, G(l, P)}{\pi \, \cos(\theta(c, P))} L_\lambda(l), \qquad (6.17)$$

where $k_s(P)$ is the specular reflection coefficient, $D(l, c, P)$ is the microfacet distribution function, $G(l, P)$ is the geometrical attenuation factor, $F_\lambda(l, c, P)$ is the Fresnel term, and $L_\lambda(l)$ is the intensity of the point light source l.

To simplify the problem, Nishino et al. [156] assumed that the normalized color vector is the same for all light sources, and it is equal to the normalized color vector of the specular reflection component at any surface point. With this assumption, we can remove the color channel index λ in Equation (6.17), and furthermore, we only have a single k_s for all surface points. Thus, Equation (6.17) can be rewritten as

$$I(c, P) = k_s \sum_{l=1}^{N_l} \frac{F(l, c, P) \, D(l, c, P) \, G(l, P)}{\pi \, \cos(\theta(c, P))} L(l). \qquad (6.18)$$

If we know the geometry of the object and the geometric relationship among the object, cameras, and the hemisphere, we can evaluate $\theta(c, P)$, $G(l, P)$, as well as $F(l, c, P)$ (assuming the refraction index is given). k_s contributes to a global scaling factor, which cannot be uniquely determined. Thus, one can simply set $k_s = 1$. The microfacet distribution function $D(l, c, P)$ is represented as (see Equation (3.7)):

$$D(l, c, P) = e^{-\frac{\beta^2(l,c,P)}{\sigma^2(P)}}, \qquad (6.19)$$

where $\beta(l, c, P)$ is the angle between the surface normal at P and the halfway vector, and $\sigma(P)$ is the specular reflectivity parameter at surface point P. A further simplification made by Nishino et al. [156] is the homogeneous reflection property, that is, the specular reflectivity is the same for all the points on the surface. With this assumption, σ is not dependent on P anymore; thus, we have just a single specular reflectance parameter σ.

In summary, the unknowns are the specular reflectance parameter σ and the light source intensities $L(1), ..., L(N_l)$. They can be determined by solving the following optimization problem:

$$\text{Min}_{\sigma,L(1),...,L(N_l)} \sum_{c=1}^{N_l} \sum_{P} |I(c,P) - I_c(P)|^2, \tag{6.20}$$

where $I_c(P)$ is the intensity of input image c at the pixel corresponding to surface point P.

Equation (6.20) can be solved in an alternating optimization scheme. For details, the readers are referred to [156].

In Figure 6.20, the image on the left is the initial lighting hemisphere. The middle image is the final result of the lighting hemisphere obtained by solving the optimization problem in Equation (6.20). The right image is the ground truth lighting hemisphere which is a photograph captured through a fish-eye lens.

6.3.4 Rendering from novel viewpoints

After the specular reflection parameter and the light hemisphere are obtained, we can generate images from arbitrary viewpoints. We first evaluate the specular reflection component using Equation (6.18) for the new camera position, and then add the diffuse reflection component. The left image of Figure 6.21 shows the face mask rendered from two novel viewpoints.

Figure 6.20. Left: Initial lighting hemisphere. Middle: Final result of the estimated lighting hemisphere. Right: Photograph of the true lighting hemisphere captured through a fisheye lens. Courtesy of Nishino et al. [156].

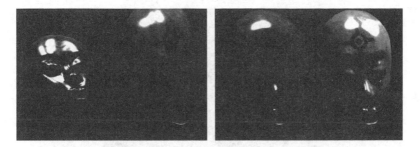

Figure 6.21. Left: The face mask rendered from two novel viewpoints. Right: The face mask relit under two novel lighting conditions. Courtesy of Nishino et al. [156].

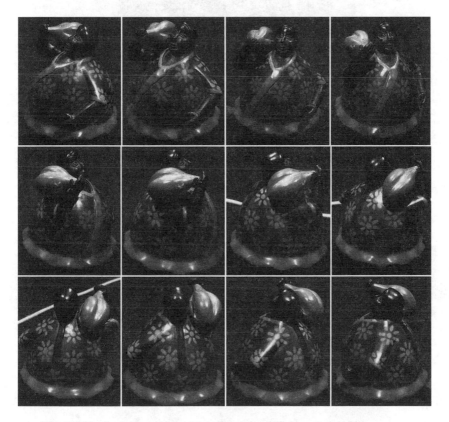

Figure 6.22. Input images of a statue. Courtesy of Nishino et al. [156].

Figure 6.23.   The diffuse texture map of the statue. Courtesy of Nishino et al. [156].

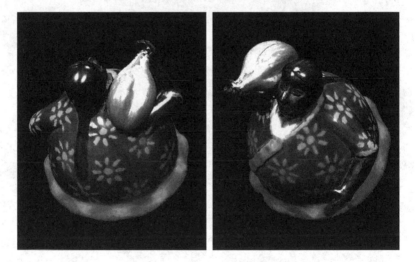

Figure 6.24.   Images of the statue rendered from two novel viewpoints. Courtesy of Nishino et al. [156].

6.3.5 *Relighting*

One can also modify the point light intensities $L(1), ..., L(L_l)$ and use Equation (6.18) to compute the new specular reflection components under the new lighting environment. To generate the diffuse reflection component

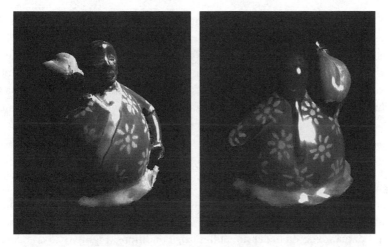

Figure 6.25. Images of the statue rendered under novel lighting conditions. Courtesy of Nishino et al. [156].

Figure 6.26. Comparison between a photograph and a relit image under the same lighting condition. Left: Photograph. Right: Image rendered under the same lighting condition as the photograph. Courtesy of Nishino et al. [156].

under the new lighting condition, we can compute the ratio between the irradiance map of the new lighting hemisphere and that of the original lighting hemisphere, and multiply the ratio with the original diffuse texture map. The right image of Figure 6.21 shows the face mask rendered from two novel lighting conditions.

An implicit assumption of this relighting scheme is that the light sources that generate the diffuse reflection components are all correctly recovered in the lighting hemisphere. This is not necessarily true in practice. For example, an area light source may not generate strong specular reflection; thus, it will not be correctly recovered from specular images. One potential remedy is to use the technique of Section 6.2 to handle diffuse reflection while using the technique presented in this section to handle specular reflection.

6.3.6 Another example

Figure 6.22 shows the input images of a statue captured from 12 different view points. Figure 6.23 shows the diffuse texture map. Figure 6.24 shows images of the statue rendered from two novel view points. Figure 6.25 shows images of the statue rendered under novel lighting conditions. Figure 6.26 compares a photograph with a relit image. On the left is the photograph. On the right is the image rendered under the same lighting condition as that of the photograph. The relit image matches quite nicely with the photograph.

7

Joint shape and appearance modeling

In this chapter, we describe techniques that model both shape and appearance. Techniques in this category have their origins in shape-from-shading. The basic idea of shape-from-shading is to use a generative imaging model (e.g., Lambertian reflectance) to fit an image and solve for the shape and illumination parameters. It is an ill-conditioned problem due to large number of unknowns. To make the problem more constrained, people usually make certain assumptions such as a constant albedo, a single directional light source, or surface smoothness. In 1999, Blanz and Vetter [19] introduced a linear space representation called face morphable model. Even though their work may not be directly motivated from shape-from-shading problem, it is interesting to look at the face morphable model from the perspective of shape-from-shading. We can think of the linear space representations of the face geometry and albedo as a regularization constraints on the shape-from-shading framework. With this representation, the number of unknowns is significantly reduced. As a result, it is possible to relax the other assumptions. For example, one does not have to assume a constant albedo anymore.

We will first give an introduction to shape-from-shading and then describe the face morphable model framework. In Sections 7.3.1 and 7.5, we describe the integration of face morphable model with spherical harmonics representation to handle general and even harsh lighting conditions.

7.1 Shape from shading

The first shape-from-shading (SFS) technique was proposed by Horn [92]. Since then, there has been a lot of research on this problem, and many different techniques have been proposed. It is beyond the scope of this book to provide detailed descriptions on various techniques. The paper [260] has a nice survey on this subject. In this section, we will give a brief introduction and point out how linear space representations of face geometry and albedo can be used for shape-from-shading.

In shape-from-shading literature, people usually assume the surface has the form $z = z(x,y)$. The normal at point (x,y) is $\mathrm{N} = \dfrac{1}{\sqrt{1+p^2+q^2}} \begin{pmatrix} -p \\ -q \\ 1 \end{pmatrix}$ where $p = \frac{\partial z}{\partial x}$, and $q = \frac{\partial z}{\partial y}$. Assume there is a single directional light source. Let $\mathrm{L} = (\sin\theta\cos\phi, \sin\theta\sin\phi, \cos\theta)^T$ denote the normalized lighting direction. Let ρ denote the albedo of the surface multiplied by the lighting intensity. Under the Lambertian assumption (Equation (3.2)), the imaging model is

$$
\begin{aligned}
I^M &= \rho\, \mathrm{N} \cdot \mathrm{L} \\
&= \rho\, \frac{-p\,\sin\theta\cos\phi - q\,\sin\theta\sin\phi + \cos\theta}{\sqrt{1+p^2+q^2}}
\end{aligned}
\tag{7.1}
$$

To make the system better constrained, ρ is assumed to be constant, and a regularization term on the surface smoothness is added. The final formulation is the following optimization problem:

$$
\begin{aligned}
\text{Minimize} \int\int \Bigg[&\left(I - \rho\, \frac{-p\,\sin\theta\cos\phi - q\,\sin\theta\sin\phi + \cos\theta}{\sqrt{1+p^2+q^2}} \right)^2 \\
&+ w_1 \left(\left(\frac{\partial p}{\partial x}\right)^2 + \left(\frac{\partial p}{\partial y}\right)^2 + \left(\frac{\partial q}{\partial x}\right)^2 + \left(\frac{\partial q}{\partial y}\right)^2 \right) \\
&+ w_2 \left(\left(\frac{\partial z}{\partial x} - p\right)^2 + \left(\frac{\partial z}{\partial y} - q\right)^2 \right) \Bigg] dx\,dy
\end{aligned}
\tag{7.2}
$$

The constant albedo ρ and lighting direction parameters θ and ϕ can be estimated based on image statistics [272]. Given ρ, θ, and ϕ, we would like to solve for p, q, z, which are functions of x and y. This is a variational problem. By using Euler's equation on variational calculus [71], we obtain the following second-order partial differential equations:

$$
\begin{aligned}
w_1 \left(\frac{\partial^2 p}{\partial^2 x} + \frac{\partial^2 p}{\partial^2 y} \right) &= -(I - R)\frac{\partial R}{\partial p} - w_2 \left(\frac{\partial z}{\partial x} - p \right) \\
w_1 \left(\frac{\partial^2 q}{\partial^2 x} + \frac{\partial^2 q}{\partial^2 y} \right) &= -(I - R)\frac{\partial R}{\partial q} - w_2 \left(\frac{\partial z}{\partial y} - q \right) \\
\frac{\partial^2 z}{\partial^2 x} + \frac{\partial^2 z}{\partial^2 y} &= \frac{\partial p}{\partial x} + \frac{\partial q}{\partial y},
\end{aligned}
\tag{7.3}
$$

where

$$R = \rho \frac{-p \sin\theta \cos\phi - q \sin\theta \sin\phi + \cos\theta}{\sqrt{1 + p^2 + q^2}}. \tag{7.4}$$

This system of differential equations can be solved numerically [93].

The main drawback of the conventional shape-from-shading approach is that there are too many unknowns, and some of the assumptions are too restrictive for some practical applications. However, if we know the object is a face, we can use this prior knowledge to constrain the parameter space. In particular, we can use the linear space representations (Sections 2.3.1 and 3.4) to parameterize both the shape and albedo. This leads to the face morphable model technique [19], which we will describe next.

7.2 Face morphable model

Face morphable model was proposed by Blanz and Vetter in 1999 [19]. The basic idea is to represent face geometry and albedo as linear combinations of example faces as described in Sections 2.3.1 and 3.4. If we look at the technique from the perspective of shape-from-shading problem, we can think of it as an effective way to dramatically reduce the number of unknowns in the shape-from-shading formulation.

Following the notation of Section 2.3.1, let $V_i = (X_i, Y_i, Z_i)^T$, $i = 1, \ldots, n$, denote the vertices of the face mesh. Let

$$\mathcal{S} = (V_1^T, \ldots, V_n^T)^T = (X_1, Y_1, Z_1, \ldots, X_n, Y_n, Z_n)^T \tag{7.5}$$

denote its geometry vector. The linear representation of $\mathcal{S}$ is

$$\mathcal{S} = \mathcal{S}^0 + \sum_{j=1}^{m} c_j \mathcal{M}^j, \tag{7.6}$$

where c_j are the shape coefficients which need to be determined.

Using the notation of Section 3.4, we can represent the face albedo ρ as

$$\rho = \rho^0 + \sum_{j=1}^{m} \beta_j T^j, \tag{7.7}$$

where β_j are albedo coefficients to be determined.

Let $\mathbf{R}$ and $\mathbf{t}$ denote the rotation and translation from the model coordinate system to the world coordinate system. Let N denote the normal map in the model coordinate system, which is a function of shape coefficients $C = (c_1, \ldots, c_m)^T$. Again, we assume a single directional light source. Let $\mathrm{L} = (l_x, l_y, l_z)^T$ denote the lighting direction multiplied by the lighting intensity. The imaging model is

$$I_{u,v}^M = \left(\rho_{u,v}^0 + \sum_{j=1}^{m} \beta_j T_{u,v}^j \right) (\mathbf{R}\mathrm{N}_{u,v}) \cdot \mathrm{L}, \tag{7.8}$$

where the subscript (u,v) denotes the pixel location.

Given a face image, we would like to estimate the shape coefficients C, the albedo coefficients $\beta = (\beta_1, \ldots, \beta_m)$, rotation matrix $\mathbf{R}$, and lighting parameters L. We first use the technique described in Section 5.4 to estimate the rotation matrix $\mathbf{R}$. Given $\mathbf{R}$, the albedo coefficients, shape coefficients, and lighting parameters can be estimated by solving the following energy minimization problem

$$\min_{C, \beta, L} \mathcal{F}, \tag{7.9}$$

where the energy function $\mathcal{F}$ is defined as the image fitting error:

$$\mathcal{F} = \sum_{u,v} [I_{u,v} - I_{u,v}^M]^2$$

$$= \sum_{u,v} \left[I_{u,v} - \left(\rho_{u,v}^0 + \sum_{j=1}^{m} \beta_j T_{u,v}^j \right) (\mathbf{R}\mathrm{N}_{u,v}) \cdot \mathrm{L} \right]^2. \tag{7.10}$$

This minimization problem can be solved in an alternating scheme. Before describing the algorithm, let us describe how to compute the partial derivative of $\mathrm{N}_{u,v}$ with respect to a shape model coefficient c_j.

Given a face mesh and a projection matrix, the normal $\mathrm{N}_{u,v}$ is computed as the normal of the mesh triangle that contains pixel (u,v) where the 2D–3D correspondence is obtained from the projection matrix. In the following, we derive the representation of the triangle normal as a (vector) function of the shape model coefficients. In addition, we derive the formula for the partial derivatives of the triangle normal with respect to the shape model coefficients.

Let $\mathcal{S}_i^0$ denote the three compoents of $\mathcal{S}^0$ that correspond to vertex i. Similarly, for each $j = 1, \ldots, m$, let $\mathcal{M}_i^j$ denote the three components of $\mathcal{M}^j$ that correspond to vertex i. From Equation (7.6), we have an per-vertex equation:

$$\mathrm{V}_i = \mathcal{S}_i^0 + \sum_{j=1}^{m} c_j \mathcal{M}_i^j. \tag{7.11}$$

Let V_{i_1}, V_{i_2}, and V_{i_3} denote the vertices of a triangle in the face mesh. Equation (7.11) yields

$$V_{i_2} - V_{i_1} = (\mathcal{S}_{i_2}^0 - \mathcal{S}_{i_1}^0) + \sum_{j=1}^{m} c_j (\mathcal{M}_{i_2}^j - \mathcal{M}_{i_1}^j),$$

$$V_{i_3} - V_{i_1} = (\mathcal{S}_{i_3}^0 - \mathcal{S}_{i_1}^0) + \sum_{j=1}^{m} c_j (\mathcal{M}_{i_3}^j - \mathcal{M}_{i_1}^j). \tag{7.12}$$

Denote

$$\mathcal{S}_{ik}^0 = \mathcal{S}_k^0 - \mathcal{S}_i^0,$$

$$\mathcal{M}_{ik}^j = \mathcal{M}_k^j - \mathcal{M}_i^j. \tag{7.13}$$

Equation (7.12) becomes

$$V_{i_2} - V_{i_1} = \mathcal{S}_{i_1 i_2}^0 + \sum_{j=1}^{m} c_j \mathcal{M}_{i_1 i_2}^j,$$

$$V_{i_3} - V_{i_1} = \mathcal{S}_{i_1 i_3}^0 + \sum_{j=1}^{m} c_j \mathcal{M}_{i_1 i_3}^j. \tag{7.14}$$

Denote

$$F_{i_1 i_2 i_3} = (V_{i_2} - V_{i_1}) \times (V_{i_3} - V_{i_1}). \tag{7.15}$$

The normal of triangle $V_{i_1} V_{i_2} V_{i_3}$ is

$$N_{i_1 i_2 i_3} = \frac{F_{i_1 i_2 i_3}}{\sqrt{F_{i_1 i_2 i_3}^T F_{i_1 i_2 i_3}}}. \tag{7.16}$$

With some albebraic manipulations, the partial derivative of $N_{i_1 i_2 i_3}$ with respect to coefficient c_j is (the subscripts are omitted to simplify notations):

$$\frac{\partial N}{\partial c_j} = \frac{1}{\sqrt{F^T F}} \left[I_{3 \times 3} - \frac{F F^T}{F^T F} \right] \frac{\partial F}{\partial c_j}, \tag{7.17}$$

where $\mathbf{I}_{3\times3}$ is a 3×3 unit matrix, and $\frac{\partial F_{i_1 i_2 i_3}}{\partial c_j}$ can be derived from (7.15) and (7.14) as

$$\frac{\partial F_{i_1 i_2 i_3}}{\partial c_j} = (\mathcal{S}_{i_1 i_2}^0 \times \mathcal{M}_{i_1 i_3}^j - \mathcal{S}_{i_1 i_3}^0 \times \mathcal{M}_{i_1 i_2}^j)$$

$$+ \sum_{k=1}^{m} (\mathcal{M}_{i_1 i_2}^k \times \mathcal{M}_{i_1 i_3}^j + \mathcal{M}_{i_1 i_2}^j \times \mathcal{M}_{i_1 i_3}^k) c_k. \qquad (7.18)$$

From (7.10), the partial derivative of $\mathcal{F}$ with respect to shape model coefficient c_j can be derived as

$$\frac{\partial \mathcal{F}}{\partial c_j} = -2 \sum_{u,v} \left\{ \left[I_{u,v} - \left(\rho_{u,v}^0 + \sum_{j=1}^{m} \beta_j \mathcal{T}_{u,v}^j \right) (\mathbf{R} N_{u,v}) \cdot \mathrm{L} \right] \right.$$

$$\left. * \left(\rho_{u,v}^0 + \sum_{j=1}^{m} \beta_j \mathcal{T}_{u,v}^j \right) \left(\mathbf{R} \frac{\partial N_{u,v}}{\partial c_j} \right) \cdot \mathrm{L} \right\}. \qquad (7.19)$$

In Equation (7.19), $\frac{\partial N_{u,v}}{\partial c_j}$ is computed by using (7.17) and (7.18).

Algorithm 2 outlines an alternating scheme for solving the minimization problem of (7.10). This scheme is a special case of the MRF-based technique of Section 7.5.2 (Algorithm 4). It might not be exactly the same as what was implemented in [19].

At the initialization, it uses the single view face-modeling method described in Section 5.4 to estimate the pose and a rough face shape. After that, we obtain the 2D–3D correspondence based on (5.20).

At Step 2, the albedo coefficients are initialied to be 0. The algorithm then enters into an iterative process.

At Step 3, it estimates the illumination parameters L (there are three unknowns) while fixing the shape and albedo coefficients. Since $\mathcal{F}$ is a quadratic function of L, the minimization problem can be solved by using a linear least-square procedure.

At Step 4, the algorithm fixes illumination parameters L and albedo coefficients β while solving for the shape coefficients C. We can use a gradient-decent approach to solve this non-linear minimization problem. The gradient of $\mathcal{F}$ with respect to the shape model coefficients C can be obtained by using (7.19).

At Step 5, the algorithm fixes the shape coefficients C and illumination parameters β while solving for the albedo parameters β. Since $\mathcal{F}$ is a quadratic function of β, the minimization problem can be solved by using a linear least-square method.

The algorithm stops if there is not enough progress between two successive iterations (or some other stop criteria is met). Otherwise, it goes to Step 3 and the iteration continues.

Algorithm 2 The algorithm for fitting a face morphable model

(1) Estimate the initial face geometry by using the technique described in Section 5.4.
(2) Initialize the albedo coefficients $\beta = (\beta_1, \ldots, \beta_m)$ to be 0.
(3) Fix albedo coeffients β and shape cofficients $C = (c_1, \ldots, c_m)$, and estimate the illumination parameters L by minimizing $\mathcal{F}$ of Equation 7.10. This is solved by using a linear least-square procedure.
(4) Fix illumination parameters L and albedo coefficients β, and estimate the shape coefficients C by minimizing $\mathcal{F}$. This is solved by using a gradient decent approach where the gradient is computed by using Equation 7.19.
(5) Fix shape coefficients C and illumination parameters L, and estimate the albedo coefficients β by mimizing $\mathcal{F}$. This is solved by using a linear least-square procedure.
(6) If the stop critera is not satisfied, go to Step 3.

Figure 7.1 shows an experiment result of face morphable model fitting obtained by Blanz and Vetter [19]. Figure 7.1a is the input image. Figure 7.1b is the resulting face mesh. Figure 7.1c is the side view of the resulting face mesh. Figures 7.1d and 7.1e are, respectively, the frontal and side views of the face mesh rendered with texture.

We would like to make a remark on why this method strongly depends on shading information. Let us consider an extreme scenario where the lighting

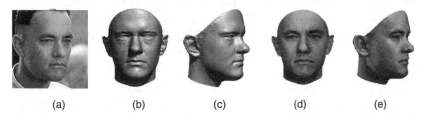

| (a) | (b) | (c) | (d) | (e) |

Figure 7.1. Face morphable model fitting. (a) Input image. (b) Face mesh obtained from face morphable model fitting. (c) The side view of the resulting face mesh. (d) Frontal view of the fitted face mesh with texture. (e) Side view of the fitted face mesh with texture. Courtesy of Blanz and Vetter [19].

environment is perfectly uniform. In other words, for any point and any direction on the face, there is an equal amount of incident light. Thus, the image intensity of any pixel on the face is the albedo times a constant (per color channel), which is indendent of the surface normal. Therefore, as long as the face mesh is aligned with the image in terms of the face features, the solution to the minimization problem in (7.9) is independent of the surface normals of the face mesh. The fitting process will become just the face albedo fitting which results in the albedo coefficients β_j while the geometry coefficients cannot be determined.

The shading dependence is also a key difference beween this approach and the struture-from-motion or stereo-based approaches (Chapter 5). In structure-from-motion or stereo-based approaches, the 3D information comes from the point matching between two views. It does not need shading information at all. In fact, in a perfectly uniform lighting environment, the point matching is actually easier.

Another remark is that the energy function in (7.10) is in general not effective for face alignment purpose. One could potentially add a term that leverages the gradient information to fit an active shape model or an active appearance model so that the extended energy function is capable of handling face alignment.

One main limitation of the formulation (7.9) is that it assumes a single directional light source. In the next two sections, we describe techniques to handle more general lighting conditions.

7.3 Spherical harmonic basis morphable model

This section extends the single point light source assumption to more general lighting environments. If we assume the face reflection is Lambertian, the irradiance can be represented by a linear combination of nine spherical harmonics basis functions as described in Section 3.2. Let N_i denote the normal of vertex V_i, $i = 1,\ldots,n$. Let $\mathcal{N} = (N_1, N_2, \ldots, N_n)^T$ denote the *normal vector* and $\mathcal{E}(\mathcal{N}) = (E(N_1), E(N_2), \ldots, E(N_n))^T$, the *irradiance vector*. Then

$$I = \rho \odot \mathcal{E}, \qquad (7.20)$$

where $\odot$ denotes component-wise multiplication.

As in Section 3.2, let h_1, h_2, ..., h_9 denote the first nine spherical harmonic basis functions. For each $j = 1,\ldots,9$, denote $H_j(\mathcal{N}) = (h_j(N_1), h_j(N_2), \ldots, h_j(N_n))^T$. Let $L = (l_1, l_2, \ldots, l_9)^T$ denote the lighting coefficients. According to Equation (3.17), we have

$$\mathcal{E} = \sum_{j=1}^{9} l_j H_j. \tag{7.21}$$

Therefore,

$$I = \sum_{j=1}^{9} l_j (\rho \odot H_j). \tag{7.22}$$

Denote

$$\mathbf{B}(\mathcal{N}) = (\rho \odot H_1(\mathcal{N}), \rho \odot H_2(\mathcal{N}), \ldots, \rho \odot H_9(\mathcal{N})), \tag{7.23}$$

which is a $n \times 9$ matrix. Equation (7.22) yields

$$I = \mathbf{B}L. \tag{7.24}$$

We call $\rho \odot H_1(\mathcal{N}), \ldots, \rho \odot H_9(\mathcal{N})$ the *textured spherical harmonic basis images* or *textured SHB images* in short, and $\mathbf{B}$ the *textured spherical harmonic basis vector* or *textured SHB vector* in short. Note that we use slightly different terminologies from the original papers [228, 258] to avoid confusion.

Suppose there are $m + 1$ exemplar faces $\{\mathcal{S}^i, \rho^i\}_{i=1}^{m+1}$ where $\mathcal{S}^i$ and ρ^i are ith face's shape and albedo vectors, respectively. From each exemplar face, we can evaluate the normals of each vertex, and let $\mathcal{N}^i$ denote the normal vector of face i. Denote

$$\mathbf{B}^i = \mathbf{B}(\mathcal{N}^i) = (\rho^i \odot H_1(\mathcal{N}^i), \rho^i \odot H_2(\mathcal{N}^i), \ldots, \rho^i \odot H_9(\mathcal{N}^i)). \tag{7.25}$$

Let $\mathbf{B}^0$ denote the mean of $\mathbf{B}^1, \ldots, \mathbf{B}^{m+1}$. Denote $\delta \mathbf{B}^i = \mathbf{B}^i - \mathbf{B}^0$, $i = 1, \ldots, m + 1$. We perform Principal Component Analysis on $\delta \mathbf{B}^1, \ldots, \delta \mathbf{B}^{m+1}$. By abuse of notation, let $\mathbf{B}^1, \ldots, \mathbf{B}^m$ denote the eigenvectors. For any given face, its spherical harmonic basis vector $\mathbf{B}$ can be represented as a linear combination of $\mathbf{B}^1, \ldots, \mathbf{B}^m$, that is,

$$\mathbf{B} = \mathbf{B}^0 + \sum_{j=1}^{m} \gamma_j \mathbf{B}^j. \tag{7.26}$$

Equation (7.26) is called *spherical harmonic basis morphable model (SHBMM)* [228, 258], and $\{\gamma_j\}_{j=1}^{m}$ are called SHBMM coefficients.

From (7.24) and (7.26), any face image I can be represented as a bilinear function of $\gamma = (\gamma_1, \ldots, \gamma_m)^T$ and L:

$$I = \left(\mathbf{B}^0 + \sum_{j=1}^{m} \gamma_j \mathbf{B}^j \right) L. \qquad (7.27)$$

Given any input face image I_{input}, its SHBMM coefficients $\gamma = (\gamma_1, \ldots, \gamma_m)^T$ and illumination coefficients L can be estimated by solving the following optimization problem:

$$\min_{\gamma, L} \left\| \left(\mathbf{B}^0 + \sum_{j=1}^{m} \gamma_j \mathbf{B}^j \right) L - I_{\text{input}} \right\|. \qquad (7.28)$$

The optimization problem of (7.28) can be solved iteratively through an alternating optimization procedure as described in Algorithm 3.

The key part of this process is the minimization of the image error as shown in Equation (7.28), where two variables γ, and L need to be recovered iteratively in an alternating fashion. Moreover, there are two methods to start the iteration: initializing γ as 0 and compute L afterwards as what is described in Algorithm 3, or starting with a random L. The first method is preferable because, as reported in [228, 258], the illumination coefficients L computed by using the mean-textured SHB vector $\mathbf{B}^0$ were close to the actual values in their synthesized experiments, and the algorithm converges fast in practice. Another important point is that, the spherical harmonic basis cannot capture specularities or cast shadows. Thus, it is better to avoid using the image pixels in the regions with strong specular reflection or cast shadow. In [228, 258], two thresholds were used to determine the regions with strong specular reflection or cast shadow.

Figure 7.2 shows the fitting process and results. The first image is the input image followed by initial fitting and the recovered textured SHB images, and the last image is the rendered image using the recovered parameters. Red points are selected major feature points, and green points are the corresponding points on the face mesh model.

7.3.1 SHBMM for face synthesis and recognition

This section describes how to use the spherical harmonic basis morphable model for face synthesis and face recognition. Section 7.3.1.1 explains how to combine the SHBMM with the ratio image technique for photorealistic face synthesis. Section 7.3.1.2 describes two face recognition methods based on the recovered SHBMM parameters and delit images, respectively.

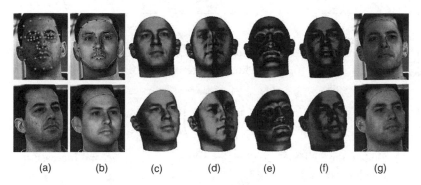

| (a) | (b) | (c) | (d) | (e) | (f) | (g) |

Figure 7.2. Fitting a 3D spherical harmonic basis morphable model to images: (a) Input image. (b) Initial result of fitting the 3D face model to the input image. Red points are selected major feature points. Green points are the corresponding points on the face mesh model. (c) Recovered first-order textured SHB images. (d–f) Recovered second-order textured SHB basis images where the red color means positive values and the green color means negative values. (g) Rendered image using the recovered parameters. (See plate section for color version.)

Algorithm 3 The algorithm for fitting a spherical harmonic basis morphable model

(1) Estimate the initial face geometry by using the technique described in Section 5.4.

(2) Initialize the SHBMM coefficients $\gamma^{(0)}$ to be 0 and set the step index $t = 1$.

(3) At step t, estimate the illumination coefficients $L^{(t)}$ by solving (7.28) with γ being fixed to $\gamma^{(t-1)}$. That is, we solve the following linear system for $L^{(t)}$:

$$\left(\mathbf{B}^0 + \sum_{j=1}^{m} \gamma_j^{(t-1)} \mathbf{B}^j \right) L^{(t)} = I_{input}$$

(4) Compute the residual error $\delta I^{(t)}$ between the input image I_{input} and the synthesized image $I^{(t)} = \left(\mathbf{B}^0 + \sum_{j=1}^{m} \gamma_j^{(t-1)} \mathbf{B}^j \right) L^{(t)}$, that is,

$$\delta I^{(t)} = I_{input} - \left(\mathbf{B}^0 + \sum_{j=1}^{m} \gamma_j^{(t-1)} \mathbf{B}^j \right) L^{(t)}$$

Algorithm 3 (cont.)

(5) Compute the update of the SHB coefficients $\delta\gamma = (\delta\gamma_1,\ldots,\delta\gamma_m)^T$ by solving the following linear system while fixing the illumination coefficients L,

$$\left(\mathbf{B}^0 + \sum_{j=1}^{m}\delta\gamma_j\mathbf{B}^j\right)L^{(t)} = \delta I^{(t)}$$

(6) Update the SHBMM coefficients $\gamma^{(t)} = \gamma^{(t-1)} + \delta\gamma$, and increase the step index t by 1.

(7) Perform Steps 1 to 6 iteratively until $\|\delta I\| < \xi_I$ or $\|\delta\gamma\| < \xi_\gamma$, where ξ_I and ξ_γ are preselected constants.

7.3.1.1 Image synthesis with SHBMM

The face synthesis problem can be stated as the following: Given a single image under unknown lighting, can we remove the effects of illumination from the image ("delighting") and generate images of the object consistent with the illumination conditions of the target images ("relighting")? The input image and target images can be acquired under different unknown lighting conditions and poses. Based on the SHBMM parameters (γ, L) from an input face I, we can combine the spherical harmonic basis morphable model and a concept similar to ratio images [180, 236] to generate photorealistic face images. In particular, we can render a face I' using the recovered parameters (γ', L') to approximate I: $I' = (\mathbf{B}^0 + \sum_{j=1}^{m}\gamma_j'\mathbf{B}^j)L'$. Thus, the face texture (delit face) can be directly computed from the estimated spherical harmonic basis, and face relighting can be performed by setting different values to the illumination coefficients L similar to [9].

Denote b_1 as the first column of $\mathbf{B}$. Since $h_1 = \frac{1}{\sqrt{4\pi}}$ (Equation (3.15)), from Equation (7.23) we have

$$\rho = \sqrt{4\pi}\,b_1. \tag{7.29}$$

After we obtain $\mathbf{B}$, we could directly obtain the delit image ρ using (7.29). The problem is that the estimated ρ is usually blurry because the high-frequency information in the albedo is difficult to accurately recover in $\mathbf{B}$. On the other hand, the irradiance map mainly consists of low-frequency information. Therefore, a better strategy is to use the ratio between the input image and the recovered irradiance map as the delit image.

Let γ' and L' denote the recovered SHBMM and illumination coefficients. Let $\mathbf{B}'$ denote the recovered textured SHB vector. We have

$$\mathbf{B}' = \mathbf{B}^0 + \sum_{j=1}^{m} \gamma_j' \mathbf{B}^j \tag{7.30}$$

and

$$I' = \mathbf{B}' L'. \tag{7.31}$$

Denote b_1' to be the first column of $\mathbf{B}'$. Denote ρ' to be the recovered albedo, and $\mathcal{E}'$ the recovered irradiance vector. Then

$$I' = \rho' \odot \mathcal{E}' = \sqrt{4\pi} b_1' \odot \mathcal{E}'. \tag{7.32}$$

Thus,

$$\mathcal{E}' = \frac{I'}{\sqrt{4\pi} b_1'}, \tag{7.33}$$

where the division is componentwise. Therefore

$$\rho = \frac{I}{\mathcal{E}} \approx \frac{I}{\mathcal{E}'} = \frac{I \odot \sqrt{4\pi} b_1'}{I'}. \tag{7.34}$$

By combining Equations (7.30), (7.31), and (7.34), we have

$$\rho \approx \frac{I \odot \sqrt{4\pi} b_1'}{(\mathbf{B}^0 + \sum_{j=1}^{m} \gamma_j' \mathbf{B}^j) L'}. \tag{7.35}$$

The right-hand side is used as the delit image I_d, that is,

$$I_d = \frac{I \odot \sqrt{4\pi} b_1'}{(\mathbf{B}^0 + \sum_{j=1}^{m} \gamma_j' \mathbf{B}^j) L'}. \tag{7.36}$$

Let I_t denote an image of the same person under a different lighting condition. Let L_t denote the illumination coefficients under the new lighting condition.

We have

$$I_t = \left(\mathbf{B}^0 + \sum_{j=1}^{m} \gamma_j \mathbf{B}^j \right) L_t. \tag{7.37}$$

Therefore,

$$\frac{I_t}{I} = \frac{(\mathbf{B}^0 + \sum_{j=1}^{m} \gamma_j \mathbf{B}^j) L_t}{(\mathbf{B}^0 + \sum_{j=1}^{m} \gamma_j \mathbf{B}^j) L}. \tag{7.38}$$

Note that the ratio in (7.38) is equal to the ratio of the irradiance maps between the two different lighting environments. Thus, we use the recovered parameters to estimate this ratio:

$$\frac{(\mathbf{B}^0 + \sum_{j=1}^{m} \gamma_j \mathbf{B}^j) L_t}{(\mathbf{B}^0 + \sum_{j=1}^{m} \gamma_j \mathbf{B}^j) L} \approx \frac{(\mathbf{B}^0 + \sum_{j=1}^{m} \gamma_j' \mathbf{B}^j) L_t'}{(\mathbf{B}^0 + \sum_{j=1}^{m} \gamma_j' \mathbf{B}^j) L'}, \tag{7.39}$$

Thus,

$$I_t \approx \frac{(\mathbf{B}^0 + \sum_{j=1}^{m} \gamma_j' \mathbf{B}^j) L_t'}{(\mathbf{B}^0 + \sum_{j=1}^{m} \gamma_j' \mathbf{B}^j) L'} I. \tag{7.40}$$

Given a target image of a different person under a different lighting condition, we can first use Algorithm 3 to recover its illumination parameters L_t'. We can then use Equation (7.40) to generate the relit image as

$$I_r = \frac{(\mathbf{B}^0 + \sum_{j=1}^{m} \gamma_j' \mathbf{B}^j) L_t'}{(\mathbf{B}^0 + \sum_{j=1}^{m} \gamma_j' \mathbf{B}^j) L'} I. \tag{7.41}$$

In the rest of the section, we describe the experiments reported in [228, 258]. They used USF data set to construct the spherical harmonic morphable model. CMU-PIE data set [198] was used to evaluate the performance of image delighting and relighting, which includes images taken under varying pose and illumination conditions. The data set contains 68 individuals, which are not included in the USF data set. Figure 7.3 shows relit images of the same input image "driven" by target images of three different subjects. For the input image and each of the three target images, Algorithm 3 is used to recover the SHBMM and illumination coefficients. Equation (7.41) is then used to compute the relit images. From Figure 7.3, we can see that the SHBMM-based method extracts and preserves illumination information consistently across different subjects and poses.

Target Images ⇨

Input image ⇩

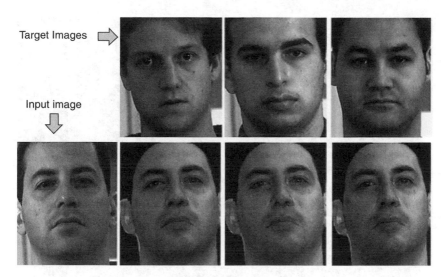

Figure 7.3. Comparison of relit images from the same input image "driven" by target images of different subjects under similar illumination conditions. The illumination information is preserved to a large extent, across different subjects.

More examples are included in Figure 7.4, which shows a series of face relighting experiments. The top row shows the images with target illumination conditions. The input images from two different subjects are listed at the leftmost column. The input image and target images can be acquired under different unknown lighting conditions and poses. The results show that high-quality images can be synthesized even if only a single input image under arbitrary unknown lighting is available.

7.3.1.2 Face recognition with SHBMM

Recognition based on SHBMM parameters: For face recognition experiments, we divide an image data set into a gallery set and a test set. The gallery set includes the prior images of people which are labeled. The test image set are used as probes. For each image I_i in the gallery set and a testing image I_t, we recover SHBMM parameters $\{\gamma^i, L^i\}$ and $\{\gamma^t, L^t\}$. Since the identity of a face is represented by $\{\gamma\}$, recognition is done by selecting the face of a subject i whose recovered parameters $\{\gamma^i\}$ are the closest to $\{\gamma^t\}$. With this method, the gallery image and the testing image can be acquired under different arbitrary illumination conditions.

Note that the initial shape estimation (Step 1 of Algorithm 3) was based on detected face features. The geometric locations of the face features are strong subject identity information which are useful for face recognition as well. In

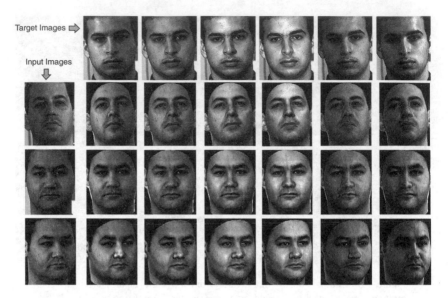

Figure 7.4. Face relighting results. First column: Input images from different subjects. Top row: Images with desired illumination conditions. Images with good
quality are synthesized even though only a single input image is available.

order to measure the effects of illumination and texture recovery on the face
recognition performance, the face recognition experiments were performed by
only using the spherical harmonic basis coefficients γ. In a complete application, both shape and texture parameters should be used for better recognition
performance.

Recognition based on delit images: Instead of using SHBMM parameters,
one can also use the delit images for face recognition. For each image I_i in
the gallery set and a testing image I_t, we first compute their corresponding
delit images I_d^i and I_d^t by using Equation (7.36). The recognition is done by
selecting the face of a subject whose delit image is closest to the delit image of
the test subject. In this method, delit images should be aligned before they are
compared against each other.

Experimental results: In order to evaluate the performance of the preceding
two methods (i.e., recognition based on SHBMM parameters and delit images),
we examined the recognition rates on the CMU-PIE Database [198]. There are
68 subjects included in the CMU-PIE Database with 13 poses and 21 directional

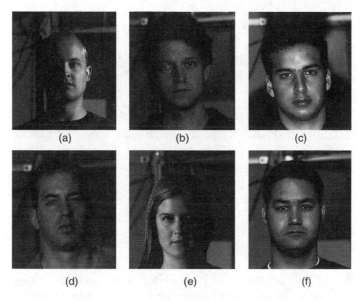

Figure 7.5. Example images from CMU-PIE Database: the lighting conditions of (a–f) are 2, 6, 8, 12, 16, and 20, respectively. The details about flash light positions can be found in [198].

illumination directions. Since we focus on the capability of handling illumination variations, face recognition results are reported on the frontal pose images only (recognition results on a subset of the PIE database under varying poses are reported in [258]). For each subject, out of the 21 directional illumination conditions, the image with certain illumination direction was included in the training set (which is referred to as the *training illumination condition*), and the remaining images were used for testing. The details about flash light positions can be found in [198]. In the experiment, the following six representative illumination conditions were selected: (i) frontal lighting: flash 08; (ii) near-frontal lighting (between 22.5 and 45 degrees): flash 06, 12, and 20; and (iii) side lighting (with the largest illumination angles in the PIE database): flash 02 and 16. The image examples under the selected six illumination conditions are shown in Figure 7.5. Figure 7.6 reports the recognition results of six representative illumination conditions with each selected as the training illumination condition. The results in Figure 7.6 show that the SHBMM-based methods, using both SHBMM parameters and delit images, can achieve high recognition rates for images under regular illumination conditions. However, their performance decreases significantly in extreme illumination cases, such as light positions 2 and 16.

Light Positions	SHBMM-Based Method	
	Using SHB Parameters	Using Delit Images
2	68.23%	70.74%
6	91.14%	97.65%
8	93.31%	98.93%
12	92.66%	99.12%
16	67.92%	69.52%
20	89.62%	98.04%

Figure 7.6. Face recognition under different illumination conditions: We evaluate and compare the recognition performance based on the SHBMM parameters and delit images. The CMU-PIE Database [198] is used in this experiment, which includes 68 subjects and 21 directional illumination conditions. For each subject, the images with the illumination directions, listed in the left column, are included in the training set and the remaining images are used for testing. The details about flash light positions listed in the left column can be found in [198], and the image examples are shown in Figure 7.5. The results show that the SHBMM-based method can achieve high recognition rates for images under a wide range of illumination conditions. However, its performance decreases significantly in extreme illumination conditions, such as light positions 2 and 16.

7.4 Data-driven bilinear illumination model

Instead of using spherical harmonics to generate illumination basis images $H_1,\ldots,H_9$, Lee et al. [118] proposed to use a data-driven approach. They used their face scanning dome as shown in Figure 6.4 (Section 6.1.3) to capture the face geometries of 33 people. For each person, they captured images of the person under 146 different lighting conditions. The captured images are all registered so that there are pixel-to-pixel correspondences between the images. For each person, they also obtained a diffuse texture (i.e., the albedo) map. They then computed the albedo-free illumination map (i.e., the irradiance map) as the pixelwise ratio between the captured images and the corresponding person's albedo map.

Similar to Section 2.4, we can use the 2D array of irradiance maps to construct a bilinear basis for the space of irradiance maps of different people under varying illumination conditions.

Let us represent an irradiance map as a vector by arranging its pixel values in a linear array[†]. Let $E_{i_1 i_2}$ denote the irradiance map for person i_1 under lighting condition i_2 where $i_1 \in [1, 33]$ and $i_2 \in [1, 146]$. Similar to (2.15), given an irradiance map of an arbitrary person under any lighting conditions, we can represent it as a bilinear combination of the example irradiance maps

$$E = \sum_{i_1=1}^{33} \sum_{i_2=1}^{146} \alpha_{i_1} \tau_{i_2} E_{i_1 i_2}. \tag{7.42}$$

Similar to (2.16), the elements of $E_{i_1 i_2}$ form an order-3 tensor, and we can perform generalized singular value decomposition to obtain a new basis $\{\mathcal{G}_{j_1 j_2}\}_{33 \times 146}$. To remove data redundancy, Lee et al. [118] chose to use only $\{\mathcal{G}_{j_1 j_2}\}_{20 \times 30}$, that is, 20 dimensions for shape and 30 dimensions for illumination.

Analogous to (2.30), we can represent E as a bilinear combination of the new basis as

$$E = \sum_{j_1=1}^{20} \sum_{j_2=1}^{30} \tilde{\alpha}_{j_1} \tilde{\tau}_{j_2} \mathcal{G}_{j_1 j_2}. \tag{7.43}$$

Let ρ_{j_1} denote the albedo map for person j_1. Let

$$\mathcal{B}_{j_1 j_2} = \rho_{j_1} \odot \mathcal{G}_{j_1 j_2}. \tag{7.44}$$

$\{\mathcal{B}_{j_1 j_2}\}$ is the albedo-weighted illumination basis. Let I denote the image of a person under arbitrary illumination conditions. We can reprepresent I as a bilinear combination of $\{\mathcal{B}_{j_1 j_2}\}$:

$$I = \sum_{j_1=1}^{20} \sum_{j_2=1}^{30} \tilde{\alpha}_{j_1} \tilde{\tau}_{j_2} \mathcal{B}_{j_1 j_2}. \tag{7.45}$$

Comparing (7.27) with (7.45), we can see that $(\mathcal{B}_{j1}, \ldots, \mathcal{B}_{j30})$ in (7.45) plays the same role as $\mathbf{B}^j$ in (7.27). In (7.45), $\tilde{\alpha}_{j_1}$ are geometry coefficients while $\tilde{\tau}_{j_2}$ are the illumination coefficients. Image fitting can be done by using a numerical procedure similar to Algorithm 3.

7.5 Spatially varying texture morphable model

Although SHBMM-based method can achieve good performance on face relighting and recognition, the performance decreases significantly under

---

[†] Lee et al. [118] actually included geometric positions in the vector. But we ignore the geometric positions here since they are illumination independent.

extreme lighting conditions. This is because the representation power of the 3D SHBMM model is inherently limited by the coupling of texture and geometry bases. For an image taken under extreme lighting conditions, the lighting approximation errors vary significantly across image regions. Such spatially varying lighting approximation errors are difficult to handle with a single set of SHBMM coefficients over the entire image region. To address this problem, Wang et al. [227, 228] proposed a spatially varying texture morphable model. It decouples the texture from shape and illumination and divides the image into multiple regions. Based on the theory of Markov random fields (MRFs), they proposed an energy minimization framework to jointly recover the lighting, the geometry (including the surface normal), and the albedo of the target face. As demonstrated by Wang et al. [227, 228], this technique is effective at handling challenging areas such as cast shadows and saturated regions and is robust to extreme lighting conditions and partial occlusions as well.

7.5.1 Subregion-based scheme

Since illumination effects in smaller image regions are more homogeneous, one can subdivide a face into smaller regions to better fit the image under an extreme lighting condition. The idea of subdivision was also used by Blanz and Vetter in [19], where a face was subdivided along face feature boundaries (e.g., eyes, nose, mouth) to increase the expressiveness of the morphable models. They estimated morphable model parameters independently over each region and performed smoothing along region boundaries to avoid visual discontinuity. However, this approach cannot be applied to images under extreme lighting conditions because of the inconsistency of the estimated textures in different regions (e.g., Figure 7.7c). Furthermore, if most pixels in a region are in cast shadows or saturated areas, there might not be enough information to recover the texture within the region itself. A principled way to address these problems, as pointed out in [227, 228], is to introduce the spatial coherence constraints to the texture model between neighboring regions.

Instead of subdividing a face along face feature boundaries as in [19], Wang et al. [227, 228] simply divided a face into regular regions with a typical size of 50×50 pixels. The subdivision is done in the image plane and projected back to the 3D face model where the relationship between the 2D input image and the 3D face model is recovered by the initialized face geometry at the first step of Algorithm 3. For each region, we represent its face texture by using a PCA texture model similar to Equation (7.7):

$$\rho^q = \overline{\rho}^q + \sum_{k=1}^{m} \beta_k^q \mathcal{T}_k^q, \quad q = 1, \ldots, Q, \tag{7.46}$$

where Q is the total number of regions, $\overline{\rho}^q$ is the mean albedo of the qth region, and $\{T_k^q\}_{k=1}^m$ are the albedo eigenvectors of the qth region, which are computed from the exemplar faces in the morphable model database by dividing them into the same regions as the target face. Then, we pose the coherence constraints on the Principal Component Analysis (PCA) coefficients β_k^q between neighboring regions: Given two neighboring regions q_i and q_j, for each PCA coefficient $k = 1, \ldots, m$, we model $\beta_k^{q_i} - \beta_k^{q_j}$ as a random variable of Gaussian distribution with mean 0 and variance $(\sigma_k^{q_i q_j})^2$. We also obtain the spatial coherence between the two neighboring regions by maximizing $\Pi_{k=1}^m Pr(\beta_k^{q_i} - \beta_k^{q_j})$, which is equivalent to minimizing

$$\sum_{k=1}^m \left(\frac{\beta_k^{q_i} - \beta_k^{q_j}}{\sigma_k^{q_i q_j}} \right)^2 . \tag{7.47}$$

It is interesting to note that the spatial coherence constraints are posed over texture PCA coefficients, not on pixel values directly. The main advantage is that even if the PCA coefficients are the same between two regions, the pixel values can be completely different.

We could potentially use a similar idea for the shape model representation. But since we are not trying to recover detailed geometry, a single shape model is sufficient. This agrees with [178], and the perception literature (such as Land's retinex theory [114]), where on Lambertian surfaces high-frequency variation is due to texture, and low-frequency variation is probably associated with illumination, which is determined by the surface geometry and the environment lighting. Given that we are mainly interested in surface normals, we directly model the surface normal as

$$\mathbf{n}_{u,v}^M = \left(\overline{\mathbf{n}}_{u,v} + \sum_{j=1}^m \lambda_j \mathbf{n}_{u,v}^j \right) \Big/ \left\| \overline{\mathbf{n}}_{u,v} + \sum_{j=1}^m \lambda_j \mathbf{n}_{u,v}^j \right\| , \tag{7.48}$$

where $\lambda = (\lambda_1, \ldots, \lambda_m)^T$ are the weighting coefficients to be estimated.

7.5.2 MRF-based framework

Following the discussion in Section 3.3, the illumination model in Equation (3.18) can be added as another constraint to fit the image I. Note that for pixels that are saturated or in cast shadows, Equation (3.18) in general does not hold. Therefore, for each pixel (u, v), we assign a weight $W_{u,v}$ to indicate the contribution of the illumination model in Equation (3.18). $W_{u,v}$ is set to a small value if the pixel is in the cast shadow or the saturated area.

Finally all the constraints can be integrated into an energy minimization problem as follows:

$$
\arg\min_{\rho,\lambda,\beta,l} \sum_{q=1}^{Q} \sum_{(u,v)\in\Omega_q} \left\{ W_{u,v}\left(I_{u,v} - \rho_{u,v} \sum_{i=1}^{9} h_i(\mathbf{n}_{u,v}^M)l_i \right)^2 + W_{MM}(\rho_{u,v} - \rho_{u,v}^q)^2 \right\}
$$

$$
+ W_{SM}N_{sr} \sum_{(q_i,q_j)\in\mathcal{N}} \sum_{k=1}^{m-1} \left(\frac{\beta_k^{q_i} - \beta_k^{q_j}}{\sigma_k^{q_i q_j}} \right)^2 \tag{7.49}
$$

where ρ is the output albedo, (u,v) is the pixel index, Ω_q denotes the qth region, $\mathcal{N} = \{(i,j)|\Omega_i$ and Ω_j are neighbors$\}$ is the set of all pairs of neighboring regions, $\mathbf{n}^M$ is constrained by the shape subspace defined in Equation (7.48), ρ^q is constrained by the texture subspace defined in Equation (7.46), and W_{MM} and W_{SM} are the weighting coefficients of the texture morphable model term, and the coherence constraint term, respectively. N_{sr} is the average number of pixels in a region and $(\sigma_k^{ij})^2$ is estimated from the exemplar texture data in the morphable models [19].

The objective function in (7.49) is an energy function of a Markov random field. The first two terms in (7.49) are the first-order potentials corresponding to the likelihood of the observation data given the model parameters, and the third term is the second-order potential, which models the spatial dependence between neighboring regions. Therefore, we have formulated the problem of jointly recovering the shape, texture, and lighting of an input face image as an MRF-based energy minimization (or maximum a posteriori) problem. Furthermore, this framework can be extended to handle different poses by replacing the normal constraint in (7.48) with the shape constraint in (5.23) where the pose matrix $\mathbf{M}$ and shape model coefficients C are unknowns.

In the implementation by Wang et al. [227, 228], they determined whether a pixel is in a cast shadow or saturated region by simple thresholding. Typically, in their experiments on a 0–255 gray-scale face image, the threshold values are 15 for the cast shadows and 240 for the saturated pixels. More sophisticated methods, such as the one in [258], could be used to detect cast shadows automatically. $W_{u,v}$ is set to 0 for the pixels in the shadow and saturated areas and 1 for the pixels in other regular areas, and $W_{MM} = 4$ and $W_{SM} = 500$ for all regions. Because the typical size of a regular region is 50×50 pixels, the average pixel number N_{sr} is 2,500. Due to the nonlinearity of the objective function (7.49), the overall optimization problem is solved in an iterative fashion. First, by fixing the albedo ρ and the surface normal $\mathbf{n}$, we solve for the global lighting l. Then, by fixing the lighting l, we solve for the albedo ρ and the surface normal $\mathbf{n}$.

To solve the minimization problem of (7.49), initial albedo values ρ are required for the nonlinear optimization. Since the linear system of (3.18) is underconstrained as the surface albedo ρ varies from point to point, it is impossible to obtain the initial lighting l_{init} directly without any prior knowledge. One solution is to approximate the face albedo ρ by a constant value ρ_{00} and to estimate the initial lighting l_{init} by solving an overconstrained linear system [227]. However, since the initial lighting l_{init} can be estimated by the previous SHBMM-based method as described in Section 7.3, we are able to obtain the initial albedo values based on the spherical harmonics representation in Equation (3.18). More specifically, we can compute ρ_{init} as follows

$$\rho_{\text{init}_{u,v}} = \frac{I_{u,v}}{\sum_{i=1}^{9} h_i(\mathbf{n}_{u,v}) \cdot l_{\text{init}_i}}, \tag{7.50}$$

where I denotes the image intensity, (u,v) is the image pixel coordinate, $\mathbf{n}$ is the surface normal, l_{init_i} is the initial lighting coefficient, and h_i is the spherical harmonic basis. In particular, given the initial shape and the associated surface normal $\mathbf{n}$ recovered by the SHBMM-based method as described in Algorithm 3 of Section 7.3, the spherical harmonic basis h_i can be evaluated by using Equation (3.15).

The outline of the optimization algorithm is presented in Algorithm 4. At Step 3, the optimization problem is solved by using a conjugate gradient method, and the gradients are computed analytically as follows.

Denote

$$\mathcal{F} = \sum_{q=1}^{Q} \sum_{(u,v)\in\Omega_q} \left\{ W_{u,v} \left(I_{u,v} - \rho_{u,v} \sum_{i=1}^{9} h_i(\mathbf{n}_{u,v}^M) l_i \right)^2 + W_{MM}(\rho_{u,v} - \rho_{u,v}^q)^2 \right\}$$

$$+ W_{SM} N_{sr} \sum_{(q_i,q_j)\in\mathcal{N}} \sum_{k=1}^{m-1} \left(\frac{\beta_k^{q_i} - \beta_k^{q_j}}{\sigma_k^{q_i q_j}} \right)^2 \tag{7.51}$$

The partial derivative of $\mathcal{F}$ with respect to l_i, $\rho_{u,v}$, λ_j, and β_k^q are, respectively,

$$\frac{\partial \mathcal{F}}{\partial l_i} = 2 \sum_{q=1}^{Q} \sum_{(u,v)\in\Omega_q} \left\{ W_{u,v} \left(\rho_{u,v} \sum_{i=1}^{9} h_i(\mathbf{n}_{u,v}^M) l_i - I_{u,v} \right) \rho_{u,v} h_i(\mathbf{n}_{u,v}^M) \right\},$$

$$\tag{7.52}$$

$$\frac{\partial \mathcal{F}}{\partial \rho_{u,v}} = 2\left\{ W_{u,v}\left(\rho_{u,v}\sum_{i=1}^{9} h_i(\mathbf{n}_{u,v}^M)l_i - I_{u,v} \right)\sum_{i=1}^{9} h_i(\mathbf{n}_{u,v}^M)l_i \right.$$

$$\left. + W_{MM}(\rho_{u,v} - \rho_{u,v}^q) \right\}, \tag{7.53}$$

$$\frac{\partial \mathcal{F}}{\partial \lambda_j} = 2\sum_{(u,v)\in\Omega_q}\left\{ W_{u,v}\left(\rho_{u,v}\sum_{i=1}^{9} h_i(\mathbf{n}_{u,v}^M)l_i - I_{u,v} \right)\left(\rho_{u,v}\sum_{i=1}^{9} \frac{\partial h_i(\mathbf{n}_{u,v}^M)}{\partial \lambda_j}l_i \right) \right\},$$

$$\tag{7.54}$$

$$\frac{\partial \mathcal{F}}{\partial \beta_k^q} = -2\sum_{(u,v)\in\Omega_q} W_{MM}(\rho_{u,v} - \rho_{u,v}^q)\mathcal{T}_k^q + W_{SM}N_{sr}\sum_{q_j:(q,q_j)\in\mathcal{N}} 2\left(\frac{\beta_k^q - \beta_k^{q_j}}{\sigma_k^{qq_j}} \right)\beta_k^q.$$

$$\tag{7.55}$$

From the spherical harmonic basis in Equation (3.15), we can derive the analytic forms for the partial derivative terms in (7.54): $\frac{\partial h_i(\mathbf{n}_{u,v}^M)}{\partial \lambda_j}$, $i = 1,\ldots,9$. For clarity purpose, we use a simplified notation $\mathbf{n}$ for the normal to substitute for the original notation $\mathbf{n}_{u,v}^M$. The formulas for the partial derivatives follow:

$$\frac{\partial h_1(\mathbf{n})}{\partial \lambda_j} = 0, \quad \frac{\partial h_2(\mathbf{n})}{\partial \lambda_j} = \frac{2\pi}{3}\sqrt{\frac{3}{4\pi}}\frac{\partial \mathbf{n}_x}{\partial \lambda_j}, \quad \frac{\partial h_3(\mathbf{n})}{\partial \lambda_j} = \frac{2\pi}{3}\sqrt{\frac{3}{4\pi}}\frac{\partial \mathbf{n}_y}{\partial \lambda_j},$$

$$\frac{\partial h_4(\mathbf{n})}{\partial \lambda_j} = \frac{2\pi}{3}\sqrt{\frac{3}{4\pi}}\frac{\partial \mathbf{n}_z}{\partial \lambda_j}, \quad \frac{\partial h_5(\mathbf{n})}{\partial \lambda_j} = \frac{3\pi}{4}\sqrt{\frac{5}{4\pi}}\mathbf{n}_z\frac{\partial \mathbf{n}_z}{\partial \lambda_j},$$

$$\frac{\partial h_6(\mathbf{n})}{\partial \lambda_j} = \frac{3\pi}{4}\sqrt{\frac{5}{12\pi}}\left(\mathbf{n}_y\frac{\partial \mathbf{n}_x}{\partial \lambda_j} + \mathbf{n}_x\frac{\partial \mathbf{n}_y}{\partial \lambda_j} \right),$$

$$\frac{\partial h_7(\mathbf{n})}{\partial \lambda_j} = \frac{3\pi}{4}\sqrt{\frac{5}{12\pi}}\left(\mathbf{n}_z\frac{\partial \mathbf{n}_x}{\partial \lambda_j} + \mathbf{n}_x\frac{\partial \mathbf{n}_z}{\partial \lambda_j} \right),$$

$$\frac{\partial h_8(\mathbf{n})}{\partial \lambda_j} = \frac{3\pi}{4}\sqrt{\frac{5}{12\pi}}\left(\mathbf{n}_z\frac{\partial \mathbf{n}_y}{\partial \lambda_j} + \mathbf{n}_y\frac{\partial \mathbf{n}_z}{\partial \lambda_j} \right),$$

$$\frac{\partial h_9(\mathbf{n})}{\partial \lambda_j} = \frac{3\pi}{4}\sqrt{\frac{5}{12\pi}}\left(\mathbf{n}_x\frac{\partial \mathbf{n}_x}{\partial \lambda_j} - \mathbf{n}_y\frac{\partial \mathbf{n}_y}{\partial \lambda_j} \right)$$

where

$$\frac{\partial \mathbf{n}_x}{\partial \lambda_j} = \frac{\mathbf{n}_x^j}{\|\mathbf{N}\|} - \frac{\mathbf{N}_x}{\|\mathbf{N}\|^3}\left(\mathbf{N}_x\mathbf{n}_x^j + \mathbf{N}_y\mathbf{n}_y^j + \mathbf{N}_z\mathbf{n}_z^j \right),$$

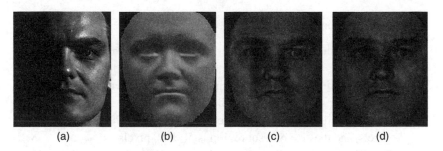

(a)   (b)   (c)   (d)

Figure 7.7. Example result: (a) the original image taken under an extreme light-ing condition. (b) the recovered surface normals by using MRF-based framework (where R, G, B color values represent the x, y, z components of the normal). (c) the recovered albedo without the spatial coherence term. (d) the recovered albedo with the spatial coherence term. Note that the region inconsistency artifacts in (c) are significantly reduced in (d). (See plate section for color version.)

$$\frac{\partial \mathbf{n}_y}{\partial \lambda_j} = \frac{\mathbf{n}_y^j}{\|N\|} - \frac{N_y}{\|N\|^3}\left(N_x \mathbf{n}_x^j + N_y \mathbf{n}_y^j + N_z \mathbf{n}_z^j\right),$$

$$\frac{\partial \mathbf{n}_z}{\partial \lambda_j} = \frac{\mathbf{n}_z^j}{\|N\|} - \frac{N_z}{\|N\|^3}\left(N_x \mathbf{n}_x^j + N_y \mathbf{n}_y^j + N_z \mathbf{n}_z^j\right),$$

$N = \bar{\mathbf{n}} + \sum_{j=1}^{m-1} \lambda_j \mathbf{n}^j$, and the subscripts x, y, and z stand for the x, y, and z components of the vector $\mathbf{n}$ (as well as N), respectively.

An example result is shown in Figure 7.7. Figure 7.7a is the original image taken under an extreme lighting condition. Figure 7.7b shows the recovered surface normal. The recovered albedo without using the spatial coherence term is shown in Figure 7.7c. Figure 7.7d shows the recovered albedo by using the spatial coherence term. As we can see, the region inconsistency artifacts in Figure 7.7c are significantly reduced in Figure 7.7d.

Algorithm 4 The outline of the MRF-based estimation algorithm

(1) **Initial Estimation, Illumination, and Albedo Estimation**: Obtain the initial values of the shape parameter α and the lighting coeffi-cient l_{init} by the SHBMM-based method as described in Algorithm 3 of Section 7.3. Compute the initial albedo value ρ_{init} by using Equation (7.50), that is,

$$\rho_{\text{init}_{u,v}} = \frac{I_{u,v}}{\sum_{i=1}^{9} h_i(\mathbf{n}_{u,v}) \cdot l_{\text{init}_i}}$$

Algorithm 4 (cont.)

(2) **Image Segmentation**: Segment the input face image into the following parts: regular shaded regions, saturated regions, and shadow regions, by thresholding the image intensity values, and further divide the image into regular subregions. Typically, on a 0–255 gray scale face image, the threshold values are 15 for the cast shadow and 240 for the saturated pixels, and the size of a subregion is 50×50 pixels.

(3) **Iterative Minimization**: Solve the optimization problem of (7.49), that is,

$$
\arg\min_{\rho,\lambda,\beta,l} \sum_{q=1}^{Q} \sum_{(u,v)\in\Omega_q} \left\{ W_{u,v} \left(I_{u,v} - \rho_{u,v} \sum_{i=1}^{9} h_i(\mathbf{n}_{u,v}^M) l_i \right)^2 \right.
$$

$$
\left. + W_{MM}(\rho_{u,v} - \rho_{u,v}^q)^2 \right\}
$$

$$
+ W_{SM} N_{sr} \sum_{(q_i,q_j)\in\mathcal{N}} \sum_{k=1}^{m-1} \left(\frac{\beta_k^{q_i} - \beta_k^{q_j}}{\sigma_k^{q_i q_j}} \right)^2
$$

in an alternating fashion:

(3a) Fixing the lighting l, solve for the albedo ρ, the texture PCA coefficients β, and the shape PCA coefficients λ for the surface normal $\mathbf{n}$. This can be solved by using the conjugate gradient method where the gradients are computed analytically.

(3b) Fixing the albedo ρ and the surface normal $\mathbf{n}$, solve for the global lighting l by using Equation (3.18), that is,

$$
I_{u,v} = \rho_{u,v} \sum_{i=1}^{9} l_i \cdot h_i(\mathbf{n}_{u,v}).
$$

This is a linear system that can be solved by using a linear least-square procedure.

7.5.3 *Image synthesis and recognition*

Using the technique described in the previous section, we can recover the albedo ρ, the surface normal $\mathbf{n}$, and the illumination parameter l from an input face image I. In this section, we will show how to perform face relighting for image synthesis and delighting for face recognition based on the recovered parameters. In compareison to the methods proposed in [236, 256], this technique can handle images with cast shadows, saturated areas, and partial occlusions and is robust to extreme lighting conditions.

7.5.3.1 Image relighting and delighting

Based on the recovered albedo ρ, the surface normal $\mathbf{n}$, and the illumination parameter l, one can render a face I' under a new lighting condition by setting desired values to the illumination parameter l' [9, 236] while using the recovered parameters ρ and $\mathbf{n}$:

$$I'_{u,v} = \rho_{u,v} \sum_{i=1}^{9} h^i(\mathbf{n}_{u,v}) \cdot l'_i, \qquad (7.56)$$

where (u,v) is the image pixel coordinate. However, certain texture details might be lost in the estimated face albedo ρ. One remedy is to use the ratio image technique to preserve the texture details.

We first smooth the original image using a Gaussian filter and then compute the pixel-wise ratio between the original image and its smoothed version. This pixel-wise ratio is then applied to the relit image computed by Equation (7.56) to capture the details of the original face texture. Typically, for a 640×480 image, the size of the Gaussian kernel is 11×11 with $\sigma = 2$. Note that the dark regions are treated in the same way as regular bright regions. Since it is possible that there are less texture details in dark regions than other regions, the relit dark regions might not have the same quality as the relit bright regions.

In order to evaluate the performance of MRF-based framework, Wang et al. [227, 228] conducted experiments on two publicly available face data sets: Yale Face Database B [72] and CMU-PIE Database [198]. The face images in both databases contain challenging examples for relighting. For example, there are many images with strong cast shadows, saturated or extremely low-intensity pixel values. More specifically, in Yale Face Database B, the images are divided into five subsets according to the angles of the light source direction from the camera optical axis, that is, (1) less than 12°, (2) between 12° and 25°, (3) between 25° and 50°, (4) between 50° and 77°, and (5) larger than 77°. Figure 7.8a shows one sample image per group of Yale Face Database B. The corresponding relit results from MRF-based method are shown in Figure 7.8d. For comparison, the results from Wen et al's method [236] are shown in Figure 7.8b, and the results from SHBMM-based method are

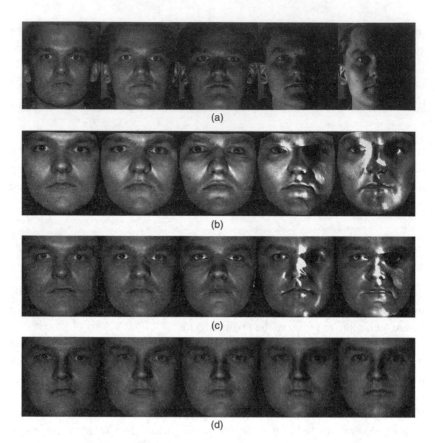

(a)

(b)

(c)

(d)

Figure 7.8. Face re-lighting experiment on Yale Face Database B [72]. (a) Example input images from group 1 to group 5. (b) The corresponding results under frontal lighting using the method proposed by Wen et al. [236]. (c) The relit results from SHBMM-based method. (d) The relit results from MRF-based method. Compared to the methods by Wen et al. [236] and the SHBMM-based method, the MRF-based method preserves photorealistic quality, especially under extreme lighting conditions such as the images in the rightmost two columns i.e., in group (4-5).

shown in Figure 7.8c. We can see that the results generated by the MRF-based method, as shown in Figure 7.8d, have much higher quality especially under extreme lighting conditions such as the images in group (4–5). Figure 7.9 shows more face relighting results on both Yale Face Database B [72] and CMU-PIE Database [198]. Despite the different extreme lighting conditions in the input images (Figure 7.9a), MRF-based method can still generate high-quality relit results as shown in Figure 7.9b.

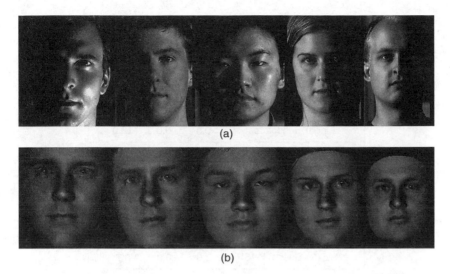

Figure 7.9. Face relighting experiment on subjects in both Yale Database B [72] and CMU-PIE Database [198]. (a) Example input images taken under different extreme lighting conditions. (b) The synthesized frontal lighting results generated by the MRF-based method with high quality.

7.5.3.2 Face recognition

In this section, we show that the MRF-based framework on face relighting from a single image can be used for face recognition. In order to normalize the illumination effects for face recognition, we relight all face images into a canonical lighting condition (i.e., the frontal lighting condition), using Equation (7.56). Once the illumination effects in images are normalized, any existing face recognition algorithms, such as Eigenfaces (Linear Discriminant Analysis or PCA) [216] and Fisherfaces (Linear Discriminant Analysis or LDA) [12], can be used on the relit face images for face recognition. In order to evaluate the face recognition performance of the MRF-based face relighting technique, Wang et al. [227, 228] tested the MRF-based method using the Yale Face Database B [72], which includes images taken under different lighting conditions, and compared the recognition results with other existing methods in the literature. The experimental results are shown in Figure 7.10.

In Yale Face Database B, there are 5,760 single-light source images of 10 subjects each seen under 576 viewing conditions (9 poses × 64 illumination conditions). In their experiments, Wang et al. [227, 228] performed face recognition for the 640 frontal pose images. Image correlation was used as the similarity measure between two images, and nearest neighbor as the classifier. For the 10 subjects in the database, they take only one frontal image per person

Methods	Error Rate (%) in Subsets		
	(1,2)	(3)	(4)
Correlation	0.0	23.3	73.6
Eigenfaces	0.0	25.8	75.7
Linear Subspace	0.0	0.0	15.0
Illum. Cones – Attached	0.0	0.0	8.6
9 Points of Light (9PL)	0.0	0.0	2.8
Illum. Cones – Cast	0.0	0.0	0.0
Zhang and Samaras [256]	0.0	0.3	3.1
BIM (30 Bases) [118]	0.0	0.0	0.7
Wen et al. [236]	0.0	1.7	30.7
MRF-Based Method	0.0	0.0	0.1

Figure 7.10. Recognition results on the Yale Face Database using various techniques. Except for Wen et al.'s method [236] and MRF-based method, the data were summarized from [118].

as the gallery image. The remaining 630 images are used as testing (probe) images.

As shown in Fig. 7.10, MRF-based method has a very low recognition error rate, compared to the rest of the recognition methods, and maintains almost the same performance even when the lighting angles become large. When the lighting direction of the test image is further away from the lighting direction of the training image, the respective illumination effects exhibit larger differences, which causes a larger recognition error rate. We can see that the MRF-based face relighting technique significantly reduces error rates, even in extreme lighting conditions (e.g., lighting angles $> 50°$).

7.6 Comparison between SHBMM- and MRF-based methods

Sections 7.3 and 7.5 described two different methods to estimate and modify the illumination conditions of a single image, namely the 3D spherical harmonic basis morphable model and the Markov random field based method. To better understand the difference and relationship between two methods, we compare them in terms of computation complexity, face synthesis, and face recognition performance.

7.6.0.3 Computational complexity

As explained in Section 7.3, the SHBMM-based method includes only three low-dimensional vectors: shape parameters, spherical harmonic basis parameters, and illumination coefficients, which are called the SHBMM parameters. However, the MRF-based method in Section 7.5 involves a more complicated optimization process to solve for a large number of shape, albedo and illumination parameters. In particular, compared to the objective function of (7.49) in the MRF-based method, the objective function of (7.28) in the SHBMM-based method is much simpler. The reduction of computational complexity mainly comes from two factors:

(i) Unlike the MRF-based method, the SHBMM-based method does not require subdividing the input face image into smaller subregions;

(ii) The objective function itself involves a much smaller number of variables to be optimized.

More specifically, given an input image, let us assume the face area has N pixels, the face region is divided into Q subregions, and the size of 3D face database is $M + 1$. Assume the number of texture PCA coefficients per subregion is M (see Equation (7.46)), and the number of geometry PCA coefficients is also M (see Equation (7.48)). Then the number of variables to be optimized in (7.49) is

$$N + Q \times M + M + 9 = N + (Q + 1) \times M + 9,$$

while the number of unknowns in (7.28) is only $M + 9$.

Since N is typically much larger than M, and Q is larger than 10, the optimization of (7.28) is much easier and less expensive than that of (7.49).

7.6.1 Face image synthesis

In Section 7.3, we showed that the simplified approach based on the 3D spherical harmonic basis morphable model can achieve good performance on delighting and relighting images. However, the representation power of the 3D SHBMM model is limited by the coupling of texture and illumination bases. Therefore, it might fail in extreme lighting conditions (e.g., in the presence of saturated areas). Figure 7.11 shows an example of the face delighting experiment using the SHBMM-based method on the CMU-PIE Database, where the four images in the first row are the input images under different unknown illuminations

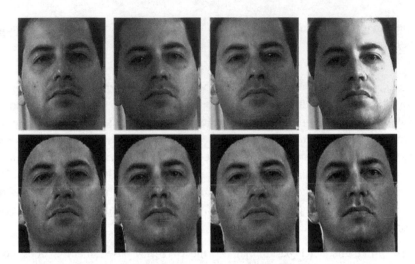

Figure 7.11. Example of delit faces using the SHBMM-based method: The images in the first row are the input images under different illumination conditions. Second row shows the corresponding delit images. The rightmost column shows a failure example where the input image is saturated.

and the images in the second row are the corresponding delit images. For regular conditions, such as the ones in the left three columns, the delit images exhibit much better invariance to illumination effects than the original images. For quantitative comparison, Wang et al. [227, 228] chose one of subjects and computed the delit images of the subject's 40 images under different illumination conditions. The variance of the 40 delit images was 6.73 intensity levels per pixel while the variance of the original images was 26.32. However, for an extreme lighting condition, such as the one in the rightmost column of Figure 7.11, where the input image is taken under an extreme illumination condition and part of the face is saturated, the delit result could not recover the saturated area faithfully.

The MRF-based method, however, decouples the estimation of the illumination and albedo and is able to handle this situation successfully. An example of high-quality synthesized results in the saturated area is demonstrated in Figure 7.12c. For comparison purposes, we also include the delit result using the SHBMM-based method in Figure 7.12b. The close-up views in Figure 7.12d–7.12f demonstrate the high quality of the images synthesized by the MRF-based method even in the presence of saturated areas.

Furthermore, because the MRF-based framework models spatial dependence, it can handle image occlusions as well. This is in spirit similar to super resolution

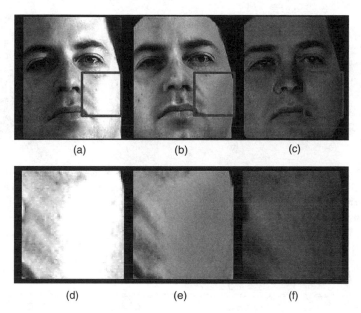

Figure 7.12. Face delighting experiment on an image with saturated regions, which is highlighted in the red boxes: (a) The original image where the left side of the face is saturated. (b) The delit result from the SHBMM-based method. (c) The delit result from the MRF-based method. (d–f) The close-up views showing that a high-quality image is synthesized by the MRF-based method even in the presence of saturated areas. Please note that because there is always a scale ambiguity between the recovered albedo and illumination, the delit faces in (c) and (f) look slightly darker than the ones in (b) and (e).

and texture synthesis [63, 273], but the technique is able to recover missing information and remove lighting effects simultaneously. Figure 7.13 shows two examples of the face delighting experiment on images under occlusions. Figures 7.13a and 7.15c are the original images under different occlusions and Figures 7.13b and 7.13d are the recovered albedos from MRF-based method. The results demonstrate that MRF-based method can generate high-quality delit images for the occluded areas as well.

7.6.2 Face recognition

In order to compare the SHBMM-based method to the MRF-method in Sections 7.3 and 7.5, Wang et al. [227, 228] examined the recognition performance on all 68 subjects in the CMU-PIE Database [198] using the same setup as in Figure 7.6 (i.e., using images taken under six representative illumination conditions). The results are reported in Figure 7.14. The details about flash light

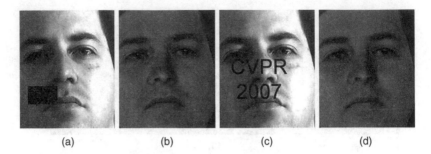

(a)   (b)   (c)   (d)

Figure 7.13. Face delighting experiment on images under occlusions: (a,c) are the original images under different occlusions and (b,d) are the recovered albedo by using MRF-based method. The MRF-based method is able to generate high-quality results for the occluded areas as well.

Light Positions	SHBMM-Based Method		MRF-Based Method
	Using SHB Parameters	Using Delit Images	
2	68.23%	70.74%	97.35%
6	91.14%	97.65%	99.55%
8	93.31%	98.93%	99.22%
12	92.66%	99.12%	99.93%
16	67.92%	69.52%	97.28%
20	89.62%	98.04%	99.86%

Figure 7.14. Face recognition under different illumination conditions: We evaluate and compare the recognition performance of the SHBMM- and MRF-based methods. The same database and experiment setting are used as in Figure 7.6. The results show that both methods achieve high recognition rates for images under a wide range of illumination conditions. However, in the extreme illumination conditions, such as light positions 2 and 16, the performance of the SHBMM-based methods decreases while the MRF-based method is more robust to illumination variation and can maintain a good recognition performance under extreme lighting conditions.

positions can be found in [198]. Figure 7.5 shows some image examples. The results in Figure 7.14 show that both the SHBMM- and MRF-based methods can achieve high recognition rates for images under regular illumination conditions. However, the performance of the SHBMM-based method decreases in the extreme illumination cases, such as light positions 2 and 16, while the MRF-based method is more robust to illumination variation and can maintain a good recognition performance under extreme lighting conditions. It is also important

Recognition Methods		Recognition Rate
SHBMM-based method	Using delit images	98.7%
	Using SHB parameters	91.9%
MRF-based method		99.3%

Figure 7.15. Recognition results on images under both single and multiple directional illumination sources from the CMU-PIE Database. There are 40 images for each subject under different illuminations. One image of each subject is randomly picked as the gallery set (prior images of people to be recognized) and the remaining images are used for testing. The random selection is performed five times, and the average recognition rates are shown. Because the SHBMM-based method could not handle extreme lighting conditions, images with large illumination angles are not included in this experiment, such as light positions 2 and 16, for fair comparison. The results show that the MRF-based method has a higher recognition rate than the SHBMM-based method.

to point out that image-based approaches, such as self-quotient images [223] and correlation filters [190, 221], can achieve comparable or even better face recognition performance without estimating the illumination conditions, albeit with the requirement of multiple training images.

Furthermore, to compare the overall performance on face recognition under a wide range of illumination conditions, Wang et al. [227, 228] tested both SHBMM- and MRF-based methods on images under both single and multiple directional illumination sources. More specifically, to study the performance of these methods on images taken under multiple directional illumination sources, they synthesized images by combining face images under different illumination conditions in the CMU-PIE Database. For each subject, they randomly selected two to four images under single directional illuminant from the training data set and combined them together with random weights to simulate face images under multiple directional illumination sources. As a result, for each subject there are 40 images under different illuminations. In the recognition step, one image of each subject was picked as the gallery set and the remaining images were used for testing. They performed the random selection five times, and the average recognition rates are shown in Figure 7.15. Because the SHBMM-based method could not handle extreme lighting conditions, they did not include images with large illumination angles, such as light positions 2 and 16.

The comparison in Figure 7.15 shows that both methods have high recognition rates on images even under multiple lighting sources. The MRF-based method has a better recognition performance and improved robustness to illumination variation than the SHBMM-based method.

Figure 5.4. Marking the lower part of the face with three points, which are shown in large yellow dots. This is an optional step. See text for explanation.

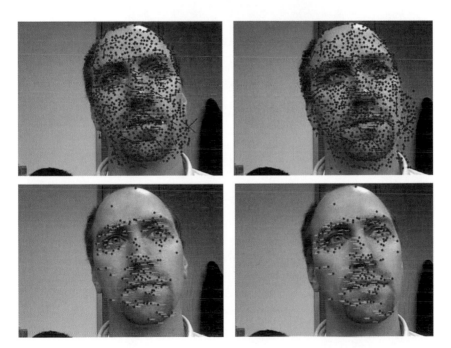

Figure 5.5. Top row: The set of matches established by correlation for the pair of images shown in Figure 5.2. Red dots are the detected corners. Blue lines are the motion vectors of the matches, with one endpoint (indicated by a red dot) being the matched corner in the current image and the other endpoint being the matched corner in the other image. Bottom row: The final set of matches after discarding automatically false matches for the pair of images shown in Figure 5.2. Green lines are the motion vectors of the matches, with one endpoint (indicated by a red dot) being the matched corner in the current image and the other endpoint being the matched corner in the other image.

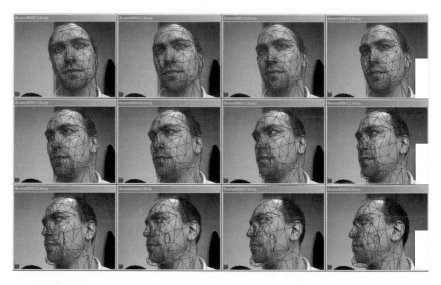

Figure 5.10. The face mesh is projected back to the automatically selected images from the video sequence where the head turns to the right.

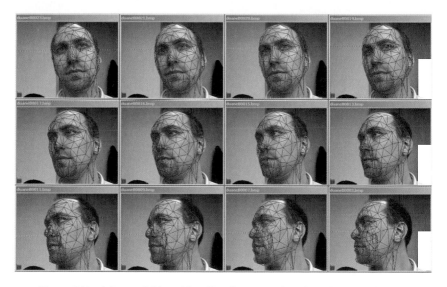

Figure 5.11. After model-based bundle adjustment, the refined face mesh is projected back to the automatically selected images from the video sequence where the head turns to the right.

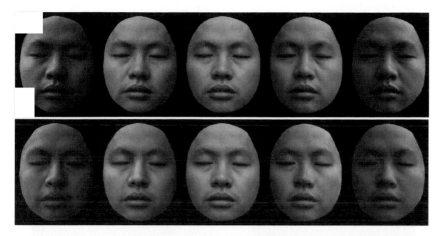

Figure 6.8. The comparison of synthesized results and ground truth. The top row is the ground truth. The bottom row is the synthesized result, where the middle image is the input.

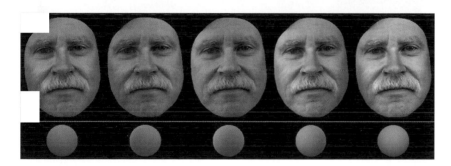

Figure 6.9. The middle image is the input. The sequence shows a 180° rotation of the lighting environment.

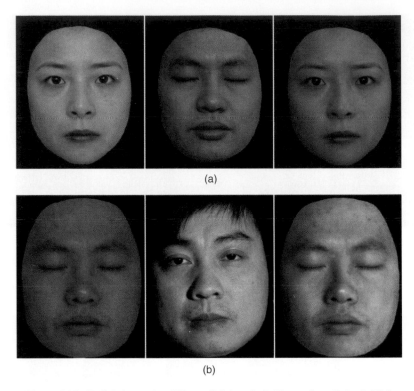

(a)

(b)

Figure 6.10. Relighting under different lighting. Left: Face to be relighted. Middle: Target face. Right: Result.

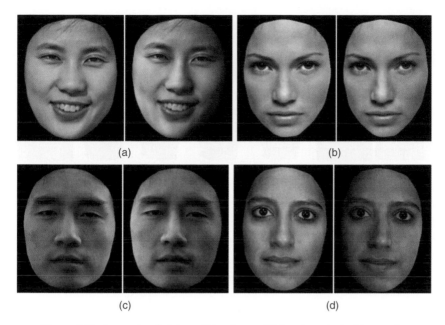

(a)   (b)

(c)   (d)

Figure 6.11. Interactive lighting editing by modifying the spherical harmonics coefficients of the pseudo irradiance environment map.

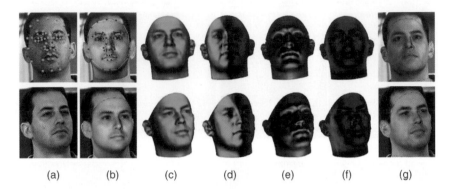

(a)   (b)   (c)   (d)   (e)   (f)   (g)

Figure 7.2. Fitting a 3D spherical harmonic basis morphable model to images (a) Input image. (b) Initial result of fitting the 3D face model to the input image. Red points are selected major feature points. Green points are the corresponding points on the face mesh model. (c) Recovered first order textured SHB images. (d–f) Recovered second-order textured SHB basis images where the red color means positive values and the green color means negative values. (g) Rendered image using the recovered parameters.

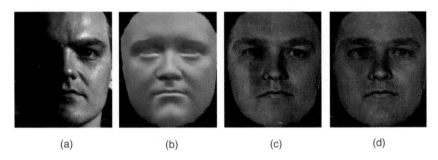

(a)   (b)   (c)   (d)

Figure 7.7. Example result: (a) the original image taken under an extreme lighting condition. (b) the recovered surface normals by using MRF-based framework (where R, G, B color values represent the x, y, z components of the normal). (c) the recovered albedo without the spatial coherence term. (d) the recovered albedo with the spatial coherence term. Note that the region inconsistency artifacts in (c) are significantly reduced in (d).

Figure 8.5. A performance-driven animation example generated by professional animators. Courtesy of Royal Winchester, Duane Molitor, and Jason Waskey.

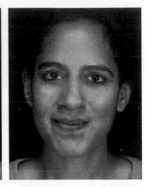

Figure 8.6. Facial expression mapping with expression details. The source image pair are displayed in Figure 8.10a. Left: neutral face. Middle: result from geometric warping. Right: result from using expression detail mapping.

Figure 8.8. An expression used to map to other people's faces. The image on the right is its expression ratio image. The ratios of the RGB components are converted to colors for display purpose.

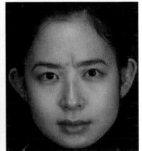

Figure 8.9. Mapping a thinking expression. Left: Neutral face. Middle: Result from geometric warping. Right: Result from ERI.

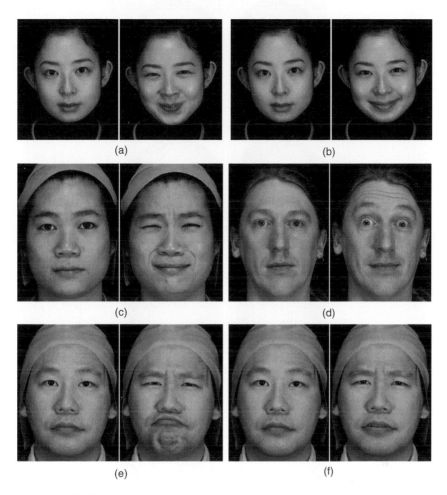

Figure 8.10. Expressions used to map to other people's faces.

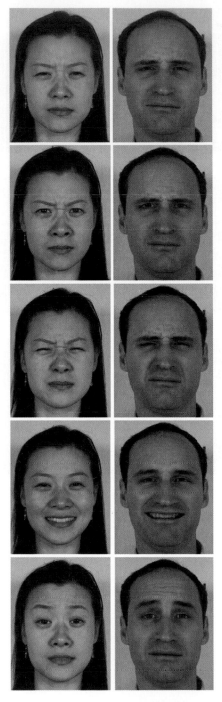

Figure 8.28. Results of the enhanced expression mapping. The expressions of the female are mapped to the male. Forty feature points are used as input for motion propagation.

Figure 9.1. Top left: synthetic sphere with many small bumps generated by using bump mapping technique. Top middle: photograph of a nectarine. Top right: result obtained by transferring the geometrical details of the sphere to the nectarine. Bottom left: photograph of an orange. Bottom middle: photograph of a nectarine. Bottom right: the synthesized image obtained by transferring the geometrical details of the orange to the nectarine.

Figure 9.2. Top row left: photograph of a tissue. Top row center: synthesized image of a rectangle. Top row right: image obtained by transferring the geometrical details of the tissue to the rectangle. Second row left: photograph of a tissue. Second row center: image of a piece of wood. Second row right: synthesized image obtained by transferring the geometrical details of the tissue to the wood. Bottom row left: image of a tissue. Bottom row center: image of a table surface. Bottom row right: synthesized image obtained by transferring the geometrical details of the tissue to the table surface.

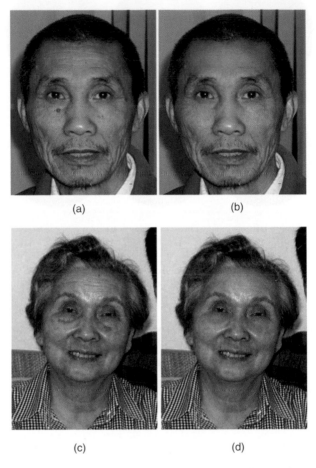

Figure 9.6. Removing wrinkles and color spots of two senior people. (a) Input image of a senior male; (b) The result after applying the touch-up tool on some of the male's color spots and his forehead area; (c) Input image of a senior female; (d) The result after applying the touch-up tool on her forehead and eye region.

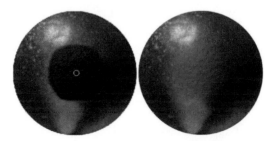

Figure 9.7. Applying Photoshop 7.0's healing brush from the bumpy sphere to the nectarine (shown in Figure 9.1). Left: the applied region. Right: the result.

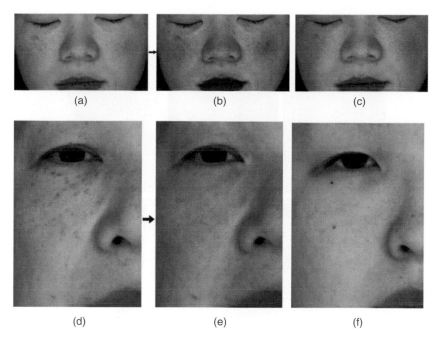

(a) (b) (c)

(d) (e) (f)

Figure 9.9. Top row: simulating the effect of alcohol consumption. (a) Original image. (b) Synthesized image. (c) Real image of the person after alcohol consumption. Bottom row: the image of a 50-year-old female is modified to match that of a 20-year-old female. (d) Original image of a 50-year-old female. (e) Synthesized image. (f) Image of a 20-year-old female. Courtesy of Tsumura et al. [214].

Figure 9.11. Images on the left are input frames captured by two different webcams. Images on the right are the enhanced frames by the proposed method.

Figure 9.14. A sample image from each class. The top left, top middle, top right, and bottom left images are, respectively, courtesies of See-Ming Lee, Aki Hanninen, Westfall, and Photoburst (http://www.flickr.com/photos/[seeminglee, hanninen,imagesbywestfall,photonburst]).

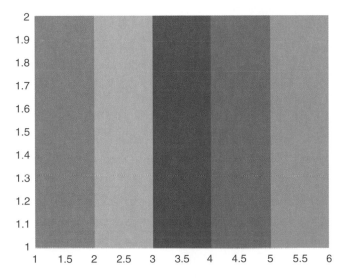

Figure 9.15. Mean colors of the five classes.

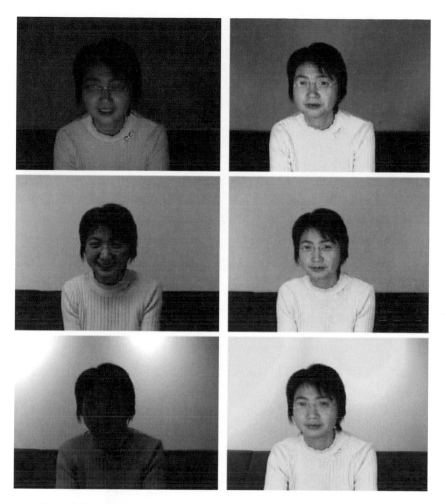

Figure 9.23. Captured video frames in three different room lighting environment: dark room lighting for the top row, normal room lighting for the middle row, and back lighting for the bottom row. In the left column are video frames captured without active lighting and with the camera auto exposure turned on. In the right columns are video frames captured with the active lighting.

SYSTEM STATUS [FPS: 1.44]
HasFloor
IsListening
InConversation

Figure 11.7. The system detects two faces which are marked with yellow rectangles. The avatar talks to the person on the left. The red dot on the left person's face is the attention of the avatar.

Figure 11.20. Final image I_F.

PART III

Applications

8

Face animation

Avatars are commonly used in virtual world and game applications. Examples include online games, Internet chat rooms, virtual communities, simulation training systems, and so on. Typically, these systems allow the users to choose an avatar as their identities in the virtual world. One interesting application of the face-modeling technology is to allow the users to build their personalized avatars and import the avatars in the virtual worlds. Face-relighting techniques can be used to make the face look consistent with the lighting conditions of the virtual worlds.

After we obtain a face model, we need to animate it to make the model look alive. In this chapter, we describe techniques to animate a face model including speech-synchronized animation and facial expression synthesis.

8.1 Talking head

The ability to talk is a basic requirement for a face animation system. The audio track can be either synthesized signals or recorded real speech. There are two different ways to drive the talking head: text or audio. If we use text, we need to synthesize the audio based on the text. This is done by a text-to-speech (TTS) system [97]. In addition to generating the audio signals, a TTS system also outputs the phonemes in real time as the audio is played. The face animation system needs to generate the mouth shapes that are consistent with the phonemes. This is called lip synchronization or lip sync in short. One drawback with a text-to-speech system is that the synthesized audio usually does not sound natural. An even more difficult problem is how to synthesize audio so that it sounds like a particular person's speech. Both are challenging research problems in the speech synthesis area.

Instead of using text, one can directly use audio (spoken by a real person) to drive the talking head. In this way, the audio will sound natural. But the

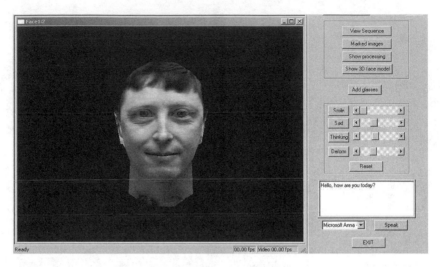

Figure 8.1. A snapshot of the talking head system developed at Microsoft Research.

system needs to analyze the audio signals to recognize the phonemes. For an offline authoring system, one could provide both the audio signals and the corresponding text. A speech-to-text alignment technique [151] can then be used to generate the phonemes associated with the audio signals. The task is much more challenging for a real-time system because the text is not available and the delay has to be very small. For techniques on phoneme analysis for lip sync application, the readers are refereed to [164, 235].

Figure 8.1 is a snapshot of the talking head system developed by Liu et al. [135]. The 3D face model is generated automatically by using the technique described in Section 5.1. It uses Microsoft Speech SDK as the text-to-speech engine. There are 21 visemes as shown in Figure 8.2. Each viseme is represented in the same format as a deformation vector (Section 2.3.2). Each time when a phoneme is uttered, the animation system deforms the face mesh by adding the corresponding viseme's deformation vector. The deformation between phonemes can be realized through interpolation between successive deformation vectors.

8.2 Facial expression synthesis

A common method for representing facial expressions was the Facial Action Coding System (FACS), which was developed by Ekman and Friesen [52]. This system describes all the possible muscle movements of a human face as *action units*. There are 46 action units. Their names and associated muscles are

Viseme	Phoneme	Viseme	Phoneme
SP_VISEME_0	silence	SP_VISEME_11	ay
SP_VISEME_1	ae, ax, ah	SP_VISEME_12	h
SP_VISEME_2	aa	SP_VISEME_13	r
SP_VISEME_3	ao	SP_VISEME_14	l
SP_VISEME_4	ey, eh, uh	SP_VISEME_15	s, z
SP_VISEME_5	er	SP_VISEME_16	sh, ch, jh, zh
SP_VISEME_6	y, iy, ih, ix	SP_VISEME_17	th, dh
SP_VISEME_7	w, uw	SP_VISEME_18	f, v
SP_VISEME_8	ow	SP_VISEME_19	d, t, n
SP_VISEME_9	aw	SP_VISEME_20	k, g, ng
SP_VISEME_10	oy	SP_VISEME_21	p, b, m

Figure 8.2. The list of visemes that are used by Microsoft Speech SDK.

described in the book by Parke and Waters [164]. A facial expression typically involve the contraction of multiple facial muscles. Thus, a facial expression can be represented as a combination of multiple action units.

In the talking head system developed by Liu et al. [135] (Figure 8.1), each action unit is stored as a mesh deformation vector. A facial expression is then created offline by linearly combining the action units and is stored as another deformation vector. At run time, given a smile strength value, the expression is generated by adding the deformation vector scaled by the strength value to the neutral face mesh. Figure 8.3 shows a smile expression with strength value 0.5.

The system allows a user to enter a text decorated with facial expressions. For example, a user can type "Well, <THINKING $t = 1.5$ s $= 0.7$/> this is really strange." The avatar will first speak "well." Afterwards, the avatar makes a think expression and at the same time speaks "this is really strange." <THINKING $t = 1.5$ s $= 0.7$/> is a simple XML-based syntax specifying the name of the expression (THINKING), the length ($t = 1.5$, in seconds), and the strength value ($s = 0.7$). During the 1.5 seconds, the avatar starts from neutral expression, gradually changes to a THINKING expression of strength value 0.7, and finally fades out to neutral expression. Each in-between frame is a linear interpolation between the neutral expression and the THINKING expression. For each frame, the deformation vector for the viseme and the deformation vector for the expression are both added to the neutral mesh thus generating speech animation with facial expression. Figure 8.4 is a snapshot of the animation where the text input is "Well, <THINKING $t = 1.5$ s $= 0.7$/> this is really strange."

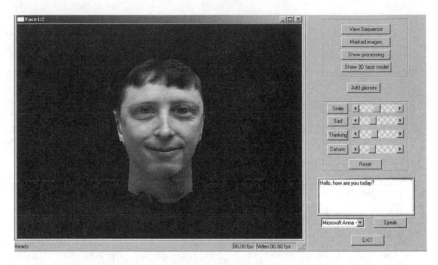

Figure 8.3. A smile expression is represented as a deformation vector of the mesh vertices. Given a smile strength value, the expression is generated by adding the smile deformation vector scaled by the smile strength to the neutral face mesh.

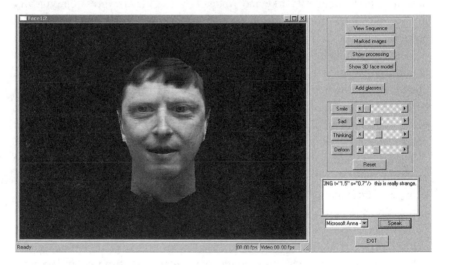

Figure 8.4. A snapshot of the avatar speaking and at the same time making an expression. The text input is "Well, <THINKING t = 1.5 s = 0.7/> this is really strange." The system generates both the lip sync animation and the facial expression. In this example, the expression name is "THINKING". The length of the expression is 1.5 seconds, and the strength value is 0.7.

There has been a lot of research on synthesizing realistic looking facial expressions. The approaches can be roughly divided into three categories: physically based approach, morph-based approach, and facial expression mapping. In the rest of the chapter, we give an overview on the techniques in each category and provide detailed descriptions on some facial expression mapping techniques.

8.3 Physically based facial expression synthesis

One of the early physically based approaches is the work by Platt and Badler [170], who used a mass-and-spring model to simulate the skin. They introduced a set of muscles where each muscle is attached to a number of vertices on the skin mesh. When a muscle contracts, it generates forces on the skin vertices, thereby deforming the skin mesh. A user generates facial expressions by controlling the muscle actions.

Waters [233] introduced two types of muscles: linear and sphincter. The lips and eye regions are better modeled by the sphincter muscles. To gain better control, they defined an influence zone for each muscle so that the influence of a muscle diminishes as the vertices are farther away from the muscle attachment point.

Terzopoulos and Waters [207] extended Waters' model by introducing a three-layer facial tissue model. A fatty tissue layer is inserted between the muscle and the skin, providing more fine grain control over the skin deformation. This model was used by Lee et al. [122] to animate dense face meshes obtained by using laser scanners.

One drawback with the physically based approaches is the difficulty of generating natural looking facial expressions. There are many subtle skin movements such as wrinkles and furrows that are difficult to model with a mass-and-spring scheme.

8.4 Morph-based facial expression synthesis

Given an existing set of facial expressions where each expression is associated with a face mesh and optionally a texture map, one could blend the meshes and texture maps to generate new expressions. This technique is called morphing or interpolation. It was first reported in Parke's pioneer work [162]. Beier and Neely [11] developed a feature-based image-morphing technique to blend images of facial expressions. Bregler et al. [26] applied the morphing technique to mouth regions to generate lip sync animations. Pighin et al. [168] used the morphing technique on both the 3D meshes and texture images to generate 3D photorealistic facial expressions. They first used a multiview stereo technique to construct the 3D geometries of a set of example facial expressions for a given person. Then they used the convex linear combination of the examples to generate new facial expression geometries and texture maps. To gain coarse-to-fine control, they allowed the user to interactively specify a small face region so that the blending affects only the specified region. The advantage of this technique is that it generates 3D photorealistic facial expression details. The disadvantage is that the possible expressions this technique can generate is limited. The local control mechanism greatly enlarges the expression space, but it puts burdens on the user. The artifacts around the region boundaries may occur if the regions are not selected properly. Joshi et al. [104] developed a technique to automatically divide the face into subregions for coarse-to-fine control. The region segmentation is based on the analysis of motion patterns for a set of example expressions.

8.5 Expression mapping

Expression mapping, also called *performance-driven animation* or *expression transfer*, has been a popular technique for generating realistic facial expressions. This technique applies to both 2D images and 3D meshes. The principle of expression mapping is quite simple. To animate a model, one just needs to track the motions of a performer, and use the performer's motion to drive the model. For example, this technique was used to produce some of the facial animations in the renowned film *Tony de Peltrie*. Figure 8.5 shows an example of performance-driven animation generated by professional animators.[†] The model is shown on the left and the performer is shown on the right. The video footage of the performer including the sound track was first recorded. The artist then created the motions of the model by observing the performer. It is interesting to note that the motion of the model does not strictly follow the motion of the performer, but the emotion of the performer is clearly mapped to the model. In some cases, the emotion of the model is exaggerated to make the animation look more appealing.

While an artist can do an amazing job of expression mapping, computational techniques are still a long way from achieving that level of quality. Below is the simplest algorithm for expression mapping. Given an image of a person's neutral face and another image of the same person's face with an expression, the positions of the face features such as eyes, eyebrows, and mouth on both images

[†] The video was created by Royal Winchester, Duane Molitor, and Jason Waskey. The actor was Mary Jo Reynolds.

Figure 8.5. A performance-driven animation example generated by professional animators. Courtesy of Royal Winchester, Duane Molitor, and Jason Waskey. (See plate section for color version.)

are located either manually or through some automatic face feature detection method. The difference vector of the feature point positions is then added to a new face's feature positions to generate the new expression for that face through geometry-controlled image warping (we call it *geometric warping*) [11, 129, 240]. In the 3D case, the expressions are meshes, and the vertex positions are 3D vectors. Instead of image warping, one needs a mesh deformation procedure to deform the meshes based on the feature point motions [80, 200, 204].

Williams [239] developed a system to track the dots on a performer's face and map the motions to the target model. Litwinowicz and Williams [129] used this technique to animate images of cats and other creatures. There has been much research done to improve the basic expression mapping technique. Pighin et al. [168] parameterized each person's expression space as a convex combination of a few basis expressions and proposed mapping one person's expression coefficients to those of another person. It requires that the two people have the same number of basis expressions and that there is a correspondence between the two basis sets. This technique was extended by Pyun et al. [172]. Instead of using convex combination, Pyun et al. [172] proposed the use of radial basis functions to parameterize the expression space. Noh and Neumann [249] developed a technique to automatically find a correspondence between two face meshes based on a small number of user-specified correspondences. They also developed a new motion mapping technique. Instead of directly mapping the vertex difference, this technique adjusts both the direction and the magnitude of the motion vector based on the local geometries of the source and target model.

One particularly interesting problem in facial expression mapping is how to transfer expression details. In 2001, Liu et al. [130] proposed an expression ratio image technique for expression detail mapping on 2D images. In 2004, Sumner and Popovic [204] proposed a technique to transfer 3D facial expression details. They modeled geometric deformations as a series of triangle-based transformations. The deformations are mapped from a source mesh to a target mesh through a globally constrained per-triangle deformation scheme. In 2006, Zhang et al. [259] developed a motion-propagation-based technique to synthesize photorealistic facial expression details based on feature point motions, which can be obtained from a performer. This technique requires example expressions of the target person. In the same year, Fu and Zheng [65] developed a system, called M-Face, that integrates expression ratio images, aging ratio images, and illumination ratio images into a single framework to synthesize faces of blended attributes: novel views, ages, and illumination conditions. In 2007, Song et al. [200] developed a general framework for facial expression detail transfer that works on both 3D meshes and 2D images. One challenging aspect in 3D expression detail mapping is that it is difficult to capture 3D facial expression details. The fine geometric deformations on human faces are difficult to capture even with laser scanners.

We will describe in more detail the expression ratio image technique [130] in the rest of this section, and the motion-propagation-based technique [259] in Section 8.6.

8.5.1 Mapping expression details

It is common knowledge that facial expressions exhibit not only facial feature motions but also subtle changes in illumination and appearance such as creases and wrinkles. These details are important visual cues, but they are difficult to capture or synthesize using geometric approaches. For instance, the conventional geometric warping approach captures face feature's geometric changes but completely ignores the illumination changes caused by skin deformations. Consequently, the resulting expressions do not have the expression details.

Figure 8.6 shows a comparison of an expression with and without the expression details. The left image is the original neutral face. The one in the middle is the expression generated using the traditional expression mapping method where the source image pair are from Figure 8.10a. The image on the right is the expression generated using the technique developed by Liu et al. [130] that preserves expression details. The face feature geometric locations on the right image are exactly the same as those on the middle image. Because there are expression details, the right image looks much more convincing than the middle one.

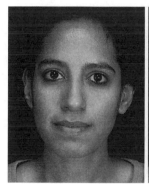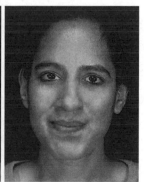

Figure 8.6. Facial expression mapping with expression details. The source image pair are displayed in Figure 8.10a. Left: neutral face. Middle: result from geometric warping. Right: result from using expression detail mapping. (See plate section for color version.)

The main idea of the technique in [130] is that the illumination changes caused by the skin deformations can be extracted in a skin albedo independent manner using an *expression ratio image (ERI)*. The ERI can then be applied to a different person's face image to generate the correct illumination changes caused by the skin deformation of that person's face.

8.5.1.1 Expression ratio image

Let I_a denote person A's neutral face image, and let I'_a denote A's expression image. We assume that I_a and I'_a are taken under the same lighting condition. Given a point on the face, let ρ_a be its albedo, and let N be its normal on the neutral face. Let N' be the normal when the face makes the expression. Assuming Lambertian reflection, we have $I_a = \rho_a E(\text{N})$ and $I'_a = \rho_a E(\text{N}')$. Taking the ratio, we have

$$\frac{I'_a}{I_a} = \frac{E(\text{N}')}{E(\text{N})}. \tag{8.1}$$

Notice that $\frac{I'_a}{I_a}$ captures the illumination changes due the changes of surface normals, and furthermore, it is independent of A's albedo. $\Re = \frac{I'_a}{I_a}$ is the (ERI).

Let I_b denote person B's neutral face image. Let ρ_b denote its albedo. By assuming that B and A are taken under similar lighting conditions and they have similar surface normals on their corresponding points, we have $I_b = \rho_b E(\text{N})$. Let I'_b denote the image of B making the same expression as A, then $I'_b = \rho_b E(\text{N}')$. Therefore,

$$\frac{I'_b}{I_b} = \frac{E(\text{N}')}{E(\text{N})}. \tag{8.2}$$

Thus,

$$I'_b = I_b \frac{I'_a}{I_a} \tag{8.3}$$

Therefore, we can compute I'_b by multiplying I_b with the expression ratio image.

In practice, the images are usually taken in different poses with different cameras. Thus, they are usually not aligned. In order to apply Equation 8.3, we have to align the images first. Given images $\tilde{I}_a$, $\tilde{I}'_a$, $\tilde{I}_b$, which have not been aligned, we use the following procedure for facial expression mapping that preserves facial expression details.

Algorithm 1 The algorithm for expression mapping using ERI

(1) Find the face features of $\tilde{I}_a$, $\tilde{I}'_a$, $\tilde{I}_b$ (either manually or using an automatic face alignment method).

(2) Compute the difference vector between the feature positions of $\tilde{I}_a$ and $\tilde{I}'_a$. Move the features of $\tilde{I}_b$ along the difference vector, and warp the image accordingly. Let I_{bg} denote the warped image, which is the result of traditional expression mapping based on geometric warping.

(3) Align $\tilde{I}_a$ and $\tilde{I}'_a$ with I_{bg} through image warping, and denote the warped images by I_a and I'_a, respectively.

(4) Compute the ERI: $\Re = \frac{I'_a}{I_a}$.

(5) Set $I'_b = \Re I_{bg}$.

Note that this algorithm requires three warping operations for each input image I_b. When applying the same expression to many people, we can save computation by precomputing the ratio image with respect to I_a or I'_a. During expression mapping for a given image I_b, we first warp that expression ratio image to align with I_{bg} and then multiply the warped expression ratio image with I_{bg}. In this way, we only need to perform warping twice for every input image.

In the preceding discussion, we only considered the monochromatic lights. For colored lights, we apply exactly the same equations to each R, G, and B component of the color images, and compute one ERI for each component. During expression mapping, each ERI is independently applied to the corresponding color component of the input image.

Equation 8.3 requires that the lighting conditions for I_a and I_b are the same. If the lighting conditions are different, the equation does not necessarily hold. If however, the main difference is just a global intensity scaling of the irradiance, the equation is still correct. This probably explains why this method works reasonably well for many images taken under different lighting environments.

In other cases, Liu et al. [130] reported that performing color histogram matching [75] before expression mapping is helpful in reducing some of the artifacts due to different lighting conditions. In addition, they found that the result is noisy if one directly applies the three color ERIs. A better solution is to first convert RGB images into the YUV space [60], compute the ERI only for the Y component, map it to the Y component of the input image, and finally convert the resulting image back into the RGB space. Of course, an even better solution is to use face-relighting techniques described in Chapers 6 and 7.

8.5.1.2 Filtering

Since image alignment is based on image warping controlled by a coarse set of feature points, misalignment between I_a and I'_a is unavoidable, resulting in a noisy expression ratio image. So we need to filter the ERI to clean up the noise while not smoothing out the wrinkles. The idea is to use an adaptive smoothing filter with little smoothing in expressional areas and strong smoothing in the remaining areas.

Since I_a and I'_a have been roughly aligned, their intensities in the nonexpressional areas should be very close (i.e., the correlation is high, even though their intensities in the expressional areas are very different). So for each pixel, we can compute a normalized cross correlation c between I_a and I'_a, and use $1 - c$ as its weight.

After the weight map is computed, an adaptive Gaussian filter is performed on the ERI. For pixels with a large weight, a small window Gaussian filter is used so that the expressional details are not smoothed out. For pixels with a small weight, a large window is used to smooth out the noises in the ERI.

8.5.1.3 Results

This section shows some experiment results of facial expression mapping with ERI. These results are extracted from [130]. Figure 8.7 shows an example of the face feature points that are used for image alignment. Liu et al. [130] used a triangulation-based method for image warping, which consists of the following steps. First, a 2D triangular mesh from the feature points is formed either manually or through Delauney triangulation. Second, the vertex coordinates are set

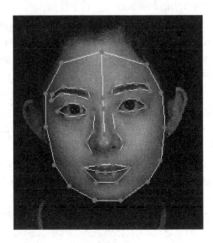

Figure 8.7. The face feature points for facial expression mapping with ERI.

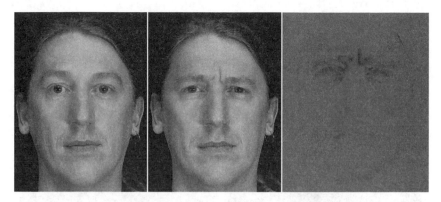

Figure 8.8. An expression used to map to other people's faces. The image on the right is its expression ratio image. The ratios of the RGB components are converted to colors for display purpose. (See plate section for color version.)

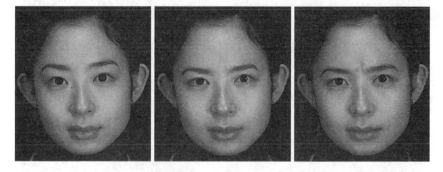

Figure 8.9. Mapping a thinking expression. Left: Neutral face. Middle: Result from geometric warping. Right: Result from ERI. (See plate section for color version.)

to be the target positions of the expression face. Third, the mesh is rendered by using the source image as the texture map.

For the first example, we map the thinking expression of the middle image in Figure 8.8 to a different person's neutral face, which is the left image of Figure 8.9. The middle image of Figure 8.9 is the result from the traditional geometrical warping. The right image is the result obtained by using ERI. We can see that the wrinkles due to the skin deformation between the eyebrows are nicely captured by ERI. As a result, the generated expression is more expressive and convincing than the middle one obtained with geometric warping.

Figure 8.10 shows six examples of facial expressions to be mapped to other people.

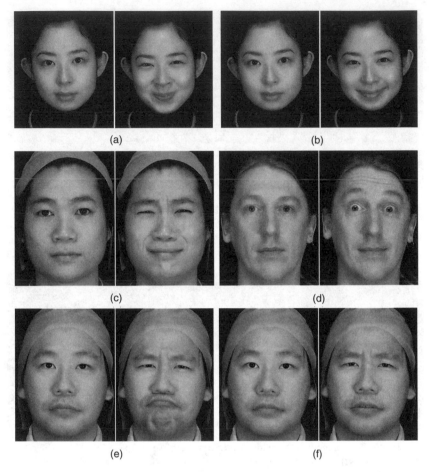

(a)   (b)

(c)   (d)

(e)   (f)

Figure 8.10. Expressions used to map to other people's faces. (See plate section for color version.)

Figure 8.11 shows the result of mapping the sad expression in Figure 8.10c. The right image in Figure 8.11 is the result generated by using ERI, while the result from geometric warping is shown in the middle. The right image clearly shows a sad/bitter expression, but we can hardly see any sadness from the middle image.

Figure 8.12 shows the result of mapping a raising-eyebrow expression in Figure 8.10d. We can see that the wrinkles on the forehead are mapped nicely to the female's face.

Figure 8.13 shows the result of mapping the frown expression in Figure 8.10e to an already smiling face (the left image in Figure 8.13). Because the frown

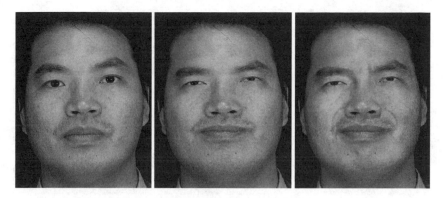

Figure 8.11. Mapping of a sad expression. Left: Neutral face. Middle: Result from geometric warping. Right: Result from ERI.

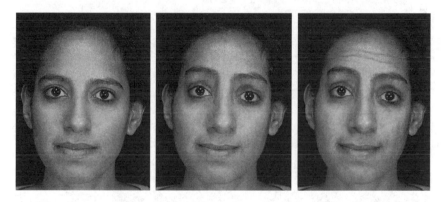

Figure 8.12. Mapping of a raising-eyebrow expression. Left: Neutral face. Middle: Result from geometric warping. Right: Result from ERI.

expression is in a separate face region from the existing smile expression, the mapping works quite well, and the resulting expression is basically the sum of the two different expressions.

Figure 8.14 shows an example of mapping expressions under different lighting conditions. The thinking expression in Figure 8.10f is mapped to the neutral face in Figure 8.14. These two images were taken in different lighting environment. Again, the image on the right is the result using ERI. We can see that the wrinkles between and above the two eyebrows are mapped quite well to the target face. The resulting expression clearly exhibits the visual effects of eyebrow crunching.

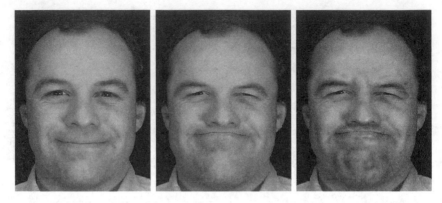

Figure 8.13. Mapping a frown expression to a smile expression. Because the two expressions are in separate face regions, the mapping is almost equivalent to the sum of the two expressions. Left: Existing expression. Middle: Result from geometric warping. Right: Result from ERI.

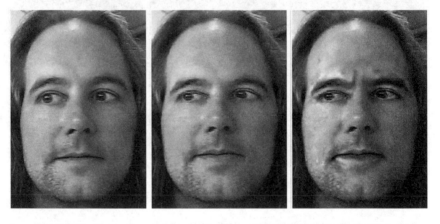

Figure 8.14. Expression mappings with different lighting conditions. Left: Neutral face. Middle: Result from geometric warping. Right: Result of ERI.

In Figures 8.15, 8.16, and 8.17, we show the results of mapping the smile expression in Figure 8.10b to different faces. Figure 8.15 shows this smile expression being mapped to a male's face. The left image is the neutral face. The middle image is generated using geometric warping, and we can see that the mouth stretching does not look natural. The image on the right is generated using ERI. The illumination changes on his two cheekbones and the wrinkles around his mouth create the visual effects of skinbulging. It exhibits a more natural and convincing smile.

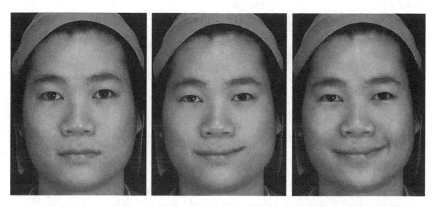

Figure 8.15. Mapping a smile. Left: Neutral face. Middle: Result from geometric warping. Right: Result from ERI.

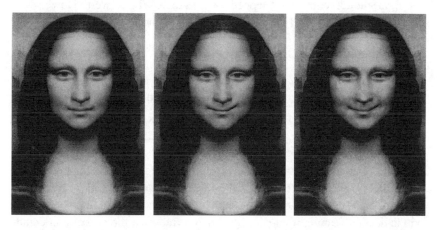

Figure 8.16. Mapping a smile to Mona Lisa's face. Left: "Neutral" face. Middle: Result from geometric warping. Right: Result from ERI.

Figure 8.16 shows the result of mapping the same smile expression in Figure 8.10b to Mona Lisa. The left image in Figure 8.16 is the image generated by Seize and Dyer [191] using their view-morphing technique. The image on the right is the result generated using ERI. The wrinkles around her two mouth corners make her smile look more natural and convincing than the one in the middle which is generated using geometric warping.

Figure 8.17 shows the results of mapping the smile expression of Figure 8.10b to two statues. The images of both statues are downloaded from the Web. The wrinkle around her left mouth corner and illumination changes on the

(a)   (b)

Figure 8.17. Mapping expressions to statues. (a) Left: Original statue. Right:
Result from ERI. (b) Left: Another statue. Right: Result from ERI.

left cheek are mapped nicely to both statues. The more subtle wrinkle around
her right mouth corner is mapped to Figure 8.17b as well. However, it
does not get mapped to Figure 8.17a because of the shadow on this statue's
right face.

8.6 Expression synthesis through feature motion propagation

One limitation of the ERI technique (Section 8.5.1) is that it requires the expression ratio image from the performer. Zhang et al. [259] proposed a technique
that only requires the feature point motions from the performer just as in the
traditional expression mapping. However, it requires a set of example expression images from the target model. They first compute the desired feature point
positions for the target model as in the traditional expression mapping. Based
on the desired feature point positions, they synthesize the expression details
for the target model from the set of example expression images of the target
model.

For each example expression, they obtain the corresponding geometry vector
and a texture image. The geometry vector consists of the 2D or 3D positions of
the face feature points. The texture images are assumed to be pixel aligned.

Let $\mathcal{E}_i = (\mathcal{G}_i, \mathcal{T}_i), i = 0, ..., m$, denote a set of example expressions where G_i
is the geometry vector and $\mathcal{T}_i$ is the texture image for the ith expression. Let
$H(\mathcal{E}_0, \mathcal{E}_1, ..., \mathcal{E}_m)$ denote the set of all possible convex combinations of these
examples. Then

$$H(\mathcal{E}_0, \mathcal{E}_1, ..., \mathcal{E}_m) = \{(\sum_{i=0}^{m} c_i \mathcal{G}_i, \sum_{i=0}^{m} c_i \mathcal{T}_i) \mid \sum_{i=0}^{m} c_i = 1, c_i \geq 0, i = 0, ..., m\}. \quad (8.4)$$

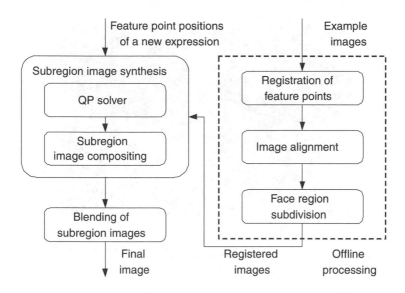

Figure 8.18. The expression texture synthesis system.

Notice that each expression in the space $H(\mathcal{E}_0, \mathcal{E}_1, ..., \mathcal{E}_m)$ has a geometric component $\mathcal{G} = \sum_{i=0}^{m} c_i \mathcal{G}_i$ and a texture component $\mathcal{T} = \sum_{i=0}^{m} c_i \mathcal{T}_i$. Since the geometric component is much easier to obtain than the texture component, Zhang et al. [259] proposed to use the geometric component to infer the texture component. Given the geometric component $\mathcal{G}$, one can project $\mathcal{G}$ to the convex hull spanned by $\mathcal{G}_0, ..., \mathcal{G}_m$, and then use the resulting coefficients to composite the example images and obtain the desired texture image.

In order to increase the space of all possible expressions, they proposed to subdivide the face into a number of subregions. For each subregion, they used the geometry associated with this subregion to compute the sub-region texture image. The final expression is then obtained by blending these subregion images together. Figure 8.18 is an overview of their expression texture synthesis system. It consists of an offline processing unit and a run time unit. The example images are processed offline only once. At run time, the system takes as input the feature point positions of a new expression. For each subregion, they solve the quadratic programming problem of Equation 8.4 by using the interior point method. They then composite the example images in this subregion together to obtain the subregion image. Finally they blend the subregion images together to produce the expression image.

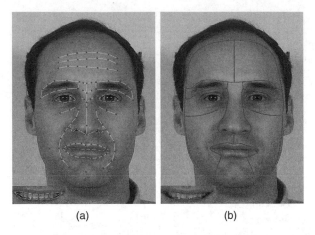

(a)   (b)

Figure 8.19. (a) Feature points. (b) Face region subdivision.

8.6.1 *Feature points and subdivision*

Figure 8.19a shows the feature points that are used in the expression texture synthesis system. Figure 8.19b shows the face region subdivision. From Figure 8.19a, we can see that the number of feature points used for their synthesis system is quite large. The reason is that more feature points are better for the image alignment and for the quadratic programming solver. The problem is that some feature points, such as those on the forehead, are quite difficult to obtain from the performer, and they are person dependent. To address this problem, they developed a motion propagation technique to infer feature point motions from a subset. Their basic idea is to learn how the rest of the feature points move from the examples. In order to have a fine-grain control, they divided the face feature points into hierarchies and performed hierarchical principal component analysis on the example expressions.

There are in total 21 feature point sets with a single feature point set in hierarchy 0, 4 sets in hierarchy 1, and 16 sets in hierarchy 2 (See Figure 8.20 for descriptions of all the feature point sets).

The single feature point set at hierarchy 0 controls the global movement of the entire face. The feature point sets at hierarchy 1 control the local movement of facial feature regions (left eye region, right eye region, nose region, and mouth region). Each feature point set at hierarchy 2 controls details of the face regions, such as eyelid shape and lip line shape. Some facial feature points belong to several sets at different hierarchies, and they are used as bridges between global and local movement of the face so that we can propagate vertex movements from one hierarchy to another.

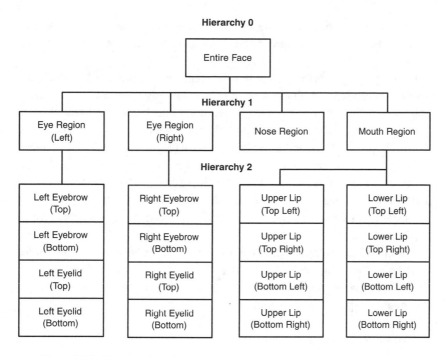

Figure 8.20. Feature point sets.

For each feature point set and each example expression, the displacement of all the vertices belonging to this feature set is evaluated. For each feature point set, the principal component analysis is applied to the vertex displacement vectors of all the example expressions. In this way, a lower dimensional vector space is generated for each feature point set.

8.6.2 Motion propagation

In this section, we describe how to use the hierarchical principal component analysis result to propagate vertex motions so that from the movement of a subset of feature points, we can infer the most reasonable movement for the rest of the feature points. The basic idea is to learn from the examples how the rest of the feature points move when a subset of the vertices move. Intuitively, we use the subspace generated by the principal components as the space that contains the most "common" feature point motions. Given the motions of a subset of the vertices, we first make a trivial guess about the motions of the rest of the vertices (e.g., by setting them to zeros). We then find its closest point in the subspace generated by the principal components. The result will

contain a better estimate for the motion of the rest of the vertices. We then
continue this process to improve the estimation. A more detailed description
follows.

Let $v_1, v_2, \ldots, v_n$ denote all the feature points on the face. Let δV denote the
displacement vector of all the feature points. For any given δV and a feature
point set F (the set of indexes of the feature points belonging to this feature
point set), we use $\delta V(F)$ to denote the subvector of those vertices that belong to
F. Let $\mathrm{Proj}(\delta V, F)$ denote the projection of $\delta V(F)$ into the subspace spanned
by the principal components corresponding to F. In other words, $\mathrm{Proj}(\delta V, F)$
is the best approximation of $\delta V(F)$ in the expression subspace. Given δV
and $\mathrm{Proj}(\delta V, F)$, we say δV is *updated* by $\mathrm{Proj}(\delta V, F)$ if for each vertex that
belongs to F, we replace its displacement in δV with its corresponding value
in $\mathrm{Proj}(\delta V, F)$.

The motion propagation algorithm takes as input the displacement vector for
a subset of the feature points, say, $\Delta v_{i_1}, \Delta v_{i_2}, ..., \Delta v_{i_k}$. Denote T to be the set
of the feature point indexes, that is, $T = \{i_1, i_2, ..., i_k\}$. Below is a description of
the motion propagation algorithm.

MotionPropagation
Begin
    Set $\delta V = 0$.
    While (stop-criteria is not met) Do
    For each $i_k \in T$, set $\delta V(i_k) = \Delta v_{i_k}$.
    For all Feature point set F, set *hasBeenProcessed*(F) to be false.
    Find the feature point set F with the lowest hierarchy such that $F \cap T \neq \emptyset$.
    MotionPropagationFeaturePointSet(F).
    End
End

The function MotionPropagationFeaturePointSet is defined as follows:

MotionPropagationFeaturePointSet(F^*)
Begin
    Set h to be the hierarchy of F^*.
    If *hasBeenProcessed*(F^*) is true, return.
    Compute $\mathrm{Proj}(\delta V, F^*)$.
    Update δV with $\mathrm{Proj}(\delta V, F^*)$.
    Set *hasBeenProcessed*(F^*) to be true.
    For each feature set F belonging to hierarchy $h - 1$ such that $F \cap F^* \neq \emptyset$.
        MotionPropagationFeaturePointSet(F).

For each feature set F belonging to hierarchy h+1 such that $F \cap F^* \neq \emptyset$.
$Motion Propagation Feature Point Set(F)$.

End

The algorithm first initializes δV to a zero vector. At the first iteration, it first sets $\delta V(i_k)$ to be equal to the input displacement vector for vertex v_{i_k}. It then finds the feature point set with the lowest hierarchy so that it intersects with the input feature point set T and calls *MotionPropagation-FeaturePointSet*. The function first uses PCA projection to infer the motions for the rest of the vertices in this feature point set. It then recursively calls *MotionPropagationFeaturePointSet* on other feature point sets. To make sure that function *MotionPropagationFeaturePointSet* is applied to each feature point set at most once, the algorithm maintains a flag named *hasBeenProcessed*. This flag is initialized to be false for all the feature point sets at the beginning of the iteration. At the end of the first iteration, δV contains the inferred displacement vectors for all the feature points. Notice that for the vertex in T, its inferred displacement vector may be different from the input displacement vector because of the PCA projection. At the second iteration, $\delta V(i_k)$ is reset to be equal to the input displacement vector for all $i_k \in T$. For the rest of the feature points that are not in T, their displacement vectors resulting from the previous iteration are used. The process is then repeated. It will result in a new δV where the displacement vectors for the vertices in T are closer to the input displacement vectors. This process continues until the stop criteria is satisfied. One can use the progress on the resulting displacement vectors in T as the stop criteria. If the average progress on the two consecutive iterations is less than a user-specified threshold, the algorithm stops.

8.6.3 Experiment results

We show some experimental results reported in [259]. They captured a number of expression images for two people: a male and a female. Each person was asked to make whatever expressions they can. There were about 30–40 expression images captured for each person. They selected the example images (see Figures 8.21 and 8.23) based on the intuitive criteria that the example expressions should be sufficiently different from each other while covering all the expressions in the captured images. The rest of the images were used as the ground truth for testing purpose. For motion propagation (Section 8.6.2), they used all the captured images (30–40 images) to perform hierarchical PCA analysis. For each feature point set, 5–10 PCA components were kept.

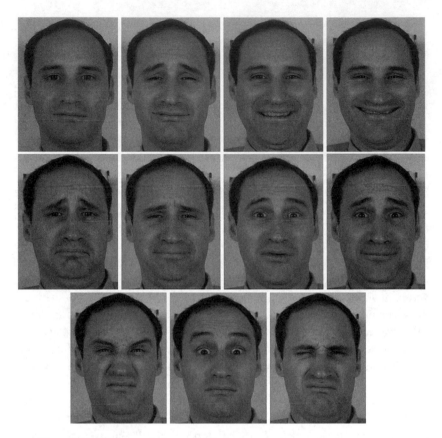

Figure 8.21. The example images of the male.

Figure 8.21 shows the selected example images for the male. The teeth examples are shown in Figure 8.22. Figure 8.24 is a side-by-side comparison where the images on the left column are ground truth, while the images on the right are the synthesized results. Even though each expression in Figure 8.24 is different from the expressions in the examples, the results from the expression synthesis system closely match the ground truth images. There is slight blurriness in the synthesized images because of the pixel misalignment resulting from the image-warping process.

Figure 8.23 shows the selected example images of the female. Figure 8.25 is the side-by-side comparison for the female where the ground truth images are on the left, while the synthesized images are on the right. Again, the synthesized results match very well with the ground truth images.

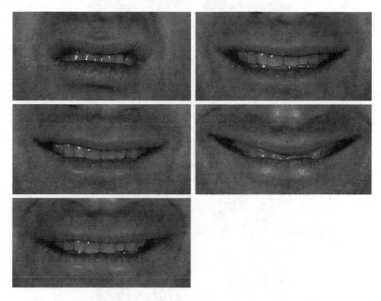

Figure 8.22. The example images of the male's teeth.

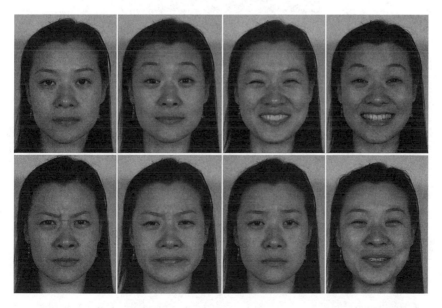

Figure 8.23. The example images of the female.

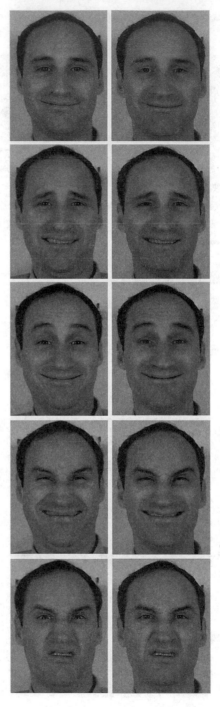

Figure 8.24. Side-by-side comparison with ground truth for the male. In each image pair, the left image is the ground truth and the right image is the synthesis result.

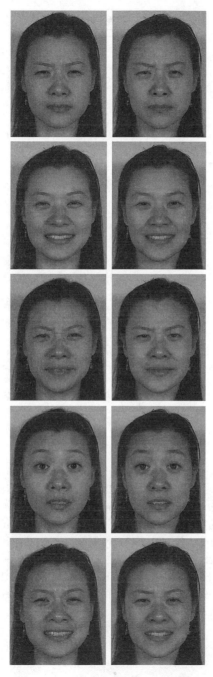

Figure 8.25. Side-by-side comparison with the ground truth of the female. In each image pair, the left image is the ground truth and the right image is the synthesis result.

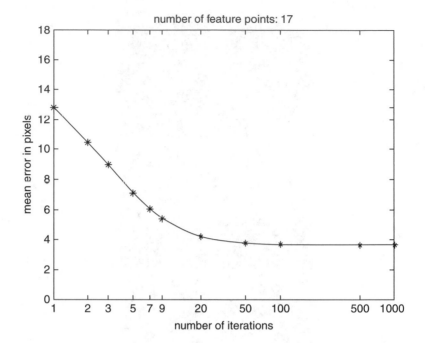

Figure 8.26. The convergence of the motion propagation algorithm with only 17 points as the input while the total number of feature points is 134. The horizontal axis is the number of iterations of the motion propagation algorithm. The vertical axis is the average error in pixels. The image size is $750 \times 1,000$.

The following experiment tests the performance of the motion propagation algorithm. The test data consists of 25 different expressions from the male actor. Only 17 feature points from the original 134 marked points are used as the input of the motion propagation algorithm to infer the motions for all of the 134 feature points (which are required by the expression synthesis system). Figure 8.26 shows the convergence of the algorithm. The horizontal axis is the number of iterations. The vertical axis is the average error in pixels for the 17 feature points and all of the 25 expressions. We can see that the error decreases quickly. It gets very close to its optimum after 50 iterations.

Figure 8.27 shows a comparison of the expression synthesis results with only 17 points and the results with all the 134 points. The images on the left are the results of using all the 134 points. The images on the right are the results of using only 17 points. We can see that the results are very close. The main difference is

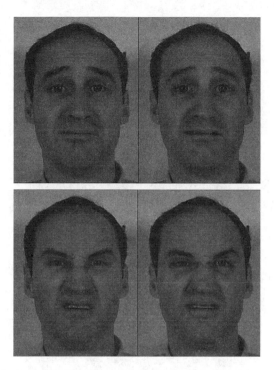

Figure 8.27. Image on the left in each pair: the result of synthesized expressions with all the feature points as input directly to the expression synthesis system. Image on the right: the result of synthesized expressions with only 17 feature points as input to the motion propagation algorithm to infer the motions of all the feature points, which are then fed into the expression synthesis system.

in the mouth region where we do not have enough examples to cover the space of all the possible mouth shapes.

Figure 8.28 shows some of the results of mapping the female's expressions to the male. Forty feature points are used as input for motion propagation. The female's expressions are the real data. The images on the right are the results of the enhanced expression mapping. We can see that the synthesized images have natural-looking expression details.

Figure 8.29 shows expression-mapping results of a live video sequence. The images on the left column are frames extracted from the input video sequence. The images on the right column are the results of mapping the expressions to a different male. The face feature points are tracked automatically by using a simple correlation-based tracking technique. Due to the difficulty of automatic face feature tracking, only 27 interior feature points are tracked. Since the

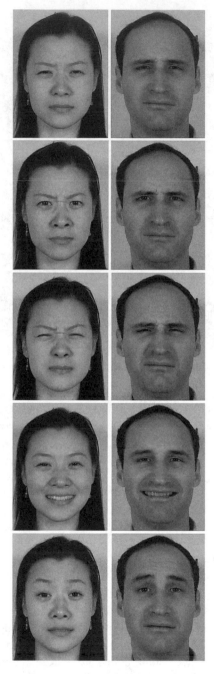

Figure 8.28. Results of the enhanced expression mapping. The expressions of the female are mapped to the male. Forty feature points are used as input for motion propagation. (See plate section for color version.)

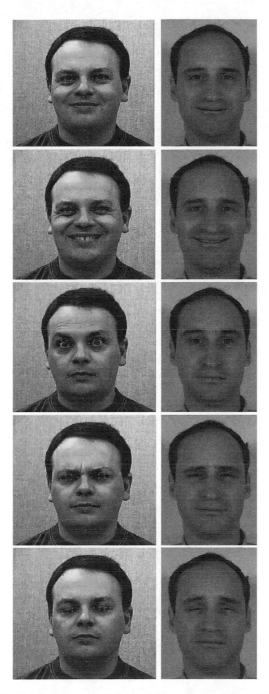

Figure 8.29. The images on the left column are frames extracted from a live video sequence of a male actor. The feature points, as shown in green, are tracked automatically. The images on the right column are the results of the enhanced expression mapping.

tracked points are noisy, a temporal smoothing procedure is used to smooth out the noises. Another problem is that there are certain amount of head pose changes in the input video. To address this problem, Zhang et al. [259] estimated the head poses and performed motion compensation to undo the head pose motion.

9

Appearance editing

Given an image of an object, if we can recover the geometry, reflectance, and lighting, we will be able to make modifications on the recovered parameters and generate a new image of the object with a different appearance. One example is to modify the lighting condition of a face image as described in Chapters 6 and 7. Such a model-based image-editing approach is powerful, but it has limitations. One important requirement for image-editing applications is that the appearance of the background needs to be consistent with that of the foreground. Unfortunately, modeling background is much more challenging than modeling the foreground object because the background is typically cluttered and has many different types of objects that occlude each other. Without background models, it is difficult to modify its appearance in a physically correct manner. An alternative is to remove the background, but foreground–background separation remains a challenging problem.

Another limitation of model-based image editing approach is that it is difficult to model and recover geometric details. For example, we would need extremely dense polygons to represent face wrinkles. How to recover such detailed geometry from images is an open problem. Thus, it is impractical to rely on recovered geometric models to edit such geometric details.

In this chapter, we describe techniques that modify an object's appearance in an image without explicitly recovering the 3D geometry or reflectance properties.

9.1 Detail transfer

In many real-world applications, it is desirable to be able to modify the geometric details of an object in an image. We might want to know, for example, how a wall would look like after adding some geometrical bumps, or how a person would look like after adding wrinkles on his or her face.

Direct methods for adding geometric details to an object require modeling the object with detailed geometry. It's usually not a trivial task to build a detailed 3D model. It's also tedious and labor intensive to model and create geometric details using existing geometric modeling tools.

Bump mapping has acted as an alternative to adding geometrical details to an otherwise smooth object. But constructing visually interesting bump maps requires practice and artistic skills.

Shan et al. [131, 192] developed a technique to transfer geometrical details from one object to another while preserving the reflectance property. The technique is capable of capturing the geometrical details of an object from a single image in a way that is independent of the object's reflectance property. Thus, the geometric details of one object can be transferred to a second object producing the new appearance of the second object with added geometrical details without modifying its reflectance property.

9.1.1 Detail transfer equation

For any given point P on a surface S, let $N(P)$ denote its normal. Assume there are m point light sources. Let $L_i(P)$, $1 \leq i \leq m$, denote the light direction from P to the ith light source and l_i be its intensity. We assume a Lambertian reflectance model, and let $\rho(P)$ denote the albedo at P. The intensity at point P in the image I is

$$I(\mathbf{p}) = \rho(P) \sum_{i=1}^{m} l_i \, N(P) \cdot L_i(P), \qquad (9.1)$$

where $\mathbf{p} = \phi(P)$ is the 2D projection of P onto the image, and $\phi(\cdot)$ is the camera projection function.

Two surfaces S_1 and S_2 are said to be *aligned* if there exists a one-to-one mapping $\mathbf{F}$ such that for all $P_1 \in S_1$ and $P_2 = \mathbf{F}(P_1) \in S_2$,

$$\|P_1 - P_2\| \leq \epsilon, \qquad (9.2)$$

where ϵ is a small positive number, and furthermore, there exist neighborhoods $\Theta(P_1)$ of P_1 and $\Theta(P_2)$ of P_2 such that

$$\|\overline{N}(P_1) - \overline{N}(P_2)\| \leq \delta, \qquad (9.3)$$

where δ is a small positive number, and $\overline{N}(P_1)$ and $\overline{N}(P_2)$ are the mean normal defined in the neighborhoods of $\Theta(P_1)$ and $\Theta(P_2)$, respectively.

The problem of geometric detail transfer can then be stated as the following. *Given images I_1 and I_2 of two aligned surfaces S_1 and S_2, respectively, what is the new image I_2' of S_2 if we modify its surface normal such that*

$$\mathbf{n}_2'(P_2) = \mathbf{n}_1(P_1), \tag{9.4}$$

where P_1 and P_2 are the corresponding points defined by the mapping **F**.

9.1.1.1 A geometric viewpoint

The following discussion assumes a single point light source to simplify the derivation. Extension to multiple light sources is straightforward. Because the distance between P_1 and P_2 is small according to Equation 9.2, it is reasonable to assume that the light is always sitting far away enough such that $\epsilon \ll d_l$, where d_l is the average distance from light to the points. This leads to the approximation $L(P_1) \approx L(P_2)$ (note that the subscript of L is omitted since we assume a single light source). From Equations 9.1 and 9.4, we then have

$$\frac{I_2'(\mathbf{p}_2)}{I_2(\mathbf{p}_2)} = \frac{\rho(P_2)\, l\, \mathbf{n}_2'(P_2) \cdot \mathbf{l}(P_2)}{\rho(P_2)\, l\, \mathbf{n}_2(P_2) \cdot \mathbf{l}(P_2)}$$

$$\approx \frac{\rho(P_1)\, l\, \mathbf{n}_1(P_1) \cdot \mathbf{l}(P_1)}{\rho(P_2)\, l\, \mathbf{n}_2(P_2) \cdot \mathbf{l}(P_2)} \frac{\rho(P_2)}{\rho(P_1)}$$

$$= \frac{I_1(\mathbf{p}_1)\, \rho(P_2)}{I_2(\mathbf{p}_2)\, \rho(P_1)}, \tag{9.5}$$

where ρ has the same meaning as in (9.1), $\mathbf{p}_1 = \phi_1(P_1)$, $\mathbf{p}_2 = \phi_2(P_2)$, and I_1, I_2, and I_2' have the same meaning as in the problem statement. Notice that the camera projections functions $\phi_1(\cdot)$ and $\phi_2(\cdot)$ are different for the two surfaces because the images I_1 and I_2 of the surfaces could be taken by two different cameras. Equation (9.5) yields

$$I_2'(\mathbf{p}_2) \approx \frac{I_1(\mathbf{p}_1)\, \rho(P_2)}{\rho(P_1)}. \tag{9.6}$$

In order to compute the ratio of $\rho(P_1)$ and $\rho(P_2)$, let us define the smoothed image of I as

$$\overline{I}(\mathbf{p}) = \sum_{\mathbf{q} \in \Omega(\mathbf{p})} w(\mathbf{q})\, I(\mathbf{q}), \tag{9.7}$$

where $\Omega(\mathbf{p}) = \phi(\Theta(P))$ is the neighborhood of $\mathbf{p}$, and $w(\cdot)$ is the kernel function of a smooth filter, say, a Gaussian filter or an average filter. Assuming that the size of $\Theta(P)$ is relatively small compared to its distance to the light source, we have $L(P) \approx L(Q), \forall Q \in \Theta(P)$. Also assuming that $\rho(P) \approx \rho(Q), \forall Q \in \Theta(P)$, from Equations 9.7 and 9.1, it is then obvious that

$$\overline{I}(\mathbf{p}) \approx \rho(P)\, l \left(\sum_{Q \in \Theta} w(\phi(Q))\, N(Q) \right) \cdot L(P), \qquad (9.8)$$

where $\sum_{Q \in \Theta} w(\phi(Q))\, N(Q) = \overline{N}(P)$, and $\overline{N}(P)$ is the mean normal as mentioned in the problem statement. For surface S_1 and S_2, we then have

$$\frac{\overline{I}_2(\mathbf{p}_2)}{\overline{I}_1(\mathbf{p}_1)} \approx \frac{\rho(P_2)\, l\, \overline{N}(P_2) \cdot L(P_2)}{\rho(P_1)\, l\, \overline{N}(P_1) \cdot L(P_1)}. \qquad (9.9)$$

Since the two surfaces are aligned, we have $L(P_1) \approx L(P_2)$, and $\overline{N}(P_2) \approx \overline{N}(P_1)$. Equation 9.9 can then be rewritten as

$$\frac{\rho(P_2)}{\rho(P_1)} \approx \frac{\overline{I}_2(\mathbf{p})}{\overline{I}_1(\mathbf{p})}. \qquad (9.10)$$

Substituting (9.10) into (9.6) leads to

$$I_2'(\mathbf{p}_2) \approx \frac{I_1(\mathbf{p}_1)}{\overline{I}_1(\mathbf{p}_1)}\, \overline{I}_2(\mathbf{p}_2). \qquad (9.11)$$

Equation (9.11) is called the *detail transfer equation*. It shows that the transfer of surface normal can be approximated by some simple operations on the images of the surfaces.

9.1.1.2 An intuitive signal-processing viewpoint

We can look at the detail transfer equation (Equation 9.11) from a different angle by treating the images as signals while not considering their underlying geometric models. Let us rewrite (9.11) as

$$I_2'(\mathbf{p}) \approx \frac{I_1(\mathbf{p})}{\overline{I}_1(\mathbf{p})}\, \overline{I}_2(\mathbf{p}) = \left(1 + \frac{I_1(\mathbf{p}) - \overline{I}_1(\mathbf{p})}{\overline{I}_1(\mathbf{p})} \right) \overline{I}_2(\mathbf{p}). \qquad (9.12)$$

From the signal-processing viewpoint, (9.12) simply substitutes the high-frequency components of I_2 with those from I_1. The high-frequency components $I_1 - \overline{I}_1$ in I_1 is normalized by $\overline{I}_1$ in order to cancel the intensity scale difference between the low-frequency components of I_2 and I_1. Generally, I_1 could be any image, regardless of the conditions given in the previous section.

But the resulting image could be meaningless because of the inconsistency between the transferred detailed components from I_1 and native low-frequency components on the I_2. This happens when I_1 and I_2 are the images of two surfaces that are not aligned.

9.1.2 Implementation

Given images I_1 and I_2 of similar shapes, to perform detail transfer, we first need to align the two images. For simple geometrical shapes such as rectangles and spheres, we usually only need to perform global transformations including rotation, translation, and scaling. For more complicated shapes such as human faces, we can use automatic face feature alignment techniques ([126, 243]) to locate face feature points on both images, and then obtain pixel alignment through image warping. The image warping can be done using a simple triangulation-based image-warping method as what is described in Section 8.5.1.3. Once the alignment is done, we can run a Gaussian filter with a user-specified σ on I_1 and I_2 to obtain $\overline{I}_1$ and $\overline{I}_2$. Finally, we apply Equation 9.11 to obtain I_2'.

Intuitively, the parameter σ of the Gaussian filter controls how much geometrical smoothing we perform on the surface of I_1. So this parameter determines the scale of the surface details to be transferred. A small σ allows fine geometrical details to be transferred while a large σ allows only large-scale geometrical deformations to be transferred.

9.1.3 Results

The top row of Figure 9.1 shows the results of transferring the geometrical details of a synthetic sphere to a real nectarine. The bumps on the synthetic sphere are generated by using the bump-mapping technique. The surface reflectance property on the synthesized sphere is set to be uniform. A point light source is placed at the top of the sphere so that its lighting condition is somewhat close to the lighting condition of the nectarine. We can see that the bumps on the synthetic sphere are transferred nicely to the nectarine except at the bottom where the synthetic sphere is basically dark. The sizes of the image are 614 by 614 pixels, and σ is 8.

The bottom row of Figure 9.1 shows the results of transferring the geometrical details of a real orange to the same nectarine as the one at the top. The bumps on the oranges are transferred faithfully to the nectarine. The image dimensions and σ are the same as what are used for the top. This example also reveals a limitation of the algorithm: the high lights on the orange are transferred to the nectarine. The reason is that the high lights are treated as being caused by geometrical variations.

Figure 9.1. Top left: synthetic sphere with many small bumps generated by using bump mapping technique. Top middle: photograph of a nectarine. Top right: result obtained by transferring the geometrical details of the sphere to the nectarine. Bottom left: photograph of an orange. Bottom middle: photograph of a nectarine. Bottom right: the synthesized image obtained by transferring the geometrical details of the orange to the nectarine. (See plate section for color version.)

The top row of Figure 9.2 shows the results of transferring the geometrical details of a real tissue to a synthetic rectangle. We can see that only the geometrical bumps on the tissues are transferred to the rectangle while the material color of the rectangle is preserved.

The second row of Figure 9.2 shows the results of geometric detail transferring from the same tissue to the image of a piece of wood. Both pictures are taken under the same lighting conditions. We can see that the small bumps on the tissue are transferred to the wood while the wood color and global texture are preserved.

The bottom row of Figure 9.2 shows the result of transferring the geometrical details of the same tissue to a table surface. This table surface has a different texture pattern than the wood on the second row. It is interesting to compare the result on the second row (the image on the right) with the result on the bottom row (the image on the right). The two images have the same geometrical bumps but different material properties.

One interesting application of the geometric detail transfer is aging effect synthesis. Geometrically speaking, the difference between an old person's skin surface and a young person's skin surface is that the old person's skin surface has more bumps than the young face. If we transfer the bumps of an old person's skin

Figure 9.2. Top row left: photograph of a tissue. Top row center: synthesized image
of a rectangle. Top row right: image obtained by transferring the geometrical details
of the tissue to the rectangle. Second row left: photograph of a tissue. Second row
center: image of a piece of wood. Second row right: synthesized image obtained
by transferring the geometrical details of the tissue to the wood. Bottom row left:
image of a tissue. Bottom row center: image of a table surface. Bottom row right:
synthesized image obtained by transferring the geometrical details of the tissue to
the table surface. (See plate section for color version.)

surface to a young person's face, the young person's face will become bumpy
and look older. Conversely, we can also replace the bumps of an old person's
skin surface with that of the young person's face so that the old person's face gets
smoother and look younger. So we can apply the details transfer technique as
described in the previous section on human faces to generate aging effects. The
alignment is done by first locating the face boundaries and face features such
as eyes, noses, and mouths, and then use triangulation-based image warping
to warp I_1 toward I_2. We only apply the detail transfer to pixels inside the
face boundary. In addition, the pixels in the regions of the two brows, the two
eyeballs, the nose top, and the mouth are not modified.

Figure 9.3 shows the aging effect synthesis results between the faces of a
young male (a) and an old male (d). Both images were taken in a room with
multiple light sources. For each face, we experiment with different σ of the
Gaussian filter during the surface detail transfer. Images in the middle (Figure
9.3b and 9.3e) are the results with $\sigma = 3$, and those on the right (Figure 9.3c

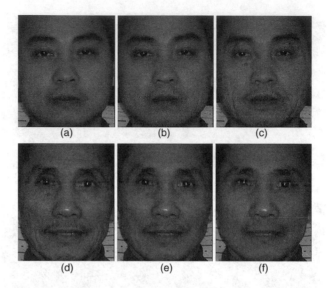

Figure 9.3. Young adult vs. senior adult. (a) The face of a young adult. (b) The simulated old face of Figure 9.3a with a small σ. (c) The simulated old face of Figure 9.3a with a large σ. (d) The face of a senior adult. (e) The simulated young face of Figure 9.3d with a small σ. (f) The simulated young face of Figure 9.3d with a large σ.

and 9.3f) with $\sigma = 8$. We can see that varying σ produces reasonable in-between aging effect such as (Figure 9.3b and 9.3e).

Obviously, surface detail transfer plays an important role when making a young person elder. However, it may be less apparent why this technique is necessary in making an old person look younger. To clarify this point, we simply smooth Figure 9.3d without transferring surface details from Figure 9.3a, while masking out the facial features as before. Figure 9.4 shows the results with $\sigma = 3$ (left image) and $\sigma = 8$ (right image). By comparing them with those shown in Figure 9.3e and 9.3f with the same σs, we can clearly see that the images in Figure 9.3 are much sharper and more convincing.

Finally, this technique can be used as a touch-up tool to remove wrinkles and color spots. The user first selects a source point on any image (which can be the same as the target image). Then he/she selects a target rectangle on the target image by clicking and dragging the mouse. When the mouse is released, the detail transfer operation is applied from the source rectangle (centered at the source point with size equal to the destination rectangle) to the destination rectangle. We then do a linear fade-in-fade-out blending along the boundary of the destination rectangle. Figure 9.5 shows an example where Figure 9.5a is the input image, Figure 9.5b shows a selected source point (the center of the small

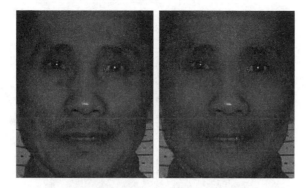

Figure 9.4. Senior adult to young adult by simple image smoothing, that is, without using detail transfer equation. Left: result with $\sigma = 3$. Right: result with $\sigma = 8$. The input face image is the one in Figure 9.3d.

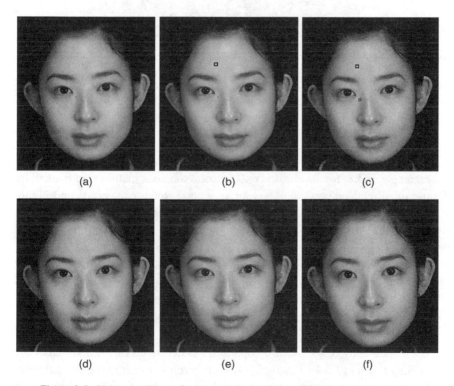

Figure 9.5. Using detail transfer as a touch-up photo-editing tool: (a) the input image; (b) the source point; (c) the destination rectangle; (d) result after applying detail transfer technique; (e) removing the second spot in the chin area; (f) removing the third spot below her right eye.

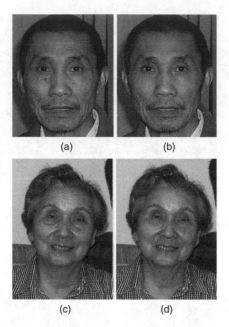

(a)   (b)

(c)   (d)

Figure 9.6. Removing wrinkles and color spots of two senior people. (a) Input image of a senior male; (b) the result after applying the touch-up tool on some of the male's color spots and his forehead area; (c) Input image of a senior female; (d) the result after applying the touch-up tool on her forehead and eye region. (See plate section for color version.)

rectangle on her forehead), Figure 9.5c shows the destination area marked by the small rectangle on top of a color spot close to her eye corner, and Figure 9.5d is the result. We can see that the color spot disappeared. In Figure 9.5e, we use the same procedure and the same source point to remove a different color spot (in her right chin area). In Figure 9.5f, we remove the color spot below her right eye. We can see that all of the three color spots are removed successfully.

Figure 9.6 shows the result of applying the touch-up tool to a senior person to remove the wrinkles on his forehead as well as some of the color spots. Figure 9.6a is the input image, and Figure 9.6b is the result.

It is worth pointing out that even though there is some similarity between the functionality of the touch-up operation as described earlier and that of the healing brush in Adobe Photoshop 7.0, the result is sometimes quite different. Figure 9.7 shows an example of using the healing brush of Photoshop 7.0 on the bumpy sphere and the nectarine as shown in Figure 9.1. In Figure 9.7, the image on the left shows the region where the brush is applied, and the image on the right is the result. The latter should be compared with the right image in

Figure 9.7. Applying Photoshop 7.0's healing brush from the bumpy sphere to the nectarine (shown in Figure 9.1). Left: the applied region. Right: the result. (See plate section for color version.)

Figure 9.1. We can see that Photoshop 7.0 does not preserve the original texture of the nectarine.

9.2 Physiologically based approach

In 2003, Tsumura et al. [214] developed a physiologically based technique for skin texture analysis and synthesis. The basic idea is to extract the hemoglobin and melanin components from an face image. One can then modify them and synthesize new images of the skin with different look. In physiology terminology, hemoglobin is a component of red blood cells that is responsible for transferring oxygen from the lungs to the rest of the body. Lower hemoglobin levels tend to make the skin look pale, while higher hemoglobin levels tend to make the skin look reddish. Melanin is a substance that gives the skin its color. For example, dark-skinned people have more melanin that light-skinned people.

As described in Section 6.1.3, human skins consist of three layers: oil layer, epidermis layer, and dermis layer. The oil layer is responsible for the specular reflectance, while the epidermis layer and dermis layer are responsible for the diffuse reflectance caused by subsurface scattering. Melanin pigments are mainly found in the epidermis layer, while hemoglobin pigments are found in the dermis layer.

Figure 9.8 is an overview of the system developed by Tsumura et al. [214]. Given a face image, its surface reflection (i.e., specular reflection) needs to be removed first. This could be done by using color–space separation techniques such as [188]. Tsumura et al. [214] used polarizing filters (one in front of the camera, and the other in front of the light source) to remove the specular reflection. The leftmost image in Figure 9.8 is the image obtained without using polarizing filters. The image with label "Body reflection" is obtained with polarizing filters. The image with label "Surface reflection" is the specular

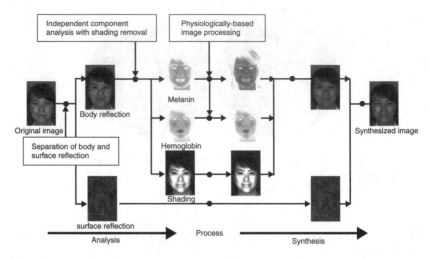

Figure 9.8. Overview of the physiologically based technique for skin texture analysis and synthesis. Courtesy of Tsumura et al. [214].

reflection component. At the end of the synthesis phase, the specular reflection component is added to the image to make the synthesized face look more natural.

A logarithm color–space analysis method is used to extract the melanin color axis and hemoglobin color axis. The analysis is based on the following assumption. If we plot the logarithm of the 3D color vectors (R,G,B) of all the skin pixels on the body reflection image, the collection of the color vectors should exhibit three axes: melanin color axis, hemoglobin color axis, and the illumination (shading) color axis. An iterative procedure is used to extract the three axes. At each iteration, a rectangular region on the body reflection is selected, and an independent component analysis is performed on the colors of the pixels within the rectangle. The resulting melanin and hemoglobin color axes are verified visually to see if they are acceptable. If not, a different rectangle is selected, and the procedure continues.

In this way, the body reflection image is decomposed into three components: melanin component, hemoglobin component, and shading component. These three components are shown at the third column from left in Figure 9.8. We can then modify these components to generate images with new skin appearance. At the fourth column from left in Figure 9.8, the melanin component is modified, and the new component looks darker. The hemoglobin and shading components are not modified. The top image at the fifth column is the result of putting the three components together. This is the new body reflection image. Finally,

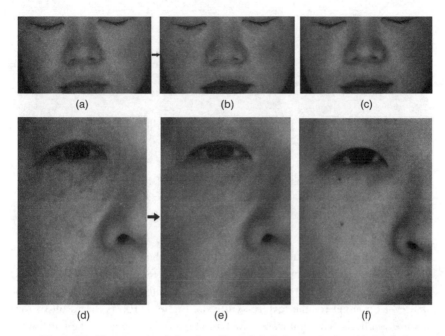

(a) (b) (c)

(d) (e) (f)

Figure 9.9. Top row: simulating the effect of alcohol consumption. (a) Original image. (b) Synthesized image. (c) Real image of the person after alcohol consumption. Bottom row: the image of a 50-year-old female is modified to match that of a 20-year-old female. (d) Original image of a 50-year-old female. (e) Synthesized image. (f) Image of a 20-year-old female. Courtesy of Tsumura et al. [214]. (See plate section for color version.)

the specular component is added to the new body reflection image to generate the final synthesized image as shown on the rightmost column.

For image synthesis, one can uniformly increase or decrease the hemoglobin and melanin components for every pixel in the image. The top row of Figure 9.9 shows an example of simulating the effect of alcohol consumption. The original image is shown in Figure 9.9a. The real image of the person after alcohol consumption is shown in Figure 9.9c. The melanin and hemoglobin components of the original image are uniformly scaled to match the real image Figure 9.9c. The resulting synthesized image is shown in Figure 9.9b. It has a realistic look of a face after alcohol consumption.

Next, we show a more complicated example where the image of a 50-year-old female is modified to match a 20-year-old female. Figure 9.9d shows the image of a 50-year-old female, and Figure 9.9f shows the image of a 20-year-old female (who is actually the daughter of the 50-year-old female). A pyramid-based texture synthesis technique ([90]) is applied to the melanin image of the

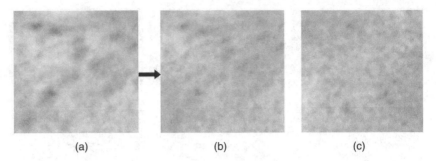

(a)   (b)   (c)

Figure 9.10. (a) Melanin texture of the 50-year-old female. (b) Synthesized melanin texture. (c) Melanin texture of the 20-year-old female. Courtesy of Tsumura et al. [214].

50-year-old female so that its texture pattern matches that of the 20-year-old female. Figure 9.10a shows the original melanin texture of the 50-year-old female, and Figure 9.9(c) is the melanin texture of the 20-year-female, which is used as a target for the texture synthesis. Figure 9.10b is the result of the texture synthesis. The synthesized melanin texture is used as the new melanin component for the 50-year-old female. In addition, the hemoglobin component is uniformly scaled to match that of the 20-year-old female. The final image is shown in Figure 9.9e. The synthesized image looks a lot younger than the original image of the 50-year-old female. One shortcoming of the result is that the skin of the synthesized image does not look as smooth as the that of the 20-year-old female. This is probably due to the fact that the skin geometry of the 50-year-old female is not modified. Given that the geometry information is contained in the shading component, we could modify the shading component to make the geometry look smoother using, for example, the detail transfer technique in Section 9.1.

9.3 Virtual lighting

In this section, we describe an interesting application of face relighting in the area of videoconferencing. In the past decade, online videoconferencing has become increasingly popular thanks to the improvement in network bandwidth, computation resources, and compression technology. The growing cost of traveling is another factor that makes videoconferencing so appealing. Webcams have become extremely popular for both home users and office workers, and most laptops have built-in video cameras. The availability of hardware, software, and network bandwidth allow people to communicate with their families, friends, and coworkers over the internet. However, the qualities of webcams vary significantly from one to another. One common issue is that webcams tend to perform poorly under challenging lighting conditions such as low light or back light. In the past several years, we have seen a lot of progress on brightness and contrast improvement in both hardware design and image processing. For example, most commercially available webcams are equipped with automatic gain control. Some webcams even perform real-time face tracking and use the face area as the region of interest to determine the gain control parameters. There have been a lot of image-processing techniques being developed that improve the brightness and contrast of the captured images [16, 146, 186, 195].

Exposure, however, is not the only factor that affects the perceptual quality of a webcam video. As shown in Figure 9.11, the images on the left are frames directly obtained from an off-the-shelf webcam. While the exposure of these frames are both very good, they look pale and unpleasant. Instead, the images on the right are much more appealing to most users. In TV show filming, it is no secret that stage lighting has to be carefully designed to make the images look visually appealing [62]. The lighting design involves not only the brightness but also the color scheme, because the color tone is essential in the perception of the look of the host and the mood of the stage.

Figure 9.11. Images on the left are input frames captured by two different webcams. Images on the right are the enhanced frames by the proposed method. (See plate section for color version.)

Since color tone is more subjective than brightness and contrast, it is difficult to come up with a quantitative formula to define what is a visually appealing color tone. Therefore, some approaches require a user to select example images. For instance, Reinhard et al. [179] proposed a color transfer technique to impose one image's color characteristics on another. The user needs to select an appropriate target image for a given input image to conduct the color transfer. Qiu [175] proposed to apply content-based image retrieval technology to obtain a set of image clusters. Given an input image, its color can be modified by selecting an appropriate cluster as target. They showed that this technique works well for color enhancement of outdoor scenes when the user is available to select an appropriate cluster.

Color-balancing-based approach is another type of techniques that modify the image colors. These approaches either use a color reference object or try to identify pixels with presumed colors (e.g., white and black) [206] and adjust the color scheme accordingly to restore the original color.

Liu et al. [132] proposed a data driven approach for video enhancement in videoconferencing applications. The basic idea is to use a set of professionally-taken face images as training examples. These images are often fine-tuned to make sure the skin tone and the contrast of the face regions are visually pleasing. Given a new image, their technique adjusts its color so that the color statistics in the face region is similar to the training examples. This procedure automates the enhancement process and is extremely efficient to compute. In the rest of this section, we describe this technique in more detail.

9.3.1 Learning-based color tone mapping

At the core of this algorithm is a *learning-based color tone mapping*. The basic idea is to select a set of training images that look good perceptually and build a Gaussian mixture model for the color distribution in the face region. For any given input image, we perform color tone mapping so that its color statistics in the face region matches the training examples.

Let n denote the number of training images. For each training image I_i, we perform automatic face detection [222] to identify the face region. For each color channel, the mean and standard deviation are computed for all the pixels in the face region. Let $\mathbf{v}_i = (m_1^i, m_2^i, m_3^i, \sigma_1^i, \sigma_2^i, \sigma_3^i)^T$ denote the vector that consists of the means and standard deviations of the three color channels in the face region. The distribution of the vectors $\{\mathbf{v}_i\}_{1 \leq i \leq n}$ is modeled as a mixture of Gaussians. Let G denote the number of mixture components. Let (μ_j, Σ_j) denote the mean vector and covariance matrix of the jth Gaussian mixture component, $j = 1, ..., G$.

Given any input image, let $\mathbf{v} = (m_1, m_2, m_3, \sigma_1, \sigma_2, \sigma_3)^T$ denote the means and standard deviations of the three color channels in the face region. Let $D_j(\mathbf{v})$ denote the Mahalanobis distance from $\mathbf{v}$ to the jth component, that is,

$$D_j(\mathbf{v}) = \sqrt{(\mathbf{v} - \mu_j)^T \Sigma_j^{-1} (\mathbf{v} - \mu_j)}, \tag{9.13}$$

The target mean and standard deviation vector for $\mathbf{v}$ is defined as a weighted sum of the Gaussian mixture component centers μ_j, $j = 1, ..., G$, where the weights are inversely proportional to the Mahalanobis distances. More specifically, denoting $\bar{\mathbf{v}} = (\bar{m}_1, \bar{m}_2, \bar{m}_3, \bar{\sigma}_1, \bar{\sigma}_2, \bar{\sigma}_3)^T$ as the target mean and standard deviation vector, we have

$$\bar{\mathbf{v}} = \sum_{j=1}^{G} w_j * \mu_j, \tag{9.14}$$

where

$$w_j = \frac{1/D_j(\mathbf{v})}{\sum_{l=1}^{G} 1/D_l(\mathbf{v})}. \tag{9.15}$$

After we obtain the target mean and deviation vector, we perform color tone mapping for each color channel to match the target distribution. For color channel c, $c = 1, 2, 3$. Let $y = f_c(x)$ denote the desired tone mapping function. In order to map the average intensity from m_c to $\bar{m}_c$, $f_c(x)$ needs to satisfy

$$f_c(m_c) = \bar{m}_c. \tag{9.16}$$

In order to modify the standard deviation σ_c to match the target $\bar{\sigma}_c$, we would like the derivative at m_c to be equal to $\frac{\bar{\sigma}_c}{\sigma_c}$, that is,

$$f_c'(m_c) = \frac{\bar{\sigma}_c}{\sigma_c}. \tag{9.17}$$

In addition, we need to make sure $f_c(x)$ is in the range of [0, 255], that is,

$$f_c(0) = 0,$$
$$f_c(255) = 255. \tag{9.18}$$

A simple function that satisfies these constraints is

$$f_c(x) = \begin{cases} 0 & \frac{\bar{\sigma}_c}{\sigma_c}(x - m_c) + \bar{m}_c < 0, \\ \frac{\bar{\sigma}_c}{\sigma_c}(x - m_c) + \bar{m}_c & 0 \le \frac{\bar{\sigma}_c}{\sigma_c}(x - m_c) + \bar{m}_c \le 255, \\ 255 & \frac{\bar{\sigma}_c}{\sigma_c}(x - m_c) + \bar{m}_c > 255. \end{cases} \quad (9.19)$$

The drawback of this function is that it saturates quickly at the low and high intensities. To overcome this problem, we instead fit a piecewise cubic spline that satisfy these constraints. To prevent quick saturation at the two ends, we add constraints on the derivatives $f_c'(0)$ and $f_c'(255)$ as follows:

$$f_c'(0) = 0.5 * \frac{\bar{m}_c}{m_c},$$

$$f_c'(255) = 0.5 * \frac{255 - \bar{m}_c}{255 - m_c}. \quad (9.20)$$

Given the constraints of Equations 9.16, 9.17, 9.18, and 9.20, we can fit a piecewise cubic spline that satisfy these constraints [54]. The details are omitted here.

Figure 9.12a shows a tone mapping curve generated by using Equation 9.19. Figure 9.12b shows the curve generated by using cubic splines.

Note that the color tone mapping function is created based on the pixels in the face region, but it is applied to all the pixels in a given input image.

9.3.2 Application to video sequences

During videoconferencing, the overall image intensity changes due to automatic gain control, lighting change, and camera movement. It is necessary to update the color tone mapping function when such change occurs. For this purpose, Liu et al. [132] used a simple technique to detect global lighting changes. It works by keeping track of the mean of the average intensity of the nonface region in the history frames. Given a new frame, if its average intensity in the nonface region differs from the accumulated mean by an amount larger than a predefined threshold, it is decided that there is a global lighting change, and subsequently the color tone mapping function is updated.

Figure 9.13 shows a flow chart of the algorithm where Y is average intensity of the nonface region of the new frame, $\bar{Y}$ is the accumulated mean of the frames in the history, Δ is a user-defined threshold for determining whether there is a global lighting change, and α is a parameter that controls the update speed

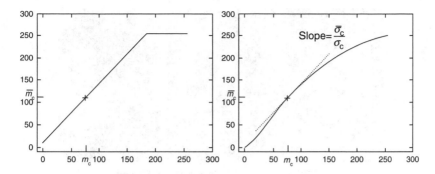

Figure 9.12. Left: Tone mapping curve by using linear function. Right: Tone mapping curve by using piecewise cubic splines.

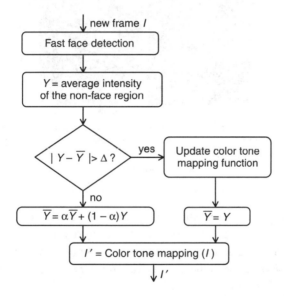

Figure 9.13. Flow diagram of the learning-based color tone mapping algorithm applied to video sequences.

of $\bar{Y}$. If the current frame does not have a global lighting change, $\bar{Y}$ is updated from the current frame Y. Otherwise, $\bar{Y}$ is reset to be equal to Y.

9.3.3 Experiment results

Liu et al. [132] collected approximately 400 professionally taken images from the Web as their training data set. It covers different types of skin colors. They used an Expectation Maximization (EM) algorithm to construct a Gaussian

Figure 9.14. A sample image from each class. The top left, top middle, top right, and bottom left images are, respectively, courtesies of See-Ming Lee, Aki Hanninen, Westfall, and Photoburst (http://www.flickr.com/photos/[seeminglee, hanninen,imagesbywestfall,photonburst]). (See plate section for color version.)

mixture model with five mixture components. Figure 9.14 shows a sample image for each class. These images are not necessarily the most representative images in their classes. In fact, images of the same person may belong to different classes because of the lighting variations. Figure 9.15 shows the mean colors of the five classes.

To reduce computation, the global lighting change detection is performed every two seconds. The color tone mapping is performed on RGB channels. When a global lighting change is detected, the color tone mapping function is recomputed for each color channel, and it is stored in a lookup table. In the subsequent frames, color tone mapping operation becomes a simple table look up which is extremely fast. As reported in Liu et al. [132], their system uses only 5% CPU time for 320×240 video with frame rate of 30 frames per second on a 3.2-GHz machine.

Liu et al. [132] tested their system with a variety of video cameras and different people. Their user study results will be described in the next section. Figure 9.11 shows an example of learning-based color tone mapping. The

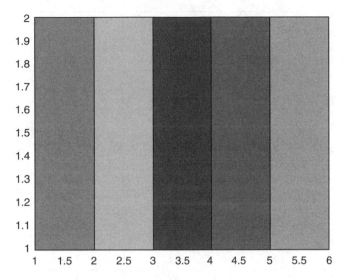

Figure 9.15. Mean colors of the five classes. (See plate section for color version.)

images on the left are input frames from two different video sequences. The images on the right are the results of learning-based color tone mapping. We can see that the resulting images are perceived as having colored lights being added to the scene that makes the scene look slightly brighter, but more importantly, having a warmer tone.

9.3.4 User study

Liu et al. [132] collected 16 teleconferencing videos with eight different cameras, including those made by Logitech, Creative, Veo, Dynex, Microsoft, and so on. Each video sequence lasts about 10 seconds. A field study was conducted, where the users were asked to view the original video and the enhanced video side by side (as shown in Figure 9.11). The orders of the two videos are randomly shuffled and unknown to the users in order to avoid bias. After viewing the video, the users shall give a score to each video, within the range of 1–5, where a score of 1 indicates very poor quality, a score of 5 indicates very good quality, and a score of 3 is considered acceptable. A total of 18 users responded in the test. All the users said they used LCD displays to watch the videos.

Figure 9.16 shows the average scores of the 18 users for the 16 video sequences. It can be seen that the enhanced video outperforms the original video in almost all the sequences. The average score of the original video is merely 2.55, which is below the acceptable level, while the proposed method

Sequence ID	Original Video	Enhanced Video
1	2.89	3.50
2	2.94	3.33
3	1.94	2.67
4	1.61	2.83
5	2.11	3.00
6	3.22	4.17
7	3.11	3.72
8	1.89	2.72
9	2.11	2.17
10	1.94	2.00
11	2.11	3.44
12	3.28	3.72
13	2.65	4.18
14	2.33	3.72
15	3.00	3.89
16	3.72	3.67
Average	**2.55**	**3.30**

Figure 9.16.   User study results.

has a score 3.30, which is now above the acceptable level. The t-test score between the two algorithms for the 16 sequences is 0.001%, which shows that the difference is statistically significant.

9.4 Active lighting

Virtual lighting technique improves the skin tone, but it does not improve the signal-to-noise ratio (SNR). If the source image is noisy (e.g., when the lighting is dark), the result enhanced by virtual lighting will still be noisy. Ideally one would like the captured images to be clean and have a good skin tone. To address this problem, Sun et al. [205] developed an active lighting system that consists of computer controllable LED lights of different colors. The intensities of the LED lights are determined through an optimization procedure that minimizes the difference between the face skin color of the captured image and the desired skin tone.

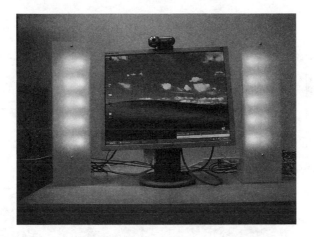

Figure 9.17. Hardware setup.

Figure 9.17 shows their hardware prototype. It consists of two light stands one on each side of the monitor so that both sides of the face are lit equally. Each light stand contains 20 LED lights in four different colors: red, green, blue, and white. The LEDs are mounted on a circuit board covered with a diffuser, which softens the lighting and makes it less intrusive. The LEDs of the same color are connected to an LED driver. The four LED drivers are connected to a data acquisition controller, which is plugged into a computer's USB port. The data acquisition controller provides a programmable interface allowing applications to adjust the voltages of the LED drivers. Each LED driver is a voltage to current converter which adjusts the brightness of the LED lights. Figure 9.18 shows the circuit design of the hardware system.

Let $\mathbf{l} = (l_r, l_g, l_b, l_w)^T$ denote the voltage vector of the system where l_r, l_g, l_b, l_w are the voltages for red, green, blue, and white LEDs, respectively. Let k denote the camera exposure, and assume the camera's white balance is fixed. Then the captured image, denoted as $I(k, \mathbf{l})$, is a function of the $\mathbf{l}$ and k.

The desired target skin color can be determined in the same way as in Equation 9.14. Let I^* denote the target skin color. We would like to determine the voltages $\mathbf{l}$ and camera exposure k to minimize the difference between the face region average color of the captured image $I(k, \mathbf{l})$ and the target mean color I^*. That is, we have the optimization problem:

$$\min_{k, \mathbf{l}} ||I(k, \mathbf{l}) - I^*||. \qquad (9.21)$$

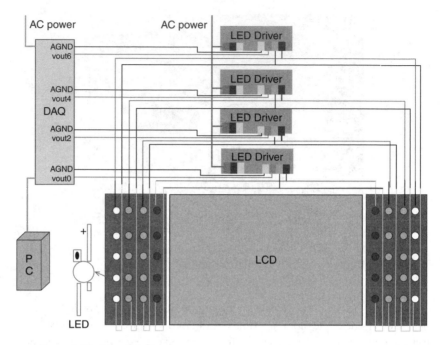

Figure 9.18. Circuit design.

In the next section, we introduce the imaging model of the system that describes the function $I(k, \mathbf{l})$ in more detail.

9.4.1 Imaging model

Based on the hardware setting, the captured image I is a function of camera exposure k and voltages $\mathbf{l}$ of LED lights. Following [86], the image intensity $I_c(x, y)$ can be modeled as

$$I_c(x,y) = f_c\left(k \int \rho(x,y,\lambda)E(x,y,\lambda)s_c(\lambda)d\lambda\right) + \epsilon_c, \qquad (9.22)$$

where (x, y) is the pixel location, c indicates the color channel, the integration on the wavelength λ is over visible spectrum, $\rho(x, y, \lambda)$ is the skin albedo, $E(x, y, \lambda)$ is the irradiance incident on point (x, y) due to the LED lights and environmental illuminant, $s_c(\lambda)$ is the camera spectral response for channel c, k is the camera exposure, and f_c is the camera response function, which maps irradiance to pixel intensity for each channel c. In addition, ϵ_c is the additive noise including sensor noise, quantization noise, and so on.

We assume that the surface reflectance ρ and the illuminant irradiance E in the face area are constant, and ignore the noise term ϵ_c. Denote $I_c = \frac{1}{|F|} \sum_{x,y \in F} I_c(x, y)$ as the average intensity in the face region where F is the set of pixels in the face region and $|F|$ denotes the cardinality of F. From (9.22), we have

$$I_c = f_c \left(k \int \rho(\lambda) E(\lambda) s_c(\lambda) d\lambda \right). \tag{9.23}$$

Furthermore, the irradiance incident on the surface $E(\lambda)$ is the sum of all LED light sources and environment illuminant. Assuming the irradiance due to each LED light is a linear function of the voltage $\mathbf{l}$, the illumination $E(\lambda)$ can be decomposed into

$$E(\lambda) = E^0(\lambda) + l_r E^r(\lambda) + l_g E^g(\lambda) + l_b E^b(\lambda) + l_w E^w(\lambda), \tag{9.24}$$

where $E^0(\lambda)$ is the environment illuminant, $E^r(\lambda)$, $E^g(\lambda)$, $E^b(\lambda)$ and $E^w(\lambda)$ are the irradiance per unit voltage due to the red, green, blue and white LED lights, respectively, and $\mathbf{l} = (l_r, l_g, l_b, l_w)$ are the input voltages.

Under the assumption that the surface reflectance ρ is effectively constant for each color channel, which is reasonable for many ordinary surfaces [28], we have

$$I_c = f_c \left(k \rho_c \int E(\lambda) s_c(\lambda) d\lambda \right)$$
$$= f_c \left(k \rho_c \int \left(E^0(\lambda) + l_r E^r(\lambda) \right. \right.$$
$$\left. \left. + l_g E^g(\lambda) + l_b E^b(\lambda) + l_w E^w(\lambda) \right) s_c(\lambda) d\lambda \right). \tag{9.25}$$

For the sake of clarity, we describe the algorithm using a YUV color format. The basic algorithm works with any color format. Denote the three color channels as y, u, v, and denote $I = (I_y, I_u, I_v)^T$. Denote $f(\mathbf{x})$ as a vector function $f(\mathbf{x}) = [f_y(\mathbf{x}_y), f_u(\mathbf{x}_u), f_v(\mathbf{x}_v)]^T$, where f_y, f_u, and f_v are the camera response function for each channel. From (9.25), we have

$$I = f(k\mathbf{P}(\mathbf{e}^0 + \mathbf{Al})), \tag{9.26}$$

where

$$\mathbf{P} = \begin{pmatrix} \rho_y & 0 & 0 \\ 0 & \rho_u & 0 \\ 0 & 0 & \rho_v \end{pmatrix},$$

$\mathbf{e^0} = (e_y^0, e_u^0, e_v^0)^T, \mathbf{l} = (l_r, l_g, l_b, l_w)^T$, and

$$\mathbf{A} = \begin{pmatrix} A_{ry} & A_{gy} & A_{by} & A_{wy} \\ A_{ru} & A_{gu} & A_{bu} & A_{wu} \\ A_{rv} & A_{gv} & A_{bv} & A_{wv} \end{pmatrix}.$$

In addition, $e_c^0 = \int E^0(\lambda) s_c(\lambda) d\lambda$, and $A_{qc} = \int E^q(\lambda) s_c(\lambda) d\lambda$, where $q \in \{r, g, b, w\}$ indicates the type of LED lights, and $c \in \{y, u, v\}$ is the color channel index.

9.4.2 Optimization

Given the optimization problem in (9.21), we write the objective function of exposure k and voltage vector $\mathbf{l}$ as

$$G = \frac{1}{2} ||I(k, \mathbf{l}) - I^*||^2 = \frac{1}{2}(I - I^*)^T(I - I^*), \qquad (9.27)$$

where $\mathbf{l} = (l_r, l_g, l_b, l_w)^T$ and l_r, l_g, l_b, l_w are the voltages for red, green, blue, and white LEDs, respectively.

For most of the webcams, the exposure can be adjusted only as a discrete number in a limited range. Each voltage ranges from 0 to 10. Based on the characteristic of the two types of variables, Sun et al. [205] used an alternating optimization scheme, which consists of two main steps: (1) Adjusting lighting $\mathbf{l}$ using gradient descent while keeping exposure k fixed and (2) adjusting the exposure k in a discrete manner while keeping lighting $\mathbf{l}$ fixed.

The lighting adjustment step optimizes the objective function of (9.27) with respect to the light voltages $\mathbf{l}$ while k is fixed. This can be solved by using a gradient descent approach. The gradient of the objective function $\frac{\partial G}{\partial \mathbf{l}} = (\frac{\partial I}{\partial \mathbf{l}})$ $(I - I^*)$ can be written as

$$\nabla G = \frac{\partial G}{\partial \mathbf{l}} = J^T(I_y - I_y^*, I_u - I_u^*, I_v - I_v^*)^T, \qquad (9.28)$$

where J is the $3*4$ Jacobian matrix representing the local changes of the image I relative to the light voltages $\mathbf{l}$, and y, u, v are the three channels of the image. By using the gradient descent approach, the update of $\mathbf{l}$ is computed as

$$(l_r, l_g, l_b, l_w)^{i+1} = (l_r, l_g, l_b, l_w)^i - \gamma \nabla G. \qquad (9.29)$$

Note that line search is not suitable because it would cause too many objective function evaluations and each objective function evaluation requires changing the voltages thus causing the LED lights to change. Frequent lighting changes are disturbing to the user. In their implementation, Sun et al. used $\gamma = \frac{1.0}{\max(1.0, ||\nabla G||_\infty)}$, which guarantee that the maximum change of the voltage of LED lights in each iteration is 1.0.

Note that, it is possible to compute Jacobian J analytically if one could obtain f and the parameters in (9.26). It would require calibration of light, surface albedo, and camera response.

Sun et al. choose to estimate Jacobian matrix J numerically. Initially, the Jacobian matrix was estimated through finite differencing by explicitly sampling around the initial voltages $\mathbf{l}^0$. Denote the image captured under the initial voltages $\mathbf{l}^0 = (l_r^0, l_g^0, l_b^0, l_w^0)^T$ as I^0. We can then increase l_r^0 by a small amount Δ, and let I^1 denote the captured image. Denote $\Delta I^1 = I^1 - I^0$, and $\Delta \mathbf{l}^1 = (\Delta, 0, 0, 0)^T$. We have the equation

$$J \Delta \mathbf{l}^1 = \Delta I^1. \tag{9.30}$$

The same procedure can be used for the other three voltages l_g^0, l_b^0, l_w^0, thus obtaining equations

$$J \Delta \mathbf{l}^i = \Delta I^i, i = 2, 3, 4, \tag{9.31}$$

where $\Delta \mathbf{l}^2 = (0, \Delta, 0, 0)^T$, $\Delta \mathbf{l}^3 = (0, 0, \Delta, 0)^T$, and $\Delta \mathbf{l}^4 = (0, 0, 0, \Delta)^T$. Denote

$$\mathbf{L}_{4*4} = \begin{pmatrix} \Delta & 0 & 0 & 0 \\ 0 & \Delta & 0 & 0 \\ 0 & 0 & \Delta & 0 \\ 0 & 0 & 0 & \Delta \end{pmatrix},$$

and $B_{3*4} = (\Delta I^1, \Delta I^2, \Delta I^3, \Delta I^4)$. Equations 9.30 and 9.31 can be written in matrix form as

$$J \mathbf{L}_{4*4} = B_{3*4}. \tag{9.32}$$

Therefore, the Jacobian J can be computed as

$$J = B_{3*4} \mathbf{L}_{4*4}^{-1}. \tag{9.33}$$

The computed Jacobian J is locally accurate around light voltages $\mathbf{l}^0$. As the LED light voltages change in the optimization procedure, reevaluating Jacobian J is necessary since the gradient is not globally constant. One way to reevaluate J is to follow the same finite differencing procedure as described before. But it takes too much time and is disturbing to the user. Referring to the imaging model in (9.26), the irradiance reaching into the camera is linear with respect to the voltages $\mathbf{l}$, and the camera response f, which maps the irradiance to image intensity, is monotonically increasing and locally close to being linear. Thus, the Jacobian J, even though not globally constant, does not vary significantly. Based on this observation, one can keep using the information obtained from the initial Jacobian estimate and update the Jacobian as we obtain new samples. More specifically, suppose we obtain a number of new images I^i under voltages $\mathbf{l}^i$, $i = 5, ..., n$. Denote $\Delta I^i = I^i - I^{i-1}$, and $\Delta \mathbf{l}^i = \mathbf{l}^i - \mathbf{l}^{i-1}$. We have new equations

$$J\Delta \mathbf{l}^i = \Delta I^i, i = 5, ..., n. \tag{9.34}$$

Combining with (9.32), we have

$$J\hat{\mathbf{L}} = \hat{B}, \tag{9.35}$$

where $\hat{\mathbf{L}} = (\mathbf{L}_{4*4}, \Delta \mathbf{l}^5, ..., \Delta \mathbf{l}^n)$, and $\hat{B} = (B_{3*4}, \Delta I^5, ..., \Delta I^n)$. Therefore, the new Jacobian is estimated as

$$J = \hat{B}\hat{\mathbf{L}}^T (\hat{\mathbf{L}}\hat{\mathbf{L}}^T)^{-1}. \tag{9.36}$$

As we sample more points near the final solution, the updated Jacobian matrix will get closer to the true value.

To summarize, we initially use finite differencing to compute the Jacobian once. After that, we update the Jacobian as we obtain more samples during the optimization procedure.

The second step of exposure adjustment optimizes (9.27) with respect to k. Given that the number of exposure levels is quite small, one can simply increase or decrease the exposure one level at a time. To avoid overexposure and underexposure, the exposure should be kept in a certain safe range.

The optimization procedure is shown as a state graph in Figure 9.19. The exposure adjustment step is contained in the state "Exposure and White Light Init" and "Exposure Adjust." The lighting adjustment step is contained in the state "∇G Init" and "∇G Update." We will describe each state in more detail in the following subsections.

9.4.2.1 Exposure and White Light Initialization

When the system is started, it goes to the state of "Exposure and White Light Init". The system first checks the overall intensity of the image (no face detection yet). If it is too dark, the system sets the voltage of the white LED light to

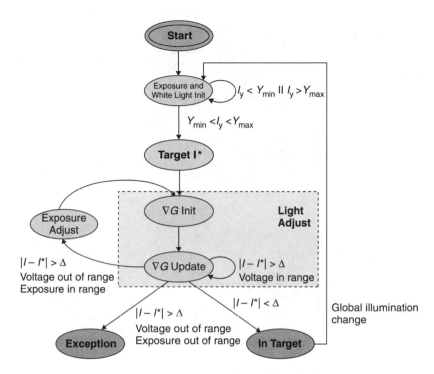

Figure 9.19. The state graph of the optimization procedure.

be an initial voltage value. Then the camera exposure is adjusted to ensure a reasonable face brightness. Denote Y_{min} as the minimal intensity value and Y_{max} as the maximal intensity value (which are set to be 70 and 170, respectively, in [205]). If the average intensity in the face region is less than Y_{min} or larger than Y_{max}, the system increases or decreases the exposure level one level at a time until the average intensity in the face region I_y falls in between Y_{min} and Y_{max}.

9.4.2.2 Setting up the target face color

After adjusting camera exposure, the system enters the state of "Target I^*." In this state, the system uses the average face color of the current frame to compute the target face color I^* based on the learned good skin tone model as in (9.14).

9.4.2.3 Adjusting voltages using gradient descent

Lighting adjustment contains two states: "∇G Init" and "∇G Update." The goal is to search for an optimal voltage vector $\mathbf{l}$ through a gradient descent procedure as described in (9.29).

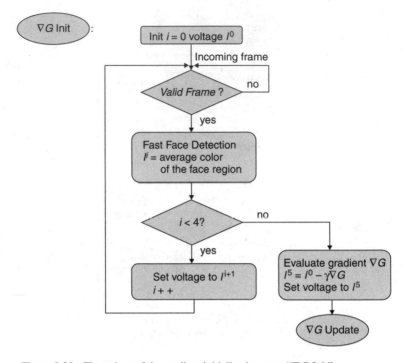

Figure 9.20. Flow chart of the gradient initialization state "∇G Init".

Gradient initialization: The state "∇G Init" is the first state of the lighting adjustment step. Figure 9.20 shows the algorithm flow in this state. A finite differencing approach can be used to compute the Jacobian, thus obtaining the gradient as described in (9.28) and (9.33). This state consists of five iterations. At iteration $i = 0$, it captures the image I^0 at the initial voltage $\mathbf{l}^0$. For each subsequent iteration $i = 1, ..., 4$, it sets the voltage $\mathbf{l}^i = \mathbf{l}^0 + \Delta \mathbf{l}^i$ and captures image I^i. Due to the delay of the LED light control device, there are a few frames of delay between the time when the LED light changes and the time when a new voltage is set. As a result, each time when the voltage is changed, the system needs to wait for a few frames before capturing the image. As shown in Figure 9.20, the systems only captures the image I^i when the current frame becomes valid, that is, several frames after the voltage is modified.

After obtaining $I^i, i = 0, ..., 4$, Equation 9.33 is used to evaluate the Jacobian, and (9.28) is used to evaluate the gradient. Finally the system sets the new voltage to be $\mathbf{l}^5 = \mathbf{l}^0 - \gamma \nabla G$ to get ready for entering the next state "∇G Update."

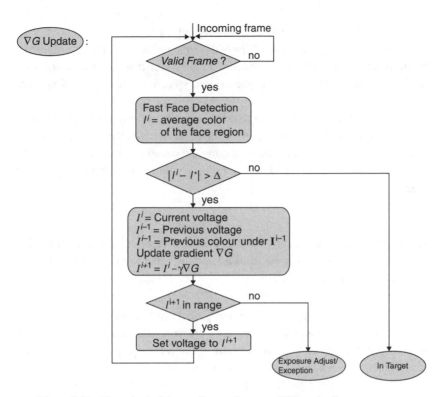

Figure 9.21. Flow chart of the gradient update state "∇G update".

Gradient Update: After gradient initialization, the system enters the state "∇G Update." In this state, a gradient descent scheme can be used to search for the optimal voltages to minimize the objective function in (9.27). The algorithm flow is illustrated in Figure 9.21. It first checks whether the average color of the face region is close to the target color. Again, due to the delay of the LED light control device, each time when a new voltage a set, the system captures the image until the frame becomes valid, that is, several frames after the new voltage is set.

If the target color is not reached within a prespecified threshold, that is, $|I^i - I^*| > \triangle$, the system updates the gradient by using the newly captured image according to (9.28) and (9.36). After that, the desired new voltage is computed as $\mathbf{l}^{i+1} = \mathbf{l}^i - \gamma \nabla G$. If the desired new voltage is out of the range of the hardware device, the system goes to either the state "Exposure Adjust" or the state "Exception" depending on whether the exposure is adjustable or not. Otherwise, the system sets the new voltage and goes to the next iteration.

9.4.2.4 Exposure adjust

If the desired voltages are out of the valid voltage range while the objective function value is still relatively large, it is an indication that the camera exposure needs to be adjusted. Therefore, the system switches to the state "Exposure Adjust."

If the desired voltages are larger than the maximum allowed value, the camera exposure is adjusted one step higher. In the opposite case, the camera exposure is adjusted one step smaller. After changing the camera exposure, the state will automatically transit to "∇G Init," and a new iteration of lighting adjustment begins.

9.4.2.5 Exception

The state "∇G Update" will transit to the state "Exception" if neither the lights nor the camera exposure can be adjusted any further. The exception case rarely happens in the experiments.

9.4.2.6 Converging at target and global illumination detection

When there are environment illumination changes after the system enters the state "In Target," the system needs to adjust the camera exposure and voltages accordingly. The environment illumination change detector can be implemented in the same way as the global lighting change detector in Section 9.3.2. After the system enters the state "In Target," the system invokes the environment illumination change detector. At each frame, the detector computes the average intensity of the entire image including the nonface area. The detector maintains a mean value and standard deviation over time and use the accumulated statistics to determine whether there is an environment illumination change in the new frame. If the environment illumination change is detected, the system goes back to the beginning state "Exposure and White Light Init" and starts the optimization loop.

9.4.3 Results

This section describes the experiment results reported by Sun et al. [205]. Figure 9.22a is an image captured by a webcam in a regular meeting room. The webcam's auto exposure and auto white balancing are turned on. Figure 9.22b is the result of virtual lighting enhancement. We can see that Figure 9.22b looks better than Figure 9.22a thanks to its improvement on brightness and skin tone. But it looks blurry because its signal to noise ratio is low. Figure 9.22c is captured when a table lamp is turned on. Even though there is enough light on the face, the image does not look appealing because the light is too harsh and not

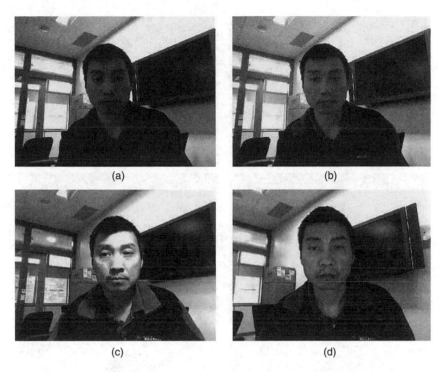

Figure 9.22. (a) Image captured by a webcam with the auto exposure enabled. (b) The result of virtual lighting enhancement on image (a). (c) Image captured when the table lamp is turned on. Again the camera auto exposure is enabled. (d) Image captured with the active lighting system.

uniform. In contrast, Figure 9.22d is captured with the active lighting system. We can see that Figure 9.22d looks significantly better than either Figure 9.22b and 9.22c.

The rest of the section shows a series of experiments with different people and different room lighting environments. The results were used by Sun et al. for their user study. In order to be able to easily switch between three different room-lighting configurations (normal, dark, and back lighting), the experiments were conducted in a room that has direct lighting sources aimed at the wall. Since the wall is white, when the direct lighting sources are on, the wall is brightened, thus creating the back-lighting effects.

Figure 9.23 shows image samples captured under three different lighting environments. In the left column are images captured without active lighting while the camera auto exposure is enabled. In the right column are images captured when the active lighting system was turned on. We can see that the

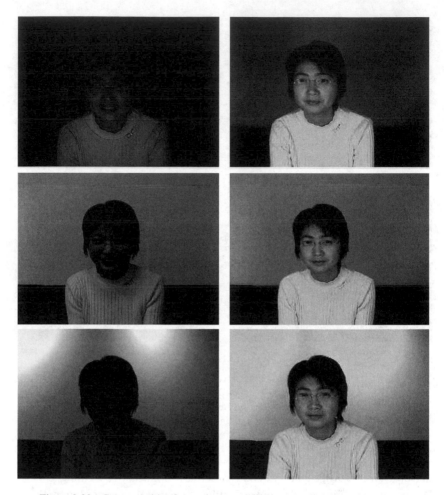

Figure 9.23. Captured video frames in three different room lighting environment: dark room lighting for the top row, normal room lighting for the middle row, and back lighting for the bottom row. In the left column are video frames captured without active lighting and with the camera auto exposure turned on. In the right columns are video frames captured with the active lighting. (See plate section for color version.)

images on the right are more appealing because the faces are lit uniformly and have a better skin tone.

Figure 9.24 compares the results of adjusting white lights only with those of adjusting color lights under normal room lighting environment. The images on the left column are captured when the white LED lights are turned on to maximum brightness, and both the camera auto exposure and auto white balance

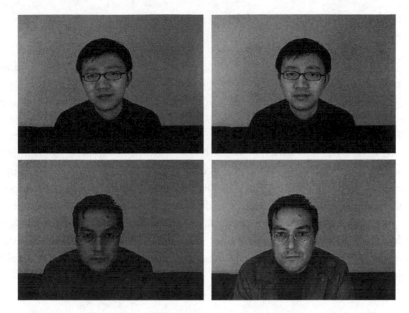

Figure 9.24. Comparison of white LED lights vs. active lighting. All the images are captured in a normal room lighting environment. The images on the left are captured when the white LED lights are turned on and set to maximum brightness and the camera auto exposure is enabled. The images on the right are captured with the active lighting system.

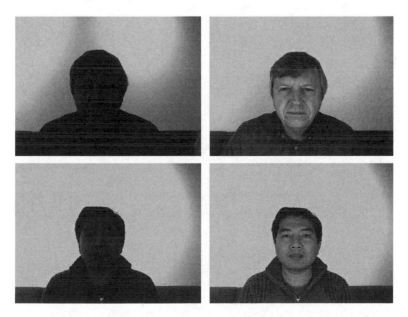

Figure 9.25. Comparison of face-tracking-based auto exposure vs. active lighting. The environment lighting is back lighting where the wall is well lit while the face is dark. The images on the left column are obtained by using face-tracking-based auto exposure control. The images on the right are captured with the active lighting system.

are turned on. The images on the right are obtained with the active lighting system. We can see that the bluish color tone on the face, which is caused by the blue background of the computer monitor, is "removed" by the active lighting system.

Figure 9.25 compares the results of active lighting with the results obtained by using face-tracking-based auto exposure control. The environment lighting is a back-lighting condition, which is regarded as the most difficult lighting condition for videoconferencing. The face-tracking-based auto exposure control system tracks the face region and uses the intensity of the face region to control the camera exposure. Thanks to this feature, the images in the left column are reasonably good considering the tough lighting condition. But the results obtained from the active lighting system, which are shown in the right column, are much better.

10

Model-based tracking and gaze correction

The problem of head pose tracking has been studied for many years. Many applications require head pose information such as attention detection, vision-based interface, head gesture recognition, and eye-gaze correction. 3D head pose is also extremely useful in face recognition and facial expression recognition in handling pose variations. Not surprisingly, there has been a wide variety of work on 3D head tracking. The paper [123] has a nice survey.

Virtually all the work on face tracking takes advantage of the constrained scenario: Instead of using a generic tracking framework that views the observed face as an arbitrarily object, a model-based approach, which incorporates knowledge about face geometry, appearance, and facial deformations, is favored. The tracking techniques can be roughly classified into the following categories.

Optical flow: Black and Yacoob [18] developed a regularized optical-flow method in which the head motion is tracked by interpretation of optical flow in terms of a planar two-dimensional patch. Basu et al. [10] generalized this approach by interpreting the optical flow field using a 3D model to avoid the singularities of a 2D model. Better results have been obtained for large angular and translational motions. DeCarlo and Metaxas [44] used optical flow as a hard constraint on a deformable detailed model. Other optical-flow-based methods include [34, 125].

Skin color: Yang et al. [244] presented a techniques of tracking human faces using an adaptive stochastic model based on human skin color. This approach is in general very fast. The drawback is that it is usually not very accurate.

Features and templates: Azarbeyajani et al. [4] presented a recursive estimation method based on tracking small facial features like the corners of the eyes

217

or mouth using an extended Kalman Filter framework. Horprasert [95] presented a fast method to estimate the head pose from tracking only five salient facial points: four eye corners and the nose top. Other template-based methods include the work of Darrell et al. [41], Saulnier et al. [189], and Tian et al. [211]. The template-based methods usually have the limitation that the same points must be visible over the entire image sequence, thus limiting the range of head motions they can track.

Lu et al. [137] developed a head pose tracking technique exploiting both face models and appearance exemplars. Because of the dynamic nature, it is not possible to represent face appearance by a single texture image. Instead, the complex face appearance space is sampled by a few reference images (exemplars). By taking advantage of the rich geometric information of a 3D face model and the flexible representation provided by exemplars, that system is able to track head pose robustly under occlusion and/or varying facial expression.

Stereo and multiple cameras: Newman et al. [155] presented a stereo vision system for head pose tracking. They first take three snapshots (frontal, 45° to the left, and 45° to the right) and reconstruct up to 32 features selected on the face. Those 3D points, together with the templates extracted from the corresponding snapshots around each feature, are used for face tracking. Yang and Zhang [247] also developed a stereo vision system for head pose tracking. Instead of selecting features from the three initial snapshots, they selected features at run time.

In this chapter, we will describe model-based head pose tracking in three different setups: (1) monocular head pose tracking, (2) stereo tracking where two pre-calibrated cameras are used, and (3) multicamera head pose tracking where the camera positions are not known a priori. In addition, we will describe an application of head pose tracking to videoconferencing: eye-gaze correction.

10.1 Head pose estimation

Head pose refers to the orientation, represented by a rotation matrix, and position, represented by a translation vector, of a person's head with respect to a world coordinate system. As mentioned in Chapter 2, we associate a coordinate system with a head model, so the head pose is the transformation (rotation and translation) between the two coordinate systems. Without loss of generality, we assume that the world coordinate system coincides with that of the camera, or one of the cameras if multiple cameras are used. In that case, the head pose is the transformation from the head coordinate system to the camera coordinate system. If this assumption is not valid, such as the case when we use a coordinate system attached to the computer screen as the world coordinate system, we can compose the two transformations: one from the head to the camera, the other from the camera to the screen.

To determine the head pose, we have to match features detected in an image with features on a person's head. Before going further, we first discuss what features we can expect. We then present various techniques of pose estimation based on either 3D–2D correspondences or 2D–2D correspondences or 3D–3D correspondences. It is worth noting that those techniques are mostly applicable to other objects, not just heads.

10.1.1 Features on a person's head

Figure 10.1 is a line drawing, illustrating some features on a person's head that we can expect to see in an image. A feature (point, line, etc.) in an image is detected due to its distinction from its neighboring pixels, but it can come from a number of different sources in the physical world. We can roughly divide features into four categories:

Stable photometric features: Those features are caused by discontinuity of reflectance on the surface. They include lip contours, eye brows, and eyelids. They also include beauty spots and blemishes, which are very personal features. We can further divide them into rigid and nonrigid features, depending on their relative rigidity with respect to the head coordinate system:

Figure 10.1. Illustration of some features on a person's head.

- *Rigid features*. These include eye corners and mouth corners.
- *Nonrigid features*. These include mouth lips as a person often talks. They also include eyelids as one closes and opens eyes. However, since eyes are open the majority of the time, we may use eyelids as rigid features in some circumstances.

Stable geometric features: Those features are caused by discontinuity in surface orientation (normal) while the surface itself is continuous. Nostrils and the sides of the nose can be considered as examples in this category. Other examples include moles and bumps, which are very personal.

Occluding contours: Those features are caused by discontinuity in distance from that particular viewpoint but the normal to the surface is continuous. Face silhouettes are a clear example. Those contours change according to head pose and camera position.

Casting shadow edges: The nose or hairs can cast shadow on the face, and the shadow produces edges. They are not stable since a person's head moves all the time, causing them to change continuously.

Different types of features are useful for different tasks. Shadow edges, for example, are useful in determining the lighting condition of an environment. For the purpose of this chapter (i.e., head pose estimation), we will consider the first three categories of features and ignore shadows.

Other features that are not as obvious as those mentioned earlier, such as those detected by Harris corner detector on the face region, can also be useful for modeling as described earlier and for pose estimation as long as they can be matched across frames or between the 3D model and the image frames.

10.1.2 Pose estimation from 3D–2D correspondences

First, let us assume that we have point correspondences $\{(P_i, \mathbf{p}_i)\}$ between the 3D head model and the image, where P_i is a 3D point such as an eye corner on the head model, and $\mathbf{p}_i$ is the corresponding point in the image plane. In the ideal case, P_i projects at $\mathbf{p}_i$, following the pinhole projection model (1.1). If the nonlinear projection function (1.2) is used, we have

$$\mathbf{p}_i = \boldsymbol{\phi}(\mathbf{M}, P_i), \tag{10.1}$$

where

$$\mathbf{M} = \begin{pmatrix} \mathbf{R} & \mathbf{t} \\ \mathbf{0}^T & 1 \end{pmatrix}$$

is the head pose matrix (remember that we assume that the world coordinate system coincides with the camera coordinate system), and $\mathbf{R}$ and $\mathbf{t}$ are the rotation matrix and the translation vector.

In reality, due to the noise in the detected image points, Equation 10.1 rarely holds. Let us denote the projected image point of 3D point P_i by $\widehat{\mathbf{p}}_i$, that is,

$$\widehat{\mathbf{p}}_i = \boldsymbol{\phi}(\mathbf{M}, P_i). \tag{10.2}$$

To estimate the head pose $\mathbf{M}$ or $(\mathbf{R}, \mathbf{t})$, we resort to minimize the squared distance between the projected and detected image points, that is,

$$\min_{\mathbf{M}} \sum_i \|\mathbf{p}_i - \widehat{\mathbf{p}}_i\|^2. \tag{10.3}$$

Any nonlinear least-squares technique, such as the Levenberg–Marquardt method, can be applied. When one has four or more noncoplanar point correspondences, the so-called POSIT algorithm [45] can be used. The idea of the POSIT algorithm is to iteratively approximate the perspective projection with a scaled orthographic projection. Under scaled orthographic projection, the pose can be estimated analytically by solving a linear system. Through iteration, the projection approximation is getting better and better, and POSIT converges to accurate pose estimation in a few iterations. If only three point correspondences are available, multiple solutions may exist, and the reader is referred to [84] for a review and analysis of solutions of the three-point perspective pose estimation problem.

In the preceding formulation, each image point has the same weight. If the detected image points do not have the same precision, they should contribute differently to the pose estimation. For example, the points at the nose sides are usually not as precise as those at the mouth corners, and thus they should contribute less than the mouth corners. One way to model the precision, or rather the uncertainty of the measurement, is to consider a detected image point $\mathbf{p}$ as a Gaussian random vector with mean at $\mathbf{p}$ (we use the same symbol to simplify the notation) and covariance matrix $\boldsymbol{\Lambda}_\mathbf{p}$. The less precise the point $\mathbf{p}$ is detected, the larger the covariance matrix $\boldsymbol{\Lambda}_\mathbf{p}$ is. The maximum likelihood estimation of the head pose is then given by minimizing the Mahalanobis distance, that is,

$$\min_{\mathbf{M}} \sum_i (\mathbf{p}_i - \widehat{\mathbf{p}}_i)^T \boldsymbol{\Lambda}_{\mathbf{p}_i}^{-1} (\mathbf{p}_i - \widehat{\mathbf{p}}_i). \tag{10.4}$$

Now let us consider a curve such as a mouth lip. This is a curve-to-curve correspondence problem. Without knowing the pose, which is what we try to determine, we cannot exactly know which point on a 3D curve matches which point on the corresponding image curve. However, we do know that for a point P on the 3D curve, its projection onto the image plane, $\widehat{\mathbf{p}}$, should lie on the 2D image curve $\mathcal{C}$ (i.e., $d(\widehat{\mathbf{p}},\mathcal{C}) = 0$, where $d(\mathbf{p},\mathcal{C})$ is the Euclidean distance of point $\mathbf{p}$ to image curve $\mathcal{C}$). For each 3D curve $\mathcal{D}_i$, we can sample sufficiently dense points, denoted by P_j^i. Given N correspondences of 3D curves $\mathcal{D}_i$ and image curves $\mathcal{C}_i$, we can thus formulate the pose estimation problem as minimizing the distance between the projected point and its corresponding image curve, that is,

$$\min_{\mathbf{M}} \sum_i \sum_j d^2(\widehat{\mathbf{p}}_j^i, \mathcal{C}_i) \tag{10.5}$$

subject to the projection of $\widehat{\mathbf{p}}_j^i$ falling into the curve segment $\mathcal{C}_i$. If $\widehat{\mathbf{p}}_j^i$ is outside of the curve segment $\mathcal{C}_i$, some special treatment needs to be performed. In Section 10.1.5, we will describe the so-called iterative closest point method to deal with the curve-to-curve matching problem.

If detected curves have different precision, they should contribute differently to the pose estimation. One way is to associate a scalar σ_i to the uncertainty of each curve, which corresponds to how uncertain the curve is located in its orthogonal direction. In that case, we can reformulate (10.5) as

$$\min_{\mathbf{M}} \sum_i \frac{1}{\sigma_i^2} \sum_j d^2(\widehat{\mathbf{p}}_j^i, \mathcal{C}_i). \tag{10.6}$$

A curve can be represented by a sequence of line segments (polygonal approximation). If a line segment is represented by $\mathcal{L}: au + bv + c = 0$ in the image plane, then the distance of point $\mathbf{p}_0 = [u_0, v_0]^T$ to line $\mathcal{L}$ is given by

$$d(\mathbf{p}_0, \mathcal{L}) = |au_0 + bv_0 + c|/\sqrt{a^2 + b^2}. \tag{10.7}$$

Finally, let us consider the case of occluding contours. Refer to Figure 10.2. Recall that an occluding contour is caused by discontinuity in distance from a particular viewpoint but the normal to the surface is continuous. There is actually no corresponding fixed contour on the surface. Consider a point $\mathbf{p}$ on the occluding contour in the image, and make a plane $\mathcal{P}$ that passes through the optical center C and is tangent to the contour at $\mathbf{p}$. Denote the normal of the plane by $\mathbf{n}$. In the normalized image coordinate system, if the tangent line at $\mathbf{p} = [u_0, v_0]^T$ is represented by $a(u - u_0) + b(v - v_0) = 0$, then the normal of the tangent plane $\mathcal{P}$ is given by $\mathbf{n} = [a, b, c]^T / \sqrt{a^2 + b^2 + c^2}$ where $c = -au_0 - bv_0$. As the tangent plane passes through the origin C of the camera

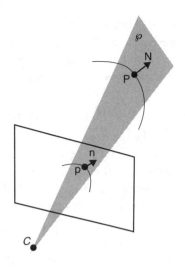

Figure 10.2. Occluding contours and 3D–2D relationship.

coordinate system, it is simply represented by $ax + by + cz = 0$, or $\mathbf{n}^T\mathbf{x} = 0$. By definition of occluding contours, the tangent plane $\mathcal{P}$ must be tangent to the surface in 3D as well. Let us denote the contact point on the surface by P, then the normal to the surface at P, denoted by N, must be parallel to the plane normal $\mathbf{n}$.

As occluding contours change with pose, they pose a chicken-and-egg problem between contour correspondence and pose estimation. With unknown pose, given a point $\mathbf{p}$ on the occluding contour in the image, we do not know which 3D point on the surface it corresponds to. Therefore, we should leverage the occluding contours for pose estimation in an iterative way. If we are given an initial pose estimate, the 3D model can be rendered for that pose, and the occluding contour can be computed, denoted by $\widehat{\mathcal{C}}$. For a point $\mathbf{p}$ on the occluding contour detected in the image, we can match it to a point, denoted by $\widehat{\mathbf{p}}$, on the projected occluding contour $\widehat{\mathcal{C}}$, with our best effort (e.g., finding the closest point, see Section 10.1.5). From $\widehat{\mathbf{p}}$, we can compute its corresponding point, denoted by $\widehat{\mathrm{P}}$, on the surface and its surface normal, denoted by $\widehat{\mathrm{N}}$. Then, the pose can be refined by minimizing the distance from $\widehat{\mathrm{P}}$ to the tangent plane $\mathcal{P}$ and the difference between $\mathbf{n}$ and $\widehat{\mathrm{N}}$. The latter can be measured by the cross product of two vectors. More precisely, the problem can be formulated as

$$\min_{\mathbf{M}} \sum_i [w_p(\mathbf{n}_i^T(\mathbf{R}\widehat{\mathrm{P}}_i + \mathbf{t}))^2 + w_n\|\mathbf{n}_i \times (\mathbf{R}\widehat{\mathrm{N}}_i)\|^2], \qquad (10.8)$$

where w_p and w_n are weighting factors for the point-to-plane distance term and for the normal vector difference term. Once the pose is refined, we can compute a better occluding contour $\widehat{C}$ with the refined pose and, in turn, refine the pose further with (10.8). The iteration process stops after convergence.

10.1.3 Pose estimation from 3D–3D correspondences

3D points of an object can be obtained with stereovision systems or range finders. When 3D-3D correspondences are available, it is relatively easier to compute the pose (or the motion). It is out of the scope of reviewing all the solutions. The interested reader is referred to [55, 138, 266, 267]. Next, we only present one technique, and briefly describe how to deal with data with uncertainty.

Let $\{P_i | i = 1, \ldots, n\}$ be the first set of n 3D points, and $\{P_i' | i = 1, \ldots, n\}$ be the second set of corresponding 3D points. Considering noise in the measurement, we have

$$P_i' = \mathbf{R}P_i + \mathbf{t} + \boldsymbol{\xi}_i. \tag{10.9}$$

If the noise $\boldsymbol{\xi}_i$ is modeled as a Gaussian noise with mean 0 and covariance matrix $\boldsymbol{\Xi}_i$, then the pose estimation problem becomes solving the following minimization problem:

$$\min_{\mathbf{M}} \sum_{i=1}^{n} (P_i' - \mathbf{R}P_i - \mathbf{t})^T \boldsymbol{\Xi}_i^{-1} (P_i' - \mathbf{R}P_i - \mathbf{t}). \tag{10.10}$$

In general, we do not have a closed-form solution.

If the covariance matrix is diagonal and the diagonal elements are equal (i.e., $\boldsymbol{\Xi}_i = \frac{1}{w_i}\mathbf{I}$), the preceding problem minimizes the following objective function:

$$\mathcal{F}(\mathbf{R}, \mathbf{t}) = \sum_{i=1}^{n} w_i \|P_i' - \mathbf{R}P_i - \mathbf{t}\|^2. \tag{10.11}$$

A closed-form solution exists, as is described later.

Recall that the rotation matrix is orthonormal. Let vector $\mathbf{r}_i$ be the ith row of the rotation matrix $\mathbf{R}$, that is,

$$\mathbf{R} = \begin{bmatrix} \mathbf{r}_1^T \\ \mathbf{r}_2^T \\ \mathbf{r}_3^T \end{bmatrix}$$

They must satisfy the following constraints:

$$\mathbf{r}_i^T \mathbf{r}_i = 1, \quad i = 1,2,3; \tag{10.12}$$

$$\mathbf{r}_i^T \mathbf{r}_j = 0, \quad i,j = 1,2,3, \text{ but } i \neq j. \tag{10.13}$$

Using Lagrange multipliers, we can convert (10.11) into the following objective function without constraint:

$$\mathcal{F}'(\mathbf{R},\mathbf{t}) = \sum_{i=1}^{n} w_i \| \mathbf{P}_i' - \mathbf{R}\mathbf{P}_i - \mathbf{t} \|^2$$

$$+ \sum_{j=1}^{3} \lambda_j (\mathbf{r}_j^T \mathbf{r}_j - 1) + 2\lambda_4 \mathbf{r}_1^T \mathbf{r}_2 + 2\lambda_5 \mathbf{r}_1^T \mathbf{r}_3 + 2\lambda_6 \mathbf{r}_2^T \mathbf{r}_3. \tag{10.14}$$

The derivative of $\mathcal{F}'(\mathbf{R},\mathbf{t})$ with respect to $\mathbf{t}$ is

$$\frac{\partial \mathcal{F}'(\mathbf{R},\mathbf{t})}{\partial \mathbf{t}} = -2 \sum_{i=1}^{n} w_i (\mathbf{P}_i' - \mathbf{R}\mathbf{P}_i - \mathbf{t}).$$

Setting it to 0 yields

$$\sum_{i=1}^{n} w_i (\mathbf{P}_i' - \mathbf{R}\mathbf{P}_i + \mathbf{t}) = \mathbf{0}.$$

So the solution to the translation is given by

$$\mathbf{t} = \overline{\mathbf{P}}' - \mathbf{R}\overline{\mathbf{P}}, \tag{10.15}$$

where $\overline{\mathbf{P}}$ and $\overline{\mathbf{P}}'$ are the centroid of the two point sets:

$$\overline{\mathbf{P}} = \frac{\sum_{i=1}^{n} w_i \mathbf{P}_i}{\sum_{i=1}^{n} w_i}, \quad \overline{\mathbf{P}}' = \frac{\sum_{i=1}^{n} w_i \mathbf{P}_i'}{\sum_{i=1}^{n} w_i}.$$

Thus, once $\mathbf{R}$ is known, the translation $\mathbf{t}$ is readily obtained.
Let's now turn to solving $\mathbf{R}$. Denote

$$\mathbf{Q}_i = \mathbf{P}_i - \overline{\mathbf{P}}, \text{ and } \mathbf{Q}_i' = \mathbf{P}_i' - \overline{\mathbf{P}}'.$$

Substituting $\mathbf{t} = \overline{\mathbf{P}}' - \mathbf{R}\overline{\mathbf{P}}$ into (10.14) gives

$$\mathcal{F}''(\mathbf{R}) = \sum_{i=1}^{n} w_i \|Q_i' - \mathbf{R}Q_i\|^2$$

$$+ \sum_{j=1}^{3} \lambda_j (\mathbf{r}_j^T \mathbf{r}_j - 1) + 2\lambda_4 \mathbf{r}_1^T \mathbf{r}_2 + 2\lambda_5 \mathbf{r}_1^T \mathbf{r}_3 + 2\lambda_6 \mathbf{r}_2^T \mathbf{r}_3. \tag{10.16}$$

The derivatives of $\mathcal{F}''(\mathbf{R})$ with respect to $\mathbf{r}_1$, $\mathbf{r}_2$ and $\mathbf{r}_3$ are

$$\frac{\partial \mathcal{F}''}{\partial \mathbf{r}_1} = -2 \sum_{i=1}^{n} w_i (q_{i,1}' - \mathbf{r}_1^T Q_i) Q_i + 2\lambda_1 \mathbf{r}_1 + 2\lambda_4 \mathbf{r}_2 + 2\lambda_5 \mathbf{r}_3,$$

$$\frac{\partial \mathcal{F}''}{\partial \mathbf{r}_2} = -2 \sum_{i=1}^{n} w_i (q_{i,2}' - \mathbf{r}_2^T Q_i) Q_i + 2\lambda_4 \mathbf{r}_1 + 2\lambda_2 \mathbf{r}_2 + 2\lambda_6 \mathbf{r}_3, \tag{10.17}$$

$$\frac{\partial \mathcal{F}''}{\partial \mathbf{r}_3} = -2 \sum_{i=1}^{n} w_i (q_{i,3}' - \mathbf{r}_3^T Q_i) Q_i + 2\lambda_5 \mathbf{r}_1 + 2\lambda_6 \mathbf{r}_2 + 2\lambda_3 \mathbf{r}_3,$$

where $q_{i,j}'$ is the jth element of vector Q_i'. Setting them to 0 gives

$$\sum_{i=1}^{n} w_i Q_i Q_i^T \mathbf{r}_1 + \lambda_1 \mathbf{r}_1 + \lambda_4 \mathbf{r}_2 + \lambda_5 \mathbf{r}_3 = \sum_{i=1}^{n} w_i q_{i,1}' Q_i,$$

$$\sum_{i=1}^{n} w_i Q_i Q_i^T \mathbf{r}_2 + \lambda_4 \mathbf{r}_1 + \lambda_2 \mathbf{r}_2 + \lambda_6 \mathbf{r}_3 = \sum_{i=1}^{n} w_i q_{i,2}' Q_i,$$

$$\sum_{i=1}^{n} w_i Q_i Q_i^T \mathbf{r}_3 + \lambda_5 \mathbf{r}_1 + \lambda_6 \mathbf{r}_2 + \lambda_3 \mathbf{r}_3 = \sum_{i=1}^{n} w_i q_{i,3}' Q_i.$$

Now introducing the following notation:

$$\mathbf{A} = \sum_{i=1}^{n} w_i Q_i Q_i^T$$

$$\mathbf{\Lambda} = \begin{bmatrix} \lambda_1 & \lambda_4 & \lambda_5 \\ \lambda_4 & \lambda_2 & \lambda_6 \\ \lambda_5 & \lambda_6 & \lambda_3 \end{bmatrix}$$

$$\mathbf{B} = [\mathbf{b}_1 \quad \mathbf{b}_2 \quad \mathbf{b}_3]$$

where

$$\mathbf{b}_k = \sum_{i=1}^{n} w_i q'_{i,k} \mathcal{Q}_i \quad \text{for } k = 1,2,3,$$

we can rewrite the above three equations in the following compact form:

$$\mathbf{A}\mathbf{R}^T + \mathbf{R}^T \mathbf{\Lambda} = \mathbf{B}. \tag{10.18}$$

Multiplying Equation 10.18 by $\mathbf{R}$ from the left gives

$$\mathbf{R}\mathbf{A}\mathbf{R}^T + \mathbf{\Lambda} = \mathbf{R}\mathbf{B}.$$

As $\mathbf{A}$ and $\mathbf{\Lambda}$ are symmetric matrices, the left side of the above equation is symmetric, which implies that the right side should also be symmetric, which leads to

$$\mathbf{R}\mathbf{B} = (\mathbf{R}\mathbf{B})^T, \text{ or } \mathbf{R}\mathbf{B}\mathbf{R} = \mathbf{B}^T. \tag{10.19}$$

Let the SVD decomposition of $\mathbf{B}$ be

$$\mathbf{B} = \mathbf{U}\mathbf{D}\mathbf{V}^T,$$

where $\mathbf{U}$ and $\mathbf{V}$ are orthonormal matrices and $\mathbf{D}$ is a diagonal matrix. Equation (10.19) now becomes

$$\mathbf{R}\mathbf{U}\mathbf{D}\mathbf{V}^T \mathbf{R} = \mathbf{V}\mathbf{D}\mathbf{U}^T.$$

The solution to $\mathbf{R}$ immediately comes as

$$\mathbf{R} = \mathbf{V}\mathbf{U}^T. \tag{10.20}$$

If $\det \mathbf{R} = 1$, then this is the correct solution; otherwise, $\det \mathbf{R} = -1$ (i.e., $\mathbf{R}$ is a reflection), and the algorithm fails. The failure happens rarely except when the 3D points are coplanar.

It is worthnoting that the matrix $\mathbf{B}$ defined above can be written in a simpler form as

$$\mathbf{B} = \sum_{i=1}^{n} w_i \mathcal{Q}_i \mathcal{Q}_i'^T.$$

10.1.4 Pose estimation from 2D–2D correspondences

In certain situations, we do not have 3D points of the model (head). We can still determine how the head pose changes from 2D observations. There is a vast volume of work reported in the literature, and it is out of the scope of this book to review them. The interested reader is referred to [55, 138, 262, 263, 264].

Next, we provide the essential elements we need for head pose estimation. The head geometry is not used, so the techniques apply to any rigid objects.

In [133], we described an algorithm specialized for head motion. In particular, physical properties such as symmetry, parallelism, and orthogonality of features were exploited to obtain more robust head motion estimation. The interested reader is referred to that paper.

10.1.4.1 Fundamental matrix and essential matrix

We are given a set of 2D–2D point correspondences $\{(\mathbf{p}_i, \mathbf{p}_i') | i = 1, \dots, n\}$. Let their unknown 3D corresponding points be $\{\mathrm{P}_i | i = 1, \dots, n\}$. Let us use $\widetilde{\mathbf{p}}_i$ and $\widetilde{\mathbf{p}}_i'$ to denote the homogeneous image coordinates, that is,

$$\widetilde{\mathbf{p}}_i = [\mathbf{p}_i^T, 1]^T \quad \text{and} \quad \widetilde{\mathbf{p}}_i' = [\mathbf{p}_i'^{\,T}, 1]^T.$$

With the pinhole camera model and assuming the world coordinate system coincide with the camera coordinate system at the first instant, we have

$$s_i \widetilde{\mathbf{p}}_i = \mathbf{A} \mathrm{P}_i, \tag{10.21}$$

$$s_i' \widetilde{\mathbf{p}}_i' = \mathbf{A}(\mathbf{R} \mathrm{P}_i + \mathbf{t}), \tag{10.22}$$

where $\mathbf{A}$ is the camera's intrinsic matrix. From the first equation, we get the unknown 3D point $\mathrm{P}_i = s_i \mathbf{A}^{-1} \widetilde{\mathbf{p}}_i$. Substitute it into the second equation, we have

$$s_i' \mathbf{A}^{-1} \widetilde{\mathbf{p}}_i' = s_i \mathbf{R} \mathbf{A}^{-1} \widetilde{\mathbf{p}}_i + \mathbf{t}.$$

To eliminate the two unknown scales s_i and s_i', we perform cross product on the preceding equation from the left by $\mathbf{t}$, which yields

$$s_i' \mathbf{t} \times \mathbf{A}^{-1} \widetilde{\mathbf{p}}_i' = s_i \mathbf{t} \times \mathbf{R} \mathbf{A}^{-1} \widetilde{\mathbf{p}}_i.$$

Then, we perform dot product on both sides with $\mathbf{A}^{-1} \widetilde{\mathbf{p}}_i'$, and the left side becomes 0, and the equation reduces to

$$\widetilde{\mathbf{p}}_i'^{\,T} \mathbf{F} \widetilde{\mathbf{p}}_i = 0, \tag{10.23}$$

where $\mathbf{F}$ is known as the *Fundamental Matrix* in the computer vision literature and is given by

$$\mathbf{F} = \mathbf{A}^{-T} [\mathbf{t}]_\times \mathbf{R} \mathbf{A}^{-1}. \tag{10.24}$$

Here we have introduced notation $[\mathbf{t}]_\times$ for an antisymmetric matrix defined by $\mathbf{t}$. If $\mathbf{t} = [t_x, t_y, t_z]^T$, then

$$[\mathbf{t}]_\times = \begin{bmatrix} 0 & -t_z & t_y \\ t_x & 0 & -t_x \\ -t_y & t_x & 0 \end{bmatrix}. \tag{10.25}$$

With that notation, we have $\mathbf{t} \times \mathbf{x} = [\mathbf{t}]_\times \mathbf{x}, \forall \mathbf{x}$. Because $\det([\mathbf{t}]_\times) = 0$, $\det(\mathbf{F}) = 0$. Note that the Fundamental Matrix can be estimated directly from image coordinates and is defined without camera calibration. The reader is referred to [263] for a review and comparative study of various techniques for estimating the fundamental matrix.

Now, let us introduce another notation:

$$\widetilde{\mathbf{m}}_i = \mathbf{A}^{-1} \widetilde{\mathbf{p}}_i \quad \text{and} \quad \widetilde{\mathbf{m}}'_i = \mathbf{A}^{-1} \widetilde{\mathbf{p}}'_i. \tag{10.26}$$

Actually, $\widetilde{\mathbf{m}}_i$ and $\widetilde{\mathbf{m}}'_i$ are the image coordinates in the normalized camera coordinate system if the camera is calibrated. In that case, Equation 10.23 can be rewritten as

$$\widetilde{\mathbf{m}}'^T_i \mathbf{E} \widetilde{\mathbf{m}}_i = 0, \tag{10.27}$$

where $\mathbf{E}$ is known as the *Essential Matrix*, and is given by

$$\mathbf{E} = [\mathbf{t}]_\times \mathbf{R}. \tag{10.28}$$

From Equation 10.27, it is clear that the magnitude of the translation cannot be determined from image points. If $\mathbf{t}$ is a solution, then any $\alpha \mathbf{t}$ ($\alpha \neq 0$) is also a solution. Geometrically, it can be understood in the following way. When the translation is α times bigger, if we multiply the 3D scene by the same factor α, we get exactly the same image points.

Note that if $\mathbf{t} = \mathbf{0}$ (i.e., a pure rotation around the optical center), (10.27) is always valid. In that case, we cannot reconstruct the scene in 3D although the rotation matrix can still be determined. In the sequel, we assume $\mathbf{t} \neq \mathbf{0}$.

The essential matrix $\mathbf{E}$ has the following properties [55]:

(i) $\det \mathbf{E} = 0$ because $[\mathbf{t}]_\times$ is an antisymmetric matrix.
(ii) $\mathbf{E}^T \mathbf{t} = \mathbf{0}$ because $([\mathbf{t}]_\times \mathbf{R})^T \mathbf{t} = \mathbf{R}^T [\mathbf{t}]^T_\times \mathbf{t} = -\mathbf{R}^T (\mathbf{t} \times \mathbf{t}) = \mathbf{0}$.
(iii) $\mathbf{E}\mathbf{E}^T = (\mathbf{t}^T \mathbf{t})\mathbf{I} - \mathbf{t}\mathbf{t}^T$ (i.e., $\mathbf{E}\mathbf{E}^T$ is only determined by the translation). This is because $([\mathbf{t}]_\times \mathbf{R})([\mathbf{t}]_\times \mathbf{R})^T = [\mathbf{t}]_\times [\mathbf{t}]^T_\times = -[\mathbf{t}]^2_\times$.
(iv) $\|\mathbf{E}\|^2 = 2\|\mathbf{t}\|^2$, where $\|\mathbf{E}\|$ is the matrix's Frobenius norm.

10.1.4.2 Estimating the essential matrix

In the following, we describe how to estimate the essential matrix from the image correspondences. Let $\mathbf{m}_i = [u_i, v_i]^T$ and $\mathbf{m}'_i = [u'_i, v'_i]^T$. Let us define a nine-dimensional vector $\mathbf{x} = [\mathbf{e}_1^T, \mathbf{e}_2^T, \mathbf{e}_2^T]^T$, where $\mathbf{e}_i^T$ is the ith row vector of $\mathbf{E}$. Equation 10.27 can be rewritten as

$$\mathbf{a}_i^T \mathbf{x} = 0,$$

where $\mathbf{a}_i = [u'_i \tilde{\mathbf{m}}_i^T, v'_i \tilde{\mathbf{m}}_i^T, \tilde{\mathbf{m}}_i^T]^T$ is a nine-dimensional vector. Given n point correspondences, we can stack the n linear equation together as

$$\mathbf{A}_n \mathbf{x} = \mathbf{0}, \tag{10.29}$$

where $\mathbf{A}_n$ is a $n \times 9$ matrix, given by

$$\mathbf{A}_n = \begin{bmatrix} \mathbf{a}_1^T \\ \mathbf{a}_2^T \\ \vdots \\ \mathbf{a}_n^T \end{bmatrix}.$$

Together with the properties of the essential matrix, a solution exists when five or more point correspondences are available. As shown in [55], when there are only five-point correspondences, maximum ten real solutions exist. When more than five-point correspondences are available, there exists in general a unique solution, but in some special cases, there may exist three solutions.

When we are given eight or more point correspondences, we can determine the essential matrix with least squares. As discussed earlier, the translation can only be determined up to a scale factor. Without loss of generality, we set $\|\mathbf{t}\| = 1$. As we know earlier, $\|\mathbf{E}\|^2 = 2\|\mathbf{t}\|^2$, so we have constraint $\|\mathbf{x}\|^2 = 2$. The pose estimation problem can then be formulated as

$$\min_{\mathbf{x}} \|\mathbf{A}_n \mathbf{x}\| \quad \text{subject to } \|\mathbf{x}\|^2 = 2. \tag{10.30}$$

With Lagrange multiplier, we transform the problem into minimizing the following unconstrained function:

$$\Phi(\mathbf{x}) = \mathbf{x}^T \mathbf{A}_n^T \mathbf{A}_n \mathbf{x} + \lambda(2 - \mathbf{x}^T \mathbf{x}). \tag{10.31}$$

Setting the derivative of $\Phi(\mathbf{x})$ with respect to $\mathbf{x}$ to 0 yields

$$\mathbf{A}_n^T \mathbf{A}_n \mathbf{x} = \lambda \mathbf{x}.$$

From this equation, it is clear that λ is the eigenvalue of the symmetric matrix $A_n^T A_n$, and $\mathbf{x}$ is the associated eigenvector. However, since $A_n^T A_n$ is a 9×9 matrix, there are potentially nine solutions. Substituting the solution back to (10.31), we have $\Phi(\mathbf{x}) = 2\lambda$. As we are minimizing $\Phi(\mathbf{x})$, we conclude that the desired solution is the eigenvector of $A_n^T A_n$ associated with the smallest eigenvalue and with magnitude equal to $\sqrt{2}$.

10.1.4.3 Determining the pose from the essential matrix

Once the essential matrix $\mathbf{E}$ is estimated, we can determine the pose parameters $(\mathbf{R}, \mathbf{t})$. Because $\mathbf{E}^T \mathbf{t} = \mathbf{0}$, we can estimate $\mathbf{t}$ by solving the following problem:

$$\min_{\mathbf{t}} \|\mathbf{E}^T \mathbf{t}\|^2 \quad \text{subject to } \|\mathbf{t}\| = 1. \tag{10.32}$$

Similar to the problem of essential matrix estimation described earlier, the solution $\mathbf{t}$ is the unit eigenvector of matrix $\mathbf{E}\mathbf{E}^T$, associated with the smallest eigenvalue.

At this point, we cannot determine the sign of $\mathbf{t}$. In fact, the essential matrix $\mathbf{E}$ was only determined up to a scale factor from the procedure, and thus the sign of $\mathbf{E}$ is undetermined. If we assume the sign of $\mathbf{E}$ is correct, we can use any point correspondence, say $(\mathbf{m}_i, \mathbf{m}_i')$, to resolve $\mathbf{t}$'s sign ambiguity. Let z_i and z_i' be the z-component of $\mathbf{m}_i$ and $\mathbf{m}_i'$, we have $\mathbf{R}(z_i \widetilde{\mathbf{m}}_i) + \mathbf{t} = z_i' \widetilde{\mathbf{m}}_i'$, that is,

$$z_i'(\mathbf{t} \times \widetilde{\mathbf{m}}_i') = z_i \mathbf{E} \widetilde{\mathbf{m}}_i.$$

Obviously, z_i and z_i' must be both positive if the sign of $\mathbf{E}$ is correct, or both negative if not. This implies that vectors $\mathbf{t} \times \widetilde{\mathbf{m}}_i'$ and $\mathbf{E}\widetilde{\mathbf{m}}_i$ must have the same direction. Therefore, if

$$(\mathbf{t} \times \widetilde{\mathbf{m}}_i') \cdot (\mathbf{E}\widetilde{\mathbf{m}}_i) > 0, \tag{10.33}$$

then $\mathbf{t}$'s sign is consistent with $\mathbf{E}$'s sign; otherwise, we must invert $\mathbf{t}$'s sign.

Now let us estimate the rotation matrix $\mathbf{R}$. By definition, we have $\mathbf{E} = [\mathbf{t}]_\times \mathbf{R}$, so we can compute $\mathbf{R}$ by solving the following problem:

$$\min_{\mathbf{R}} \|\mathbf{E} - [\mathbf{t}]_\times \mathbf{R}\|^2 \quad \text{subject to } \mathbf{R} \text{ is a rotation matrix.} \tag{10.34}$$

Since $\mathbf{E} - [\mathbf{t}]_\times \mathbf{R} = (\mathbf{E}\mathbf{R}^T - [\mathbf{t}]_\times)\mathbf{R}$, we have $\|\mathbf{E} - [\mathbf{t}]_\times \mathbf{R}\|^2 = \|\mathbf{E}\mathbf{R}^T - [\mathbf{t}]_\times\|^2$, and the problem becomes

$$\min_{\mathbf{R}} \sum_{j=1}^{3} \|\mathbf{R}\boldsymbol{\epsilon}_j - \boldsymbol{\tau}_j\|^2 \quad \text{subject to } \mathbf{R} \text{ is a rotation matrix,} \tag{10.35}$$

where ϵ_j and τ_j are, respectively, the jth *row* vector of matrix $\mathbf{E}$ and $[\mathbf{t}]_\times$. This is exactly the same problem as minimizing Equation 10.16, and the solution is already given in Section 10.1.3.

Now, we can determine the sign of $\mathbf{E}$. Using any point correspondence, say $(\mathbf{m}_i, \mathbf{m}'_i)$, we can reconstruct their corresponding 3D point. If the reconstructed point has a negative z value, then the sign of $\mathbf{E}$ is wrong, and we need to invert the sign of $\mathbf{t}$; otherwise, the sign is already correct. More precisely, the z value can be computed in the following way. Since $\mathbf{R}(z_i \widetilde{\mathbf{m}}_i) + \mathbf{t} = z'_i \widetilde{\mathbf{m}}'_i$, we can eliminate z'_i by performing cross product $\widetilde{\mathbf{m}}'_i$ with both sides, which gives $z_i [\widetilde{\mathbf{m}}'_i]_\times \mathbf{R}\widetilde{\mathbf{m}}_i + [\widetilde{\mathbf{m}}'_i]_\times \mathbf{t} = \mathbf{0}$. Performing now the dot product with $[\widetilde{\mathbf{m}}'_i]_\times \mathbf{R}\widetilde{\mathbf{m}}_i$ yields z_i, given by

$$z_i = -\frac{([\widetilde{\mathbf{m}}'_i]_\times \mathbf{t}) \cdot ([\widetilde{\mathbf{m}}'_i]_\times \mathbf{R}\widetilde{\mathbf{m}}_i)}{([\widetilde{\mathbf{m}}'_i]_\times \mathbf{R}\widetilde{\mathbf{m}}_i) \cdot ([\widetilde{\mathbf{m}}'_i]_\times \mathbf{R}\widetilde{\mathbf{m}}_i)}.$$

Note that we do not need to re-estimate $\mathbf{R}$ because inverting the sign of both $\mathbf{E}$ and $\mathbf{t}$ produces the same rotation matrix $\mathbf{R}$.

10.1.4.4 Nonlinear optimization

Given a point correspondence $(\mathbf{p}_i, \mathbf{p}'_i)$, from (10.23), we have

$$f_i \equiv \widetilde{\mathbf{p}}'^T_i \mathbf{F}\widetilde{\mathbf{p}}_i = 0.$$

However, the points extracted from the images are noisy, and f_i is rarely equal to 0. Assuming noise is modeled as Gaussian, we will show next how to compute the variance of f_i, denoted by σ_i^2. Using the maximum likelihood estimation method, the pose $(\mathbf{R}, \mathbf{t})$ can be estimated by solving the following nonlinear optimization problem:

$$\min_{\mathbf{R},\mathbf{t}} \sum_i f_i^2/\sigma_i^2 \quad \text{with } f_i = \widetilde{\mathbf{p}}'^T_i \mathbf{F}\widetilde{\mathbf{p}}_i \text{ and } \mathbf{F} = \mathbf{A}^{-T}[\mathbf{t}]_\times \mathbf{R}\mathbf{A}^{-1}. \quad (10.36)$$

Before proceeding further, we define

$$\mathbf{l}'_i = \mathbf{F}\widetilde{\mathbf{p}}_i \equiv [\alpha'_i, \beta'_i, \gamma'_i]^T, \quad (10.37)$$

$$\mathbf{l}_i = \mathbf{F}^T \widetilde{\mathbf{p}}'_i \equiv [\alpha_i, \beta_i, \gamma_i]^T. \quad (10.38)$$

In the computer vision literature, $\mathbf{l}_i$ and $\mathbf{l}'_i$, respectively, represent the epipolar line defined by point $\mathbf{p}'_i$ and $\mathbf{p}_i$. We can now compute the derivatives of f_i with respect to $\mathbf{p}_i$ and $\mathbf{p}_i'$:

$$\frac{\partial f_i}{\partial \mathbf{p}_i} = [\alpha_i', \beta_i'], \tag{10.39}$$

$$\frac{\partial f_i}{\partial \mathbf{p}_i'} = [\alpha_i, \beta_i]. \tag{10.40}$$

Assuming point $\mathbf{p}_i$ is a Gaussian random vector with mean $\mathbf{p}_i$ and covariance matrix $\mathbf{\Lambda}_{\mathbf{p}_i}$ and point $\mathbf{p}_i'$ is a Gaussian random vector with mean $\mathbf{p}_i'$ and covariance matrix $\mathbf{\Lambda}_{\mathbf{p}_i'}$, then under the first-order approximation, the variance of f_i can be computed as

$$\sigma_i^2 = [\alpha_i', \beta_i'] \mathbf{\Lambda}_{\mathbf{p}_i} [\alpha_i', \beta_i']^T + [\alpha_i, \beta_i] \mathbf{\Lambda}_{\mathbf{p}_i'} [\alpha_i, \beta_i]^T. \tag{10.41}$$

The nonlinear minimization needs an initial guess of the pose parameters, which can be obtained from the previous least-squares solution.

There are many other optimization criteria. The interested reader is referred to [264] for a comparative study of those criteria, including (10.36).

10.1.5 Iterative closest point matching

Iterative closest point is a popular algorithm employed to register two sets of curves, two sets of surfaces, or two clouds of points. It was proposed independently by Besl and McKay [15] and Zhang [261] in two different contexts. Besl and McKay [15] developed the ICP algorithm to register partially sensed data from rigid objects with an ideal geometric model, prior to shape inspection. So this is a subset–set matching problem because each sensed point has a correspondence in the ideal model. Zhang [261] developed the ICP algorithm in the context of autonomous vehicle navigation in rugged terrain based on vision. His algorithm is used to register a sequence of sensed data in order to build a complete model of the scene and to plan a free path for navigation. So this is a subset–subset matching problem because a fraction of data in one set does not have any correspondence in the other set. To address this issue, Zhang's ICP algorithm has integrated a statistical method based on the distance distribution to deal with outliers, occlusion, appearance, and disappearance. However, both algorithms share the same idea: Iteratively match points in one set to the closest points in another set, and refine the transformation between the two sets, with the goal of minimizing the distance between the two sets of point clouds.

The ICP algorithm is very simple, and can be summarized as follows.

- **Input:** two point sets, initial estimation of the transformation.
- **Output:** optimal transformation between the two point sets.
- **procedure:** Iterate the following steps
    - (i) Apply the current estimate of the transformation to the first set of points;
    - (ii) Find the closest point in the second set for each point in the first transformed point set;
    - (iii) Update the point matches by discarding outliers;
    - (iv) Compute the transformation using the updated point matches;
    until convergence of the estimated transformation.

Here are a few comments on this general algorithm:

- Depending on the nature of the point sets, various pose estimation techniques described in the earlier sections can be used to compute the transformation between the two sets.
- The step of finding the closest point to a given point is generally the most time-expensive one. However, this step can be easily parallelized.
- Many data structures can be used to accelerate the finding of the closest point. They include k-D tree and octree.
- Instead of using all points from the first set, a selected subset of points (such as high curvature points) can be used to speed up the process, with only moderate sacrifice of the final accuracy.
- The above algorithm is not symmetric. Let point $\hat{\mathbf{p}}'_i$ in the second set be the closest point to a point $\mathbf{p}_i$ in the first set. In the other direction, point $\mathbf{p}_i$ is, in general, not necessarily the closest point to $\hat{\mathbf{p}}'_i$. In order to make the algorithm symmetric, we can find the closest point in the first transformed point set for each point in the second set, and add these point matches to the overall set of matches. Better results can then be obtained at the expense of additional computational cost.
- When the ICP algorithm is applied to register curves or surfaces, they need to be sampled. The final accuracy depends on the density of sampling. The denser the sampling is, the higher the registration quality will be, but the more the computation will be required.

For more detailed and extensive discussions on ICP, the interested reader is referred to Sections 7 and 8 of Zhang's paper [261].

There are several variants to the ICP algorithm. A useful variation is to substitute the point-to-point distance with point-to-plane distance [33]. The point-to-plane distance allows one surface to slide tangentially along the other surface, making it less likely get stuck in local minima. Consider a point $\mathbf{p}_i$ in the first set. Let point $\hat{\mathbf{p}}_i'$ in the second set be its closest point. Let the surface normal at point $\mathbf{p}_i$ be $\mathbf{n}_i$ (a unit vector). Then, the point-to-plane distance measure is given by

$$d_i = \mathbf{n}_i^T (\hat{\mathbf{p}}_i' - \mathbf{p}_i).$$

Surface normals can be precomputed to save computation.

10.2 Monocular head pose tracking

This section describes a monocular tracking technique along the line of [217, 226]. The algorithm combines information from preceding frames as well as keyframes. The advantage of using keyframes is that it effectively prevents drifting.

The tracker can be initialized by using a face detector [242] and a face alignment algorithm [128]. The face alignment algorithm outputs a number of face feature points. Each feature point is in fact a semantic point and we can obtain its corresponding vertex on the 3D face model. Thus, we obtain a set of 3D–2D correspondences. The head pose can be obtained by using the technique described in Section 10.1.2. This frame is typically stored as a keyframe. As the tracking continues, the algorithm maintains a set of keyframes by inserting newly tracked frames whose head poses are sufficiently different from those in the existing keyframes. To ensure that the poses for the inserted keyframes are accurate, one could use a face alignment program to recompute its head pose.

Given a new frame, the algorithm estimates its head pose by using a number of preceding frames and a number of keyframes selected from the keyframe pool. The number of preceding frames is usually fixed and is typically set to be a value between 1 and 5 in the implementation. The number of selected keyframes usually varies from frame to frame, and it depends on how many keyframes in the keyframe pool are reasonably close to the current frame.

Once the keyframes are selected, they are used in a similar way as the preceding frames to estimate the pose of the current frame. In the following, we use the term reference frames to refer to both keyframes and preceding frames.

Let I^t denote the current frame where t is the frame index. Let I^r denote a reference frame that could be either a preceding frame or a keyframe. Let $\{(\mathbf{u}_k^r, \mathbf{u}_k^t)\}_{k=1}^K$ denote a set of matched image points between I^r and I^t, where $\{\mathbf{u}_k^r\}_{k=1}^K$ are the points on image I^r and $\{\mathbf{u}_k^t\}_{k=1}^K$ are the points on image I^t. The corner detection and matching can be done in a way similar to what is described in Section 5.1.2.2. For each point $\mathbf{u}_k^r$ on the reference frame, since we know its head pose, we back-project the point to the 3D face model, and let U_k^t

denote the corresponding 3D position on the model. Let $\mathbf{M}^t$ denote the 4×4 transformation matrix of the head pose at frame t with respect to the camera coordinate system. According to (10.1), the projected point of $\mathbf{U}_k^t$ on image I^t is

$$\hat{\mathbf{u}}_k^t = \boldsymbol{\phi}(\mathbf{M}^t, \mathbf{U}_k^t). \tag{10.42}$$

Therefore, the total projection errors between reference frame I^r and current frame I^t is

$$e_r^t = \sum_{k=1}^K \rho(\mathbf{u}_k^t - \boldsymbol{\phi}(\mathbf{M}^t, \mathbf{U}_k^t)), \tag{10.43}$$

where $\rho(.)$ is an M-estimator [98] for robustness against noises.

The overall error function is a weighted sum of the projection errors across all the reference frames, that is,

$$e^t = \sum_r w_r e_r^t, \tag{10.44}$$

where r ranges over all the reference frames, and w_r is the weight for reference frame I^r. For preceding frames, w_r can be specified as an aging function, that is, $w_{t-j} = \alpha^j$ where $0 < \alpha < 1$ is an aging factor. For keyframes, w_r usually depends on the similarity between the pose of I_r and the pose of the previous frame I^{t-1}. If the two poses are similar, it is likely that we can obtain better corner matchings between I^r and I^t, thus we want to use a larger weight. In this way, the pose estimation problem becomes an optimization problem: solving for $\mathbf{M}^t$ to minimize e^t. If we ignore the M-estimator (i.e., setting $\rho(x) = x^2$), then the problem becomes a pose estimation problem with 3D–2D correspondences. As described in Section 10.1.2, one can use the POSIT algorithm to obtain an initial estimate. After that, we can use a nonlinear optimization procedure such as the Levenberg–Marquardt method to refine the solution.

10.3 Stereo head pose tracking

In this section, we describe a technique to use a stereo pair for head pose tracking. One such system was developed by Yang and Zhang [247]. In their setup, one camera is mounted at the top of the monitor, and the other camera is mounted at the bottom. The technique described in this section closely follows their work.

We assume the two cameras of the stereo pair are precalibrated so that their intrinsic and extrinsic parameters are known. Let $\mathbf{A}_1$ and $\mathbf{A}_2$ denote the intrinsic camera parameters of the two cameras where $\mathbf{A}_1$ and $\mathbf{A}_2$ are 3×3 matrices. Without loss of generality, we use the first camera's coordinate system as the world coordinate system. The second camera's coordinate system is related to the first one by a rigid transformation

$$\mathbf{M}_{21} = \begin{pmatrix} \mathbf{R}_{21} & \mathbf{t}_{21} \\ \mathbf{0}^T & 1 \end{pmatrix},$$

where $\mathbf{R}_{21}$ is a 3×3 rotation matrix, and $\mathbf{t}_{21}$ is a 3 dimensional translation vector. A point P in 3D space is projected to the image planes of the two cameras by

$$\mathbf{p}_1 = \phi(\mathbf{A}_1, \mathbf{1}_{4\times 4}, \mathrm{P}), \tag{10.45}$$

$$\mathbf{p}_2 = \phi(\mathbf{A}_2, \mathbf{M}_{21}, \mathrm{P}), \tag{10.46}$$

where $\mathbf{1}_{4\times 4}$ is a 4×4 identity matrix, and $\mathbf{p}_1$ and $\mathbf{p}_2$ are the image coordinates in the two cameras. Note that these two equations are similar to (1.2) except that the intrinsic parameters are explicit. The parameters $\mathbf{A}_1$, $\mathbf{A}_2$, $\mathbf{R}_{21}$, and $\mathbf{t}_{21}$ can be obtained by using the camera calibration method described in [265].

Again, a face model is used in the tracking. The face model can be either a generic face model or a personalized face model constructed by using the face-modeling technique described in Section 5.1. The rigid motion of the head, that is, the head pose in the world coordinate system at frame t is represented by

$$\mathbf{M}^t = \begin{pmatrix} \mathbf{R}^t & \mathbf{t}^t \\ \mathbf{0}^T & 1 \end{pmatrix}.$$

The goal of head pose tracking is to determine $\mathbf{R}^t$ and $\mathbf{t}^t$. The problem can be formally stated as follows.

Given: (1) A pair of stereo images I_1^{t-1} and I_2^{t-1} at frame $t-1$; (2) two sets of matched 2D points $S_1^{t-1} = \{\mathbf{p}_{1,k}^{t-1}\}_{k=1}^{K^{t-1}}$ and $S_2^{t-1} = \{\mathbf{p}_{2,k}^{t-1}\}_{k=1}^{K^{t-1}}$ from the image pair, and their corresponding 3D model points $Q^{t-1} = \{\mathrm{P}_k^{t-1}\}_{k=1}^{K^{t-1}}$; (3) a new image pair I_1^t and I_2^t at frame t.

Determine: (1) A subset $Q^t = \{\mathrm{P}_k^t\}_{k=1}^{K^t} \subset Q^{t-1}$ whose corresponding image points in I_1^t and I_2^t are denoted by $S_1^t = \{\mathbf{p}_{1,k}^t\}_{k=1}^{K^t}$ and $S_2^t = \{\mathbf{p}_{2,k}^t\}_{k=1}^{K^t}$; (2) the head pose $\mathbf{R}^t$ and $\mathbf{t}^t$ so that the projections of P_k^t in I_1^t and I_2^t are, respectively, $\mathbf{p}_{1,k}^t$ and $\mathbf{p}_{2,k}^t$.

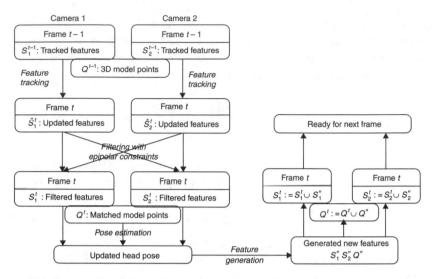

Figure 10.3. Model-based stereo head pose tracking.

Figure 10.3 is a diagram showing the outline of the stereo-tracking algorithm. It first performs feature point tracking from frame $t-1$ to frame t for each camera independently. One can use the KLT tracker [196]. However, there are usually drifts and errors in the matched points. Therefore, it is helpful to use epipolar constraints to filter out any stray points. The epipolar constraint states that if a point $\mathbf{p}_1$ in the first image and a point $\mathbf{p}_2$ in the second image correspond to the same 3D point P, they must satisfy the following equation:

$$\widetilde{\mathbf{p}}_2^T \mathbf{F} \widetilde{\mathbf{p}}_1 = 0. \tag{10.47}$$

where $\mathbf{F} = \mathbf{A}_2^T [\mathbf{t}_{21}]_\times \mathbf{R}_{21} \mathbf{A}_1$ is the fundamental matrix, $\widetilde{\mathbf{p}}_1$ and $\widetilde{\mathbf{p}}_2$ are the homogeneous coordinates of $\mathbf{p}_1$ and $\mathbf{p}_2$, respectively. Geometrically, $\mathbf{F}\widetilde{\mathbf{p}}_1$ defines the epipolar line in the second image; thus, (10.47) means that the epipolar line $\mathbf{F}\widetilde{\mathbf{p}}_1$ must pass through the point $\widetilde{\mathbf{p}}_2$. By transposing (10.47), we obtain a symmetric equation from the second image to the first image. $\mathbf{F}\widetilde{\mathbf{p}}_2$ defines the epipolar line on the first image, and (10.47) says that point $\widetilde{\mathbf{p}}_1$ must lie on the epipolar line.

In practice, due to inaccuracy in camera calibration and feature localization, we cannot expect the epipolar constraint to be satisfied exactly. For a triplet $(\mathbf{p}_{1,k}, \mathbf{p}_{2,k}, P_k)$, if the distance from $\mathbf{p}_{2,k}$ to $\mathbf{p}_{1,k}$'s epipolar line is larger than a certain threshold (typically set to a few pixels), this triplet is considered to be an outlier and is discarded.

After we filter out all the stray points that violate the epipolar constraint, we estimate the head pose $\mathbf{M}^t$ so that the reprojection error of P_k to $\mathbf{p}_{1,k}$ and $\mathbf{p}_{2,k}$ is minimized. The total reprojection error for all the points is defined as

$$e(\mathbf{R}^t, \mathbf{t}^t) = \sum_{k=1}^{K^t} (||\mathbf{p}_{1,k}^t - \phi(\mathbf{A}_1, \mathbf{M}^t, P_k^t)||^2 + ||\mathbf{p}_{2,k}^t - \phi(\mathbf{A}_2, \mathbf{M}_{21}\mathbf{M}^t, P_k^t)||^2).$$

$$(10.48)$$

Thus the estimation of $(\mathbf{R}^t, \mathbf{t}^t)$ minimize the objective function $e(\mathbf{R}^t, \mathbf{t}^t)$. The minimization problem can be solved by using the Levenberg–Marquardt algorithm, and the head pose at frame $t - 1$: $(\mathbf{R}^{t-1}, \mathbf{t}^{t-1})$ can be used as an initial guess.

10.3.1 Feature generation

After the head pose is determined, we need to replenish the matched point sets S_1^t, S_2^t, and Q^t by adding more good feature points. The feature points can be selected based on the following three criteria:

- **Texture:** The feature points in the images must have rich texture information to facilitate tracking. We can first select 2D points in the images using the criteria in [196] and then back-project them onto the face model to obtain their corresponding model points.
- **Visibility:** The feature points must be visible in both images. An intersection routine is implemented in [247] that returns the first visible triangle given an image point. A feature point is visible if the intersection routine returns the same triangle for its projections in both images.
- **Rigidity:** We must be careful not to add feature points in the nonrigid regions of the face, such as the mouth region. One can use a bounding box around the tip of the nose that covers the forehead, eye, nose, and cheek regions. Any points outside this bounding box will not be added to the feature set.

This feature regeneration scheme improves the tracking system in two ways. First, it replenishes the features points which are lost due to occlusions or nonrigid motion, so that the tracker always has a sufficient number of features to start with in the next frame. This improves accuracy and stability. Second, it alleviates the problem of tracker drift by adding new features at every frame.

10.3.2 Tracker initialization and recovery

The tracker needs to know the head pose at the initial frame to start tracking. One method for the initialization is to use a face detector [242] and a face alignment program [128] to locate face features on the two images. The detected face features can be used to estimate the head pose. Since the detected face features may not be accurate, we can use the epipolar constraints to refine the matching. This method can also be used for tracking recovery when the tracker loses tracking. The tracker may lose tracking when the user moves out of the camera's field of view or rotates his/her head away from the camera. When the user moves his/her head back, the system can use the same procedure as in the initialization to estimate the head pose and resume the tracking process.

We can also use keyframes as in Section 10.2 to avoid drifting during stereo tracking. For each keyframe, we store both images from the two cameras as well as their feature points and the head pose. Given a new frame, its head pose can be estimated based on a keyframe by using the same method as what is described in Figure 10.3 where we treat the keyframe as the frame $t - 1$. Furthermore, we can use multiple keyframes as well as multiple preceding frames as in (10.44).

10.3.3 Stereo-tracking experiments

We show some stereo tracking experiment results which were obtained by Yang and Zhang [247]. There are three video sequences with resolution 320×240 at 30 frames per second.

Figure 10.4 shows the results for the first video sequence. The 3D face mesh is projected according to the estimated head pose and is overlayed on the input stereo images. This sequence contains large head rotations close to 90 degrees.

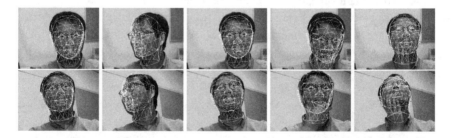

Figure 10.4. Stereo-tracking result for the first vide sequence (320×240 at 30 frames per second). Images from the first camera are shown at the upper row, while those from the second camera are shown at the lower row. From left to right, the frame numbers are 1, 130, 325, 997, and 1,256.

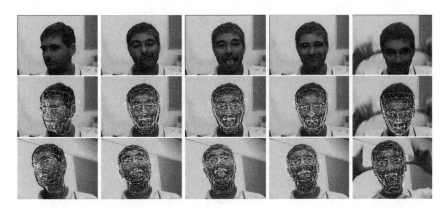

Figure 10.5. Stereo-tracking result for the second vide sequence (320 × 240 at 30 frames per second). The first row shows the input images from the upper camera. The second and third rows show the projected face model overlayed on the images from the upper and lower camera, respectively. From left to right, the frame numbers are 56, 524, 568, 624, and 716.

Figure 10.6. Stereo-tracking result for the third sequence (320 × 240 at 30 frames per second). All of the images are from the top camera. The frame numbers, from left to right and from top to bottom, are 31, 67, 151, 208, 289, 352, 391, 393, 541, 694, 718, and 737.

This type of out-of-plane rotation is usually difficult for monocular head pose tracking. But the stereo-tracking algorithm is able to estimate the head pose quite accurately.

The second sequence, shown in Figure 10.5, contains predominantly nonrigid motions caused by dramatic facial expressions. The original images are shown to make it easier to visualize the nonrigid motions. Because the face is classified into rigid and nonrigid regions and the features are selected from the rigid region, the tracker is quite robust to nonrigid motion.

Figure 10.6 shows the third sequence where large occlusions and out-of-plane head motions frequently occur. Note that only the images from the top camera are shown here.

10.4 Multicamera head pose tracking

In the setup of stereo tracking described in Section 10.3, the relative geometry of the two cameras is assumed to be known a priori. In practice, this assumption may not hold because people may move cameras around. It is not feasible to ask the user to recalibrate cameras whenever the cameras are moved. In this section, we describe a technique that does not have this limitation. It assumes that the camera placements are unknown. In addition, it can handle an arbitrary number of cameras.

Suppose there are N cameras. We assume their intrinsic parameters are known, but their relative placements (extrinsic parameters) are not known. We also assume that the cameras do not move during the tracking process. As it will become clear later, when one or more cameras move, the tracker will discard the tracking history and restart the tracking process.

One of the cameras is used as a reference camera, and we use c to denote the index of the reference camera. Note that c is not fixed, and it may change from frame to frame. Let $\mathbf{M}_i^t$ denote the head pose at frame t in the coordinate system of camera i. Let $\mathbf{M}_{i,j}$ denote the transformation from the coordinate system of camera i to that of camera j. Then $\mathbf{M}_j^t = \mathbf{M}_{i,j}\mathbf{M}_i^t$. In particular, $\mathbf{M}_j^t = \mathbf{M}_{c,j}\mathbf{M}_c^t$. The pose-tracking problem is to estimate the relative camera geometry $\mathbf{M}_{c,j}$ and the head pose with respect to the reference camera $\mathbf{M}_c^t$.

Similar to Section 10.2, we maintain a set of keyframes that are shared among the cameras. A keyframe is an image captured by one of the cameras. Both the intrinsic parameter matrix ($\mathbf{A}$) of the camera and the head pose ($\mathbf{M}$) with respect to the camera are stored. In addition to keyframes, we also use a few preceding frames per camera for the pose estimation of the current frame. As in Section 10.2, given a new frame, for each camera we use a fixed number of preceding frames as well as a number of dynamically selected keyframes to match with the new frame. We use the term reference frame to refer to both the preceding frames and the keyframes. We use the index r to refer to a reference frame.

The objective function consists of three terms. The first term is the matching error between the current frame of the reference camera and the reference frames. The second term is the matching error between the cameras. The third term is a smoothness term.

The first term is similar to (10.43) and (10.44). For each reference frame I^r, we can find a set of matched image points between I^r and the current frame I_c^t of the reference camera. Let $\{(\mathbf{u}_k^r, \mathbf{u}_{c,k}^{t,r})\}_{k=1}^{K_r}$ denote the matched points. For each point $\mathbf{u}_k^r$ on I^r, since we know $\mathbf{A}^r$ and $\mathbf{M}^r$, we can back-project $\mathbf{u}_k^r$ to the 3D face model. Let $\mathbf{U}_k^r$ denote the corresponding 3D position on the model.

According to (10.1), the projected point of $\mathtt{U}_k^r$ on image I_c^t is

$$\hat{\mathbf{u}}_{c,k}^{t,r} = \boldsymbol{\phi}(\mathbf{A}_c, \mathbf{M}_c^t, \mathtt{U}_k^r). \tag{10.49}$$

If we assume that the distribution of $\mathbf{u}_{c,k}^{t,r}$ is Gaussian with mean $\hat{\mathbf{u}}_{c,k}^{t,r}$ and covariance matrix $\sum_{r,c,k}$, the likelihood of $\mathbf{u}_{c,k}^{t,r}$ is inversely proportional to $(\mathbf{u}_{c,k}^{t,r} - \hat{\mathbf{u}}_{c,k}^{t,r})^T \Sigma_{r,c,k}^{-1} (\mathbf{u}_{c,k}^{t,r} - \hat{\mathbf{u}}_{c,k}^{t,r})$. This leads to the following minimization term:

$$e_1 = \sum_r \omega_r \sum_k (\mathbf{u}_{c,k}^{t,r} - \hat{\mathbf{u}}_{c,k}^{t,r})^T \Sigma_{r,c,k}^{-1} (\mathbf{u}_{c,k}^{t,r} - \hat{\mathbf{u}}_{c,k}^{t,r}). \tag{10.50}$$

The second term measures the image-matching errors between the cameras. Let I_i^t denote the image of camera i at frame t. Let $\{(\mathbf{u}_{i,k}^t, \mathbf{u}_{c,k}^{t,i})\}_{k=1}^{K_i}$ denote the matched points between I_i^t and I_c^t, $i \neq c$. For each point $\mathbf{u}_{c,k}^{t,i}$ on I_c^t, we back-project $\mathbf{u}_{c,k}^{t,i}$ to the 3D face model. Let $\mathtt{U}_{c,k}^{t,i}$ denote the corresponding 3D position on the model. According to (10.1), the projected point of $\mathtt{U}_{c,k}^{t,i}$ on image I_i^t is

$$\hat{\mathbf{u}}_{i,k}^{t,c} = \boldsymbol{\phi}(\mathbf{A}_i, \mathbf{M}_i^t, \mathtt{U}_{c,k}^{t,i}). \tag{10.51}$$

If we assume the distribution of $\mathbf{u}_{i,k}^t$ is Gaussian with mean $\hat{\mathbf{u}}_{i,k}^{t,c}$ and covariance matrix $\sum_{c,i,k}$, the likelihood of $\mathbf{u}_{i,k}^t$ is inversely proportional to $(\mathbf{u}_{i,k}^t - \hat{\mathbf{u}}_{i,k}^{t,c})^T \Sigma_{c,i,k}^{-1} (\mathbf{u}_{i,k}^t - \hat{\mathbf{u}}_{i,k}^{t,c})$. This leads to the following minimization term:

$$e_2 = \sum_{i,i \neq c} \omega_i \sum_k (\mathbf{u}_{i,k}^t - \hat{\mathbf{u}}_{i,k}^{t,c})^T \Sigma_{c,i,k}^{-1} (\mathbf{u}_{i,k}^t - \hat{\mathbf{u}}_{i,k}^{t,c}). \tag{10.52}$$

The third term is a smoothness term on the relative geometry $\mathbf{M}_{i,j}$ between the cameras. Let $\mathbf{M}_{i,j}^{old}$ denote the estimated transformation matrix between cameras i and j in the previous frame. Let $\Lambda_{i,j}$ denote the covariance matrix of $\mathbf{M}_{i,j}$. Since we assume the cameras do not move, we can minimize the Mahalanobis distance between $\mathbf{M}_{c,j}$ and $\mathbf{M}_{i,j}^{old}$. This leads to the third term:

$$e_3 = \sum_{i,j,i \neq j} \omega_{i,j} (\mathbf{M}_{i,j} - \mathbf{M}_{i,j}^{old})^T \Lambda_{i,j}^{-1} (\mathbf{M}_{i,j} - \mathbf{M}_{i,j}^{old}). \tag{10.53}$$

The covariance matrix $\Lambda_{i,j}$ controls the amount of adaptation for the relative geometry $\mathbf{M}_{i,j}$. Initially $\Lambda_{i,j}$ is set to be a diagonal matrix with large values at the diagonal. It is updated at each frame by the newly estimated $\mathbf{M}_{i,j}$. Note that $\mathbf{M}_{i,j}$ is a function of $\mathbf{M}_{c,i}$ and $\mathbf{M}_{c,j}$. In fact, $\mathbf{M}_{i,j} = \mathbf{M}_{c,j}(\mathbf{M}_{c,i})^{-1}$.

The overall objective function is

$$
\begin{aligned}
e^t &= e_1 + e_2 + e_3 \\
&= \sum_r \omega_r \sum_k (\mathbf{u}_{c,k}^{t,r} - \hat{\mathbf{u}}_{c,k}^{t,r})^T \Sigma_{r,c,k}^{-1} (\mathbf{u}_{c,k}^{t,r} - \hat{\mathbf{u}}_{c,k}^{t,r}) \\
&+ \sum_{i,i\neq c} \omega_i \sum_k (\mathbf{u}_{i,k}^t - \hat{\mathbf{u}}_{i,k}^{t,c})^T \Sigma_{c,i,k}^{-1} (\mathbf{u}_{i,k}^t - \hat{\mathbf{u}}_{i,k}^{t,c}) \\
&+ \sum_{i,j,i\neq j} \omega_{i,j} (\mathbf{M}_{i,j} - \mathbf{M}_{i,j}^{old})^T \Lambda_{i,j}^{-1} (\mathbf{M}_{i,j} - \mathbf{M}_{i,j}^{old}).
\end{aligned}
\tag{10.54}
$$

10.4.1 Initialization

To initialize tracking, each camera independently initializes its head pose estimation by using the initialization method described in Section 10.2. Let $\mathbf{M}_i^0$ denote the head pose in the coordinate system of camera i. The relative geometry between camera i and camera j is set to $\mathbf{M}_{i,j} = \mathbf{M}_j^0 (\mathbf{M}_i^0)^{-1}$. The camera close to the frontal view of the face is selected as the reference camera, and the image is inserted into the reference frame pool. If a camera fails to initialize (e.g., no face is detected on the image), the camera does not participate in the tracking initially. For each subsequent frame, the initialization procedure continues to be invoked until it succcessfully finds a face and estimates the head pose. After that, the camera is included in the tracking process.

10.4.2 Tracking procedure

The tracking procedure is outlined in Algorithm 6. Before we run a numerical procedure to minimize (10.54), we need to obtain $\mathbf{u}_{i,k}^t$ and $\mathsf{U}_{c,k}^{t,i}$. Given that the baseline between camera i and camera c may be relatively large, it is better to perform image matching after correcting the head pose for image I_i^t so that its head pose is close to $\mathbf{M}_c^t$. This requires the knowledge of $\mathbf{M}_i^t$ and $\mathbf{M}_c^t$. For this purpose, we use a single-camera head pose estimation method to obtain an initial estimate of $\mathbf{M}_i^t$ for each camera i. This is the initialization step of the multicamera head pose tracking algorithm. The single-camera head pose estimation method is similar to the monocular head pose tracking algorithm described in Section 10.2. The difference is that the head poses for the preceding frames of each camera are obtained jointly from all the cameras, and the keyframe pool is shared by all the cameras.

After the initialization, the algorithm goes into an iterative loop.

At the first step of the loop, the algorithm performs corner matching between image I_i^t and image I_c^t. As we mentioned before, the image matching is performed on the head pose corrected image of I_i^t so that its head pose is similar to that of I_c^t. We then back-project the points on I_c^t to the face model to obtain the 3D model points $U_{c,k}^{t,i}$. Again, we use the current estimate of $\mathbf{M}_c^t$ for the back-projection. In this way, we obtain image points $\mathbf{u}_{i,k}^t$ on I_i^t and model points $U_{c,k}^{t,i}$.

At the second step, the algorithm performs corner matching between the reference camera and each reference frame (i.e., preceding frames of the reference camera and the selected keyframes) to obtain $\mathbf{u}_{c,k}^{t,r}$ on I_c^t and model points U_k^r. This is the same as described in Section 10.2.

The third step minimizes the objective function of (10.54). We can use a nonlinear optimization technique such as Levenberg–Marquardt method to solve for head pose $\mathbf{M}_c^t$ and relative camera geometry $\mathbf{M}_{c,i}$.

The fourth step updates $\mathbf{M}_i^t$ based on $\mathbf{M}_c^t$ and $\mathbf{M}_{c,i}$.

Finally the algorithm checks whether the stop criteria is met or not. If not, it goes back to Step 1, and the iteration continues. A simple stop criteria is to check the amount of decrease in the objective function between two consecutive iterations. The iteration stops if the amount of decrease is smaller than a prespecified threshold.

The benefit of iterating within each time instant is to refine the corner matching in Steps 1 and 2 which depends on head pose and camera geometry estimation to warp images.

Algorithm 6 The algorithm for multicamera head pose tracking

Input: Images I_i^t of the cameras at current frame t;
              Preceding frames for each camera;
              The set of keyframes;
              The reference camera index c.

Output: Head pose $\mathbf{M}_i^t$ in each camera's coordinate system.

Initialize: For each camera i, perform single-camera pose estimation
              to obtain an initial estimate of $\mathbf{M}_i^t$.
              Select a new reference camera c if necessary.

Algorithm 6 (cont.)

Loop:

(1) For each camera i, perform feature matching between I_i^t and I_c^t and obtain 2D image points $\mathbf{u}_{i,k}^t$ on I_i^t and 3D model points $\mathsf{U}_{c,k}^{t,i}$.

(2) For each reference frame r, perform feature matching between I^r and I_c^t and obtain 2D image points $\mathbf{u}_{c,k}^{t,r}$ on I_c^t and 3D model points U_k^r.

(3) Minimize the objective function (10.54) to obtain $\mathbf{M}_c^t$ and relative camera geometry $\mathbf{M}_{c,i}$.

(4) Update head poses $\mathbf{M}_i^t$ for all the cameras $i \neq c$ based on newly estimated $\mathbf{M}_c^t$ and $\mathbf{M}_{c,i}$.

(5) Go to Step 1 if the stop criteria is not satisfied.

10.4.3 Experiment results

Cai et al. [27] implemented a multicamera pose-tracking system. The implemented algorithm is a simplified version of Algorithm 6. It only performs a single iteration of the loop. The system runs in real time on a PC with a dual core 3GHz processor with three cameras of resolution 320×240 at 15 frames per second. In this section, we show some experiment results obtained by Cai et al. [27].

Figure 10.7 shows three frames selected from a two-camera tracking sequence. The top three images are from the first camera. The bottom three images are from the second camera. In the left frame, the first camera is blocked. In the third frame, the right camera is blocked. In the middle frame, each camera can see half of the face. The multicamera tracking system is capable of handling occlusions like these because the two cameras work together.

To evaluate the tracking accuracy, a three-camera tracking sequence was captured with the user wearing a hexagonal cap (Figure 10.8). The sequence was 1 minute long at 30 frames per second. The ground truth was estimated by calibrating each view independently where the patterns on the hexagonal cap were used for feature matching and the incorrect matchings were corrected manually. The estimated head poses by the multicamera tracking system was matched against the ground truth allowing for a global scale, rotation, and translation between the two sets of head poses. Figure 10.9 shows the tracking results overlayed on the ground truth. The top diagram shows the Euler angles of the rotation matrices (roll in red, pitch in green, and yaw in blue). The bottom diagram shows the translation (x in red, y in green, z in blue). The

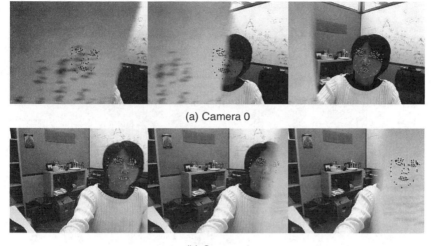

Figure 10.7. Three frames selected from a two-camera tracking sequence. The two cameras help each other to handle occlusions. Each column corresponds to a frame.

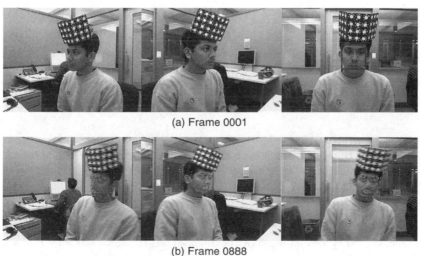

Figure 10.8. A three-camera tracking sequence for ground truth comparison. The hexagonal cap on the person's head was used to obtain ground truth for the head pose as well as the camera placement. Each row is a frame.

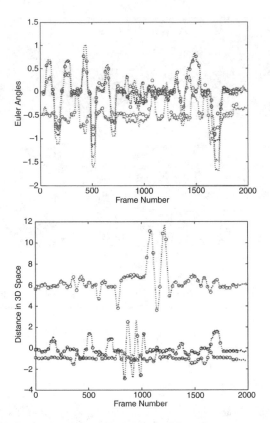

Figure 10.9. Comparison of head poses estimated from three-camera pose tracking (shown in dotted line) against the ground truth (shown in circles). They coincide well as the dotted lines mostly pass through the circles. The results were obtained over the video shown in Figure 10.8.

mismatches between ground truth and tracking results occur only at the extreme translations.

Figure 10.10 shows the ground truth comparison of the estimated relative camera geometry from the video sequence of Figure 10.8.

Figure 10.11 shows a comparison with monocular tracking. There are three cameras used by the multicamera tracking system. The video sequence is about 30 seconds long at 30 frames per second. The top figure shows an example frame where the face is completely blocked from one camera and half blocked from the other. The bottom diagram shows the estimated head pose translations with respect to the middle camera, which is the camera used for the monocular tracking. The thick lines are the results from monocular tracking,

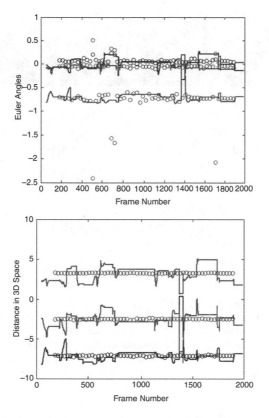

Figure 10.10. Ground truth comparison of the relative geometry between cameras in a three-camera pose-tracking sequence. The estimated transformation parameters (translation and Euler angles) between camera 1 and camera 2 are shown in dotted lines. The ground truth are shown in circles.

and the thin lines are the results from multicamera tracking. There is a period with severe occlusions and the single camera tracking fails (no thick lines are drawn).

Table 10.1 compares the pose-tracking performances between using a single camera, two cameras, three cameras, and three cameras with pre-calibrated camera geometry. The video sequence is the one shown in Figure 10.8. The evaluation metric is the difference between the estimated head pose and the ground truth. The second to fourth columns are the median angle errors, median translation errors, mean angle errors, and mean translation errors, respectively. As expected, the errors decrease as the number of cameras increases. It is interesting

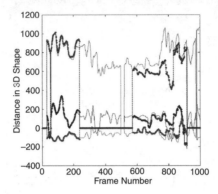

Figure 10.11. Comparison of single-camera and multicamera head pose tracking when there are severe occlusions. The top image shows an example frame of the three-camera tracking sequence. The red, green and blue thick lines in the bottom diagram represent the x, y, and z components of the head translation estimated by the single-camera tracking. The thin lines are results obtained from the multi-camera tracking.

Table 10.1. *Comparison of the pose tracking performances between using a single camera, two cameras, three cameras, and three cameras with precalibrated camera geometry*

Number of Cameras	Median Angle Error	Median Translation Error	Mean Angle Error	Mean Translation Error
1	5.9754	0.4138	19.0132	0.5504
2	5.4878	0.3481	11.8039	0.4885
3	4.4671	0.3404	11.0915	0.4634
3 (calib.)	4.0827	0.3132	11.0577	0.4540

to see that the three-camera tracking performance (the second row from the bottom) is almost the same as that when the cameras are precalibrated (the bottom row). The large mean rotation error in the single-camera tracking case is mainly due to the loss of tracking for profile poses where the frontal poses are used as default.

10.5 Eye-gaze correction for videoconferencing

In a typical desktop video-teleconferencing setup, the camera and the display screen cannot be physically aligned, as depicted in Figure 10.12. A participant looks at the image of the remote party displayed on the monitor but not directly into the camera while the remote party looks at her through the camera. Therefore, she does not appear to make eye contact with the remote party. Research [203] has shown that if the divergence angle (α) between the camera and the display is greater than 5 degrees, the loss of eye-contact is noticeable. If we mount a small camera on the side of a 21-inch monitor, and the normal viewing position is 20 inches away from the screen, the divergence angle will be 17 degrees, well above the threshold at which the eye-contact can be maintained. Under such a setup, the video loses much of its communication value and becomes ineffective compared to telephone. We will describe a prototype system developed by Yang and Zhang [246] to overcome this eye-gaze divergence problem. One important component of the system is the stereo head-pose-tracking technique described in Section 10.3.

10.5.1 System overview

Figure 10.13 is an illustration of the block diagram of the eye-gaze correction system. There are two digital video cameras mounted vertically. One camera is mounted on top of the screen monitor, while the other camera is mounted on the bottom. The cameras are precalibrated. The advantage of the vertical setup is that it provides wider coverage of the subject and the higher disambiguation capability in feature matching since matching ambiguity usually involves symmetric facial features such as eyes and lip contours that are aligned horizontally. The user's personalized face model is acquired by using the face modeling system described in Section 5.1. Use of the face model helps overcome the difficulty of matching a pair of wide baseline stereo images and produce an accurate head pose estimation. The outcome of the system is a synthesized video of the user as if it were taken behind the display, thus maintaining the correct gaze awareness among teleconferencing participants.

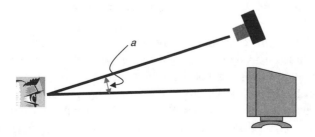

Figure 10.12. Camera-screen displacement causes the lose of eye-contact.

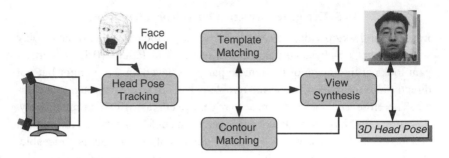

Figure 10.13. Overview of the eye-gaze correction system.

For each frame, the eye-correction algorithm consists of four steps: (1) head pose estimation, (2) correlation-based stereo feature matching, (3) stereo silhouette matching, and (4) hardware-assisted view synthesis.

The head pose is estimated by using the stereo head-pose-tracking technique described in Section 10.3. The result from the head pose tracking provides a set of good matches between the stereo pair in the rigid region of the face. To generate convincing and photorealistic virtual views, it is necessary to obtain more matching points over the entire foreground images, especially in the nonrigid face region, and along the contours.

The second step of the algorithm aims at finding more feature matches on the face especially in the non-rigid face region. During this matching process, the reliable information obtained from tracking is used to constrain the search range. In areas where such information is not available, such as on the hands and shoulders, the search threshold is relaxed and the disparity gradient limit is used to remove the false matches. To facilitate the matching and the view synthesis, the images are first rectified so that the epipolar lines are horizontal.

The feature-matching method at the second step usually does not work well for face contours especially along the silhouettes. Yet face contours are very important visual cues for view synthesis. The lack of matching information along the contours will result in excessive smearing or blurring in the synthesized views. The third step of the algorithm extracts and matches the contours across the two views.

For each view, the contour of the foreground object is extracted after background subtraction. A dynamic programming-based algorithm is then used to find the global optimal matching between the contours on the two views. The core of the algorithm is the design of the cost function. The cost functions consist of two parts: matching cost and transition cost. The matching cost measures the spatial consistency between the two views and accounts for epipolar constraint, the orientation difference, and the disparity gradient limit. The transition cost measures the consistency over time. In contour matching, when two segments are continuous in one image, we would expect that their matched segments in the other image are continuous too. But this is not always the case due to changes in visibility: Some part of the contour may only be seen in one image. The transition cost is designed to favor smooth matching from one segment to the next, while taking into account the discontinuities caused by occlusions.

The fourth step is the view synthesis. One possibility is to use view morphing [191]. This technique allows to synthesize virtual views along the path connecting the optical centers of the two cameras. A view-morphing factor λ controls the exact view position. It is usually between 0 and 1, whereas a value of 0 corresponds exactly to the first camera view, and a value of 1 corresponds exactly to the second camera view. Any value in between represents a virtual viewpoint somewhere along the path from the first camera to the second. By changing the view-morphing factor λ, one can synthesize correct views with desired eye gaze.

In their system, Yang and Zhang [246] used a hardware-assisted rendering method. First, a 2D triangular mesh is created through Delauney triangulation in the top camera's image space. Each vertex's coordinates are offset by the disparity modulated by the view morphing factor λ. The offset mesh is fed to the hardware renderer with two sets of texture coordinates, one for each camera image. Note that all the images and the mesh are in the rectified coordinate space. For each vertex, a texture-blending weight for each view is computed based on the areas of its adjacent triangles on the two views.

Note that the view synthesis only works for the foreground object. For the background, it is very difficult to obtain a reliable set of matches because the baseline between the two views is very large. There are two possible solutions for the background. The first is to treat the background as unstructured and add image boundary as matches. The result will be ideal if the background has a uniform color; otherwise, it will be fuzzy as shown in the synthesized view of Figure 10.14 where the image in the middle is synthesized. The second solution is to replace the background by anything appropriate. In that case, view synthesis is only performed for the foreground objects. This is how the results in the next section were produced. The synthesized foreground objects are overlayed on the image of the first camera.

10.5.2 Experiment results

Figure 10.15 shows the intermediate results at various stages of eye-gaze correction algorithm. It starts with a pair of stereo images in Figure 10.15a. Figure

Figure 10.14. Eye-gaze correction. The first and the third image were taken from the stereo cameras mounted on the top and bottom sides of a monitor while the person was looking at the screen. The picture in the middle is a synthesized virtual view that preserves eyecontact.

 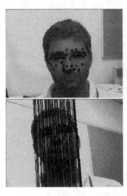 

(a) The input image pair

(b) Tracked feature points with epipolar line superimposed

(c) Extracted fore-ground contours

 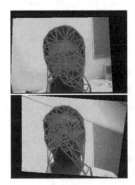 

(d) Rectified images for stereo matching

(e) Delaunay tri-angulation over matched points

(f) Final synthesized view (uncropped)

Figure 10.15. Intermediate results of the eye-gaze correction algorithm.

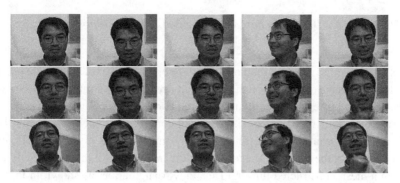

Figure 10.16. Sample frames from an eye-gaze correction video sequence. The top and bottom rows show the images from the top and bottom cameras. The middle row displays the synthesized images from a virtual camera located in the middle of the two real cameras. The frame numbers from left to right are 1, 51, 220, 272, and 1,010.

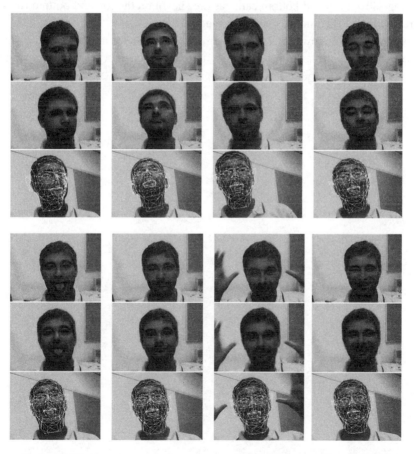

Figure 10.17. Eye-gaze correction sequence of another person. The upper and lower rows are the original stereo images, while the middle rows are the synthesized ones. The triangular face model is overlayed on the bottom images. From left to right and from top to bottom, the frame numbers are 159, 200, 400, 577, 617, 720, 743, and 830.

10.15b shows the matched feature points. The epipolar lines of the feature points in the first image are drawn on the second image (bottom). Figure 10.15c shows the extracted foreground contours. The red contour (typically a few pixels far away from the "true" contour) is the initial contour after background subtraction. The blue contour is the refined contour using the "snake" technique. Figure 10.15d shows the rectified images for feature matching. All the matched points form a mesh constructed through Delaunay triangulation, as shown in Figure 10.15e. The last image (Figure 10.15f) shows the synthesized view. The eye-gaze in the synthesized view appears to be looking forward, achieving the effect of eye-gaze correction.

Figure 10.16 shows some frames selected from a video sequence. The images from top and bottom cameras are shown on the top and bottom rows, respectively. The middle shows the synthesized view.

Figure 10.17 shows the eye-gaze correction results for another person. This sequence contains large head motions, dramatic facial expression changes, and hand waving.

11

Human computer interaction

Ever since the birth of the computer, people have been fascinated by the problem of how to improve the interaction between human users and computers so that it feels natural to users. People would love the computers to behave more like humans instead of machines as it will make computers easier to use and more receptive to a user's needs. To achieve natural interaction, the computer needs to be intelligent enough to understand the world and to behave like a human. One type of systems that many researchers have developed to showcase natural interaction is conversational agents. A conversational agent has a visual representation, which is typically a photorealistic-looking avatar. It is capable of understanding the user's needs through audio and visual sensors, and furthermore, it provides audio and visual feedback to the user. We will describe a conversational agent in Section 11.1.

This chapter will describe another related but very different technology, called human interactive proof (HIP). In some sense, the goal of the HIP system is exactly the opposite of that of the conversational agent. It assumes that there is a gap between the intelligence of the computer and the intelligence of human users. A HIP system exploits this gap to tell a computer program from a human user so that Web services that are designed for human users are not abused by malicious computer programs. One interesting technology that is related to faces is the face-based HIP system, which will be described in Section 11.2.

11.1 Conversational agent

The basic requirement of a conversational agent is that it is capable of understanding a user's speech and talking back to the user. Figure 11.1 is the system architecture of a basic conversational agent. The user's voice is captured by a microphone. The captured audio is passed to an automatic speech recognition

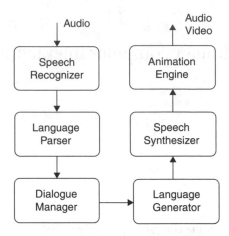

Figure 11.1. The system architecture of a basic conversational agent.

engine. A language parser analyzes the text output of the speech recognition engine and generates semantic description. Based on the semantic description of the user's speech, the dialogue manager selects appropriate actions. A language generator executes the verbal action and generates the text for the avatar to speak. A speech synthesizer such as a text-to-speech engine generates audio signals, and at the same time notifies the animation engine for each phoneme it generates. The animation engine generates the appropriate mouth shapes, facial expressions, and head movements.

11.1.1 Video-rewrite-based conversational agent

Figure 11.2 is a snapshot of the virtual tour guide system developed at Microsoft Research Asia [252, 253]. The name of the tour guide is "Maggie," and she resides at the lower right corner of the screen. A user talks to Maggie through a microphone. Maggie answers questions often asked by tourists in Beijing. Maggie speaks English, and the user is required to speak English as well. Besides speaking, she also presents multimedia materials such as images and videos to the user. The multimedia materials are shown in the content window located at the upper left corner of the screen.

The same architecture was used to develop another conversational agent named "Cherry." Cherry speaks Chinese. She acts as an information guide to the visitors of Microsoft Research Asia.

The animation was generated by using the video rewrite technique, which was proposed by Bregler et al. [26]. Unlike the talking head system described

Figure 11.2. A snapshot of the virtual tour guide system developed at Microsoft Asia.

in Section 8.1, which uses a 3D face model, video rewrite technique does not use 3D mesh representation. It uses a data-driven approach.

The basic idea of the video rewrite technique is to prerecord a sufficient number of video sequences with an actor speaking many different sentences to cover a variety of mouth shapes and articulations. Given a sequence of phonemes, the animation is generated by searching the prerecorded database to find, for each phoneme, the video frames that match the phoneme. In the following, we describe in more detail the animation module that is used in both the virtual tour guide and the information guide system.

Figure 11.3 is a diagram of their animation module. The bottom is offline data capturing and analysis phase. The top is the online synthesis phase. For each of the two characters (Maggie and Cherry), a 15 to 20-minute database of video sequences was captured by filming an actress reading a number of predesigned articles.

The audio data together with the text are used as input by a speech recognition engine to generate the phoneme labels for the audio signals. In order to make sure the synthesized lip motion is smooth, we need to take into account the coarticulation between adjacent phonemes: the mouth shape for the same phoneme

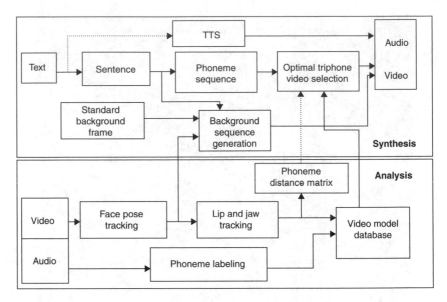

Figure 11.3. Face animation system for the virtual tour guide and visitor guide system developed at Microsoft Research Asia. It is based on the video rewrite technique. The bottom is the offline data capture and analysis phase. The top is the online synthesis phase.

may vary depending on the phonemes before or after it. For example, the mouth shape for phoneme *G* in the word *big* is different from the mouth shape for the same phoneme in the word *dog*. For this reason, the audio and video are segmented into triphones where each triphone is a sequence of three phonemes. During synthesis when we match a viseme to a triphone, we emphasize the middle phoneme and cross-fade the overlapping portions (in time domain) of the adjacent triphones.

Video analysis includes head pose tracking and lip and jaw tracking. Similar to [26], 2D affine transformation was used as the head motion model. For head motions with relatively large out-of-plane rotations, a 3D motion model is preferable, and the 3D head pose tracking can be done in a similar way as what was described in Section 5.1.2.6. After the head pose tracking, the images are warped to transform all the images into a canonical head pose. Lip and jaw tracking are performed on the warped images. The tracked feature points along the lip and jaw area used in the synthesis phase to warp the overlapping videos so that they have the same lip shape and to superimpose the lip portion on the correct location of the background face.

The synthesis phase consists of four steps. The first step converts the input text to a phoneme sequence and a wave file using a text-to-speech engine. The second step generates an appropriate background sequence from a database of prerecorded background video footage. The third step searches for an optimal triphone video sequence that best fits the input phoneme sequence. The final step time-aligns the triphone video sequence with the wave file, and rewrites the mouth region of the time-aligned video sequence to the background video sequence.

The background video provides the environment setting of the talking head. The background behind the subject during the video recording is used as it is in the synthesized video. In addition, the head motion, eyebrow movement, and eye blinks are all copied from the actual video recording. In this way, the synthesized video gives the appealing of photorealism. The mouth region of the background video is overwritten by the time-aligned triphone video sequence.

In the offline, the video data are segmented into short clips such that all the beginning and ending frames of all the short clips are similar. This is done by finding a frame, called standard frame, which has the largest number of similar frames in the video data. The similarity between two frames is measured by how close their head poses are. In the synthesis phase, for any given sentence, a video clip whose length best matches the length of the sentence is selected as the corresponding background video sequence.

Step 3 is to search for a triphone video sequence from the database that best matches an input phoneme sequence. Let n denote the length of the input phoneme sequence. For any triphone video sequence of length n synthesized from the database, its distance from the input phoneme sequence is a weighted sum of two terms: (1) the phoneme-context distance, and (2) the smoothness measurement. We can think of each phoneme in the input phoneme sequence as a triphone that consists of the phoneme itself plus the one before and the one after. The phoneme-context distance is the sum of the distance between each triphone in the input phoneme sequence and its corresponding triphone in the synthesized triphone sequence. Bregler et al. [26] computed the distance between two triphones based on phoneme confusion matrices [160]. Zhang et al. used a different approach [252, 253]. They first define a canonical viseme for each phoneme by computing the mean of all the lip shapes with the same phoneme label in the video database. Therefore, a triphone in the input sequence corresponds to three canonical visemes. Note that each triphone in the video database also corresponds to three visemes. Therefore, the distance between a triphone in the input sequence and a triphone in the synthesized sequence can be defined as a weighted sum of the three viseme distances where the middle viseme has larger weight than the other two. The distance between two visemes is simply the Euclidean distance between the corresponding vertices on the contour. The second term of smoothness measurement is the distance between the lip shapes in the overlapping triphones.

The triphone sequence synthesis problem becomes a combinatorial optimization problem where the objective is to minimize the distance between the synthesized triphone sequence and the input phoneme sequence. This can be solved by using dynamic programming.

Finally at Step 4, the selected optimal triphone video sequence is time-aligned with the synthesized audio, and the mouth region is rewritten back to the background video. In case two triphone frames are written back to the same background frame, the two frames need to be blended to ensure a smooth transition. On the other hand, if a background frame has no corresponding triphone frames, we need to interpolate the two triphone frames on its left and right to fill in this frame.

Figure 11.4 shows 16 frames selected from a synthesized video sequence. Three frames are shown for each second.

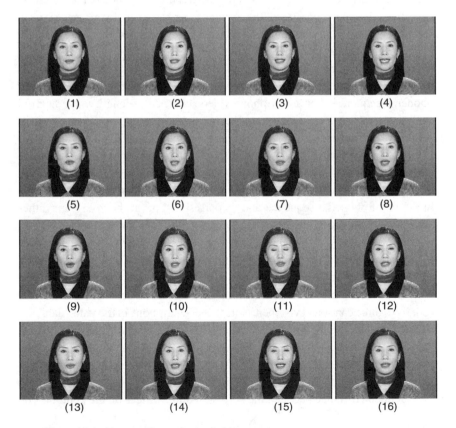

Figure 11.4. Frames of a synthesized video sequence.

Video rewrite technique has the advantage that the synthesized results look photorealistic, but it has a number of limitations. The first limitation is that a new database needs to be recollected for each new character. Capturing and analyzing a new database is expensive and time consuming. Second, due to the difficulty of pose tracking, the actor is usually asked not to have large head motions. As a result, the synthesized video exhibits little head movement. In addition, it is difficult to synthesize a video with desired head gestures. Third, generating facial expressions requires the actor to repeat each sentence multiple times with different expressions. In addition, the eyebrow, eyes, and nose regions need to be synthesized as well. It would require a large amount of training data, and both the analysis and synthesis are much more challenging. In the next section, we describe a 3D-model-based conversational agent system that is more flexible in terms of generating desired head gestures and facial expressions but does not have the same kind of photorealism as the video rewrite system has.

11.1.2 3D-model-based conversational agent

Most of the conversational agent systems that have been developed use a synthetic model to represent the character. Some systems use a 2D cartoon model, while others use a 3D face model. The animation system is much easier to develop than a video rewrite system because there is no need for data capturing and analysis, and the animation is more flexible. In this section, we describe a 3D-model-based conversational agent, called virtual receptionist, which was developed by Bohus et al. at Microsoft Research. Compared to other conversational agent systems, the virtual receptionist system has two interesting properties. First, its character (i.e., the receptionist) is personalized. Second, the system performs audio/visual scene analysis, and the action of the avatar is determined based on the scene understanding.

Figure 11.5 shows a snapshot of the system. The avatar was constructed from two images of an actual receptionist by using the technique described in Section 5.3. People can talk to the virtual receptionist to make shuttle reservations. Shuttle reservation is one of the major work items of the actual receptionists in Microsoft office buildings. The goal of developing a virtual receptionist system is not to replace human receptionists but to use this simple task as a test bed to study human–machine interactions.

There are a camera and a linear microphone array on top of the screen. The microphone array has two functionalities. First, it performs beamforming to enhance the quality of the audio signal, thus improving the speech recognition accuracy. Second, it is used to determine the direction of the sound source. This

Figure 11.5. A snapshot of the virtual receptionist system. A camera and linear microphone array are installed on the top of the monitor.

information is combined with the face detection results to determine who is talking.

The system has a face detection component that detects the number of faces in the current frame [254]. The detected face rectangle is used as a coarse estimation of how close the person is to the screen. Whenever a face is detected, the system performs head pose tracking. Based on the head pose and the position trajectory of each face, the system determines whether it should engage in a conversation with the user. The system is capable of engaging in a conversation with more than one person. It uses face detection and face-tracking information to determine whether one person is in the same group as another person (if so, they will book the same shuffle).

Figures 11.6 through 11.11 are snapshots of a live video recording of the virtual receptionist interacting with three users. For each frame, the virtual receptionist image is shown on the left. The image on the right is what the virtual receptionist sees, that is, the image captured by the camera. The image on the bottom left is a global view shot of the interaction scene.

Initially as shown in Figure 11.6, two people approach the virtual receptionist. The system detects two faces, and the avatar first talks to the person on the left as shown in Figure 11.7 where the red dot on the left person's face shows the attention of the avatar. She then talks to the person on the right confirming that the two people are together. This is shown in Figure 11.8. In Figure 11.9, a third person walks into the view of the system. The system detects the new face,

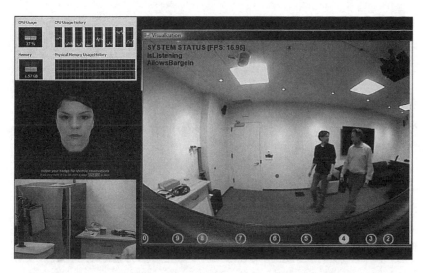

Figure 11.6. Two people approach the virtual receptionist to reserve a shuttle.

Figure 11.7. The system detects two faces which are marked with yellow rectangles. The avatar talks to the person on the left. The red dot on the left person's face is the attention of the avatar. (See plate section for color version.)

and the avatar looks at the person and tells him that she will be with him in a second. The avatar then turns her attention back to the first two people to finish their shuttle reservation. This is shown in Figure 11.10. Finally the first two people walk away, and the avatar engages in conversation with the third person as shown in Figure 11.11.

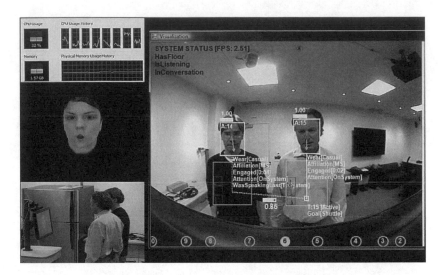

Figure 11.8. The avatar talks to the person on the right. Her attention is now on the right person's face.

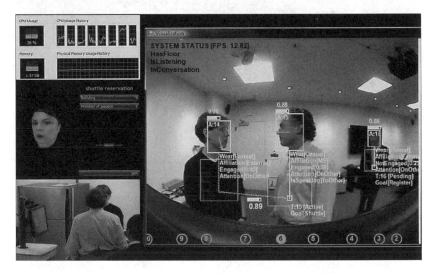

Figure 11.9. A third person walks into the view of the virtual receptionist. The system detects his face. The avatar turns to the person and tells him that she will be with him in a second.

Even though it is a simple task, there are significant challenges to develop a virtual receptionist that behaves as naturally as a real person. First of all, the system needs to understand the scene. For example, it needs to know how many people there are, whether two people are together, who is talking, whether a

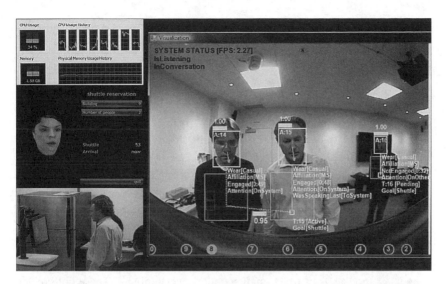

Figure 11.10. The avatar turns her attention back to the first two people to finish their shuttle reservation.

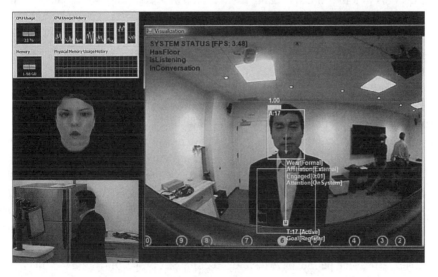

Figure 11.11. The first two people walk away. The avatar engages in conversation with the third person.

person is talking to the virtual receptionist, and so on. Second, the system needs to decide what the avatar needs to do based on the analysis of the scene. For example, if two people approach the avatar and they appear to be together, the avatar may ask, "Are you two together?" Otherwise, the avatar may tell them that she will help one person first and have the second person wait. Third, the system needs to animate the avatar so that her movement look realistic.

11.2 Face-based human interactive proof system

Web services have become part of people's daily life. Many people use free Web e-mail accounts to send and receive e-mails. Many organizations use online polls to gather people's opinions. People use social network services to share photos and stay in touch with friends. Online shopping and information search have become our daily activities. But all these Web services, which are designed for human use, are being abused by computer programs (bots).

Free e-mail services: There are many free Web e-mail services such as Hotmail, Yahoo, Gmail, and others. Malicious programmers have designed bots to register thousands of free e-mail accounts every minute. These bot-created e-mail accounts not only waste large amounts of disk space of the service providers, but they are also being used to send thousands of junk e-mails [1, 5].

Online polls and recommendation systems: Online polling is a convenient and cost-effective way to obtain people's opinions. But if the polls are abused by bots, their credibility is ruined. In 1998, http://www.slashdot.com released an online poll asking for the best computer science program in the United States [1]. This poll turned into a bots-voting competition between MIT and CMU. Clearly, in this case the online poll has lost its intended objectives. A similar situation arises in online recommendation systems. For example, at Expedia.com, people write reviews for the hotels in which they stayed. At Amazon.com, people write reviews for the books they purchased and recommend that others buy or not buy a particular book. If malicious bots start to write hotel and book reviews, such online recommendation systems will become useless.

Chat rooms: Online chat rooms are designed for human users to socialize with others. But some people have developed computer programs (bots) to join chat rooms and point people to advertisement sites.

Meta services and shopping agents: Meta service is unwelcome among e-commerce sites and search engines [101]. In the case of e-commerce, a malicious programmer can design a bot whose task is to aggregate prices from other e-commerce sites. Based on the collected prices, the malicious programmer can make his/her price slightly cheaper, thus stealing away other sites' customers.

Meta services are good for consumers, but e-commerce owners do not like them because they consume a site's resources without bringing in any revenue. Similar situations arise with search engine sites.

These real-world issues have generated a research area called human interactive proofs whose goal is to defend services from malicious attacks by differentiating bots from human users. The design of HIP systems turns out to have a significant relationship with the famous Turing test.

In 1950, Turing proposed a test whose goal was to determine if a machine had achieved artificial intelligence (AI) [215]. The test involves a human judge who poses questions to a human and to a machine and decides which of them is human based on their answers. So far, no machine has passed the Turing test in a generic sense, even after decades of active research in AI. This fact implies that there still exists a considerable intelligence gap between humans and machines.We can therefore use this gap to design tests to distinguish bots from human users. HIP is a unique research area in that it creates a win–win situation. If attackers cannot defeat a HIP algorithm, that algorithm can be used to defend Web services. On the other hand, if attackers defeat a HIP algorithm, then they have solved a hard AI problem, thus advancing AI research.

The first idea related to HIP can be traced back to Naor who wrote an unpublished note in 1996 [158]. The first HIP system in action was developed in 1997 by researchers at Alta Vista. Its goal was to prevent bots from adding URLs to the search engine to skew the search results. Since then, many HIP algorithms and systems have been developed, most of which are based on characters [1, 5]. Variations of these character-based HIPs have been deployed in many commercial Web services (e.g., Yahoo mail, MSN Passport, Gmail). They mainly explore the gap between human and bots in terms of reading poorly printed or manipulated characters. Figure 11.12 shows a character HIP used in MSN Passport, which consists of distorted characters and random arcs. A user needs to recognize the characters and correctly types in the space below the HIP to prove he/she is a human.

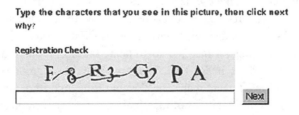

Figure 11.12. An example of character HIP,which was used in MSN Passport around 2005.

Character HIPs are the mostly widely used HIPs in today's commercial sites because of their ease of use, ease of implementation, and universality. The universality property requires a HIP to be usable by people from different countries. An English-digit-based audio HIP, for example, does not satisfy the universality property as people who do not understand English cannot use the HIP. Universality is especially important in practice as it eliminates the localization effort for sites such as Yahoo or MSN. (See [184] for other good HIP properties.)

As the state-of-the-art on optical character recognition technology advances, it is becoming increasingly difficult to design a character-based HIP that is difficult for computers yet easy for humans. For example, the Gimpy HIP that was used earlier at Yahoo site was broken by Mori and Malik [152], and an earlier version of MSN Passport HIP was also broken [30]. In fact, over the past few years, the HIPs used at many commercial Web sites have become increasingly difficult for human users.

Rui and Liu [184] developed a face-base HIP, called ARTiFACIAL (Automated Reverse Turing test using FACIAL features), which is completely different from character HIPs yet also satisfies the universality property. This new HIP is based on human face and facial feature detection. In fact, it is even more universal than character HIPs, as people all know human faces, regardless of where they come from. On the other hand, the accurate detection of facial features (e.g., eyes, mouth, nose) has been very difficult for computers, even after decades of research. Nonfrontal faces, asymmetrical faces, poor lighting conditions, and cluttered background make the task especially difficult for machines, while human users have no problem in those situations. The basic idea of ARTiFACIAL system is to take advantage of the limitations of face feature detection techniques to generate test images so that they are difficult for computer programs but easy for human users.

The face HIP works as follows. Per each user request, it automatically synthesizes an image with a distorted face embedded in a clustered back-ground. The user is asked to first find the face and then click on four points (two eyes and two mouth corners) on the face. If the user can correctly identify these points, the face HIP concludes the user is a human; otherwise, the user is a machine.

We next use a concrete example to illustrate how to automatically generate an ARTiFACIAL test image. For clarity, we use F to indicate a foreground object in an image (e.g., a face), B to indicate the background in an image, I to indicate the whole image (i.e., foreground and background), and T to indicate a cylindrical texture map. The design of the algorithm aims at taking advantage of the four limitations of face feature detection techniques: (1) head pose variations, (2) violation of face symmetry, (3) lighting variations, and (4) cluttered background.

Figure 11.13. A cylindrical texture map of a person's face, which is used as an input to the ARTiFACIAL test image generation algorithm. It is denoted as T_m.

ARTiFACIAL test image generation algorithm

Input: The only inputs to the algorithm are the 3D wireframe model of a generic face mesh (Figure 2.1) and a 512×512 cylindrical texture map T_m of an arbitrary person (Figure 11.13). Note that any person's texture map will work in this system, and from that single texture map one can in theory generate an infinite number of test images.

Output: A 512×512 ARTiFACIAL test image (Figure 11.20) with ground truth (i.e., face location and facial feature locations).

Step 1. Confusion texture map T_c generation: This process takes advantage of the cluttered background limitation to design the HIP test. The 512×512 confusion texture map T_c (Figure 11.14) is obtained by moving the facial features (e.g., eyes, nose, mouth) in Figure 11.13 to different places such that the "face" no longer looks like a face.

Step 2. Global head transformation: Because we have the 3D wireframe model (Figure 2.1), we can easily generate any global head transformations we want. Specifically, the transformations include translation, scaling, and rotation of the head. Translation controls where we want to position the head in the final image, scaling controls the size of the head, and rotation can be around all three axes. At run time, we randomly select the global head transformation parameters and apply them to the 3D wireframe model texture-mapped with the input texture T_m. This process takes advantage of the head pose limitation to design the HIP test.

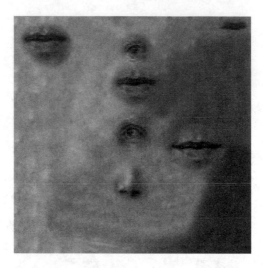

Figure 11.14. The confusion texture map T_c is generated by randomly moving the facial features (e.g., eyes, nose, mouth) in Figure 11.13 to different places such that the image no longer looks like a face.

Step 3. Local facial feature deformations: The local facial feature deformations are used to modify the facial feature positions so that they are slightly deviated from their original positions and shapes. This deformation process takes advantage of the face symmetry limitation to design the HIP test. Each geometric deformation is represented as a vector of vertex differences. Rui and Liu [184] designed a set of geometric deformations including the vertical and horizontal translations of the left eye, right eye, left eyebrow, right eyebrow, left mouth corner, and right mouth corner. Each geometric deformation is associated with a random coefficient uniformly distributed in $[-1, 1]$, which controls the amount of deformation to be applied. At run time, the geometric deformation coefficients can be randomly selected and applied to the 3D wireframe model. An example of a head after Steps 2 and 3 is shown in Figure 11.15. Note that the head has been rotated and facial features deformed.

Step 4. Confusion texture map transformation and deformation: In this step, we repeat Steps 2 and 3 to the confusion texture map T_c, instead of to T_m. This step generates the transformed and deformed confusion head F_c, as shown in Figure 11.16.

Step 5. Stage 1 image I_1 generation: Use the confusion texture map T_c as the background B and use F_h as the foreground to generate the 512×512 Stage 1 image I_1 (Figure 11.17).

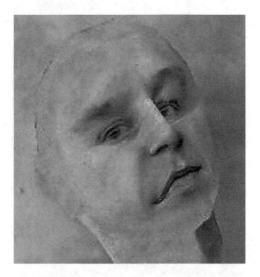

Figure 11.15. The head after global transformation and facial feature deformation. We denote this head by F_h.

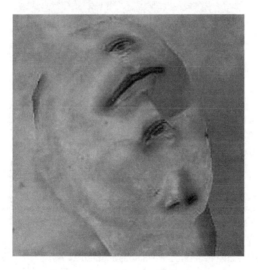

Figure 11.16. The confusion head after global transformation and facial feature deformation. We denote this head by F_c.

Step 6. Stage 2 image I_2 generation: Make L copies of randomly shrunk T_c and randomly put them into image I_1 to generate the 512×512 Stage 2 image I_2 (Figure 11.18). This process takes advantage of the cluttered background limitation to design the HIP test. Note that none of the copies should occlude the key face regions including eyes, nose, and mouth.

Figure 11.17. Image generated at Stage 1, denoted as I_1.

Figure 11.18. Image generated at Stage 2, denoted as I_2.

Step 7. Stage 3 image I_3 generation: There are three steps in this stage. First, make M copies of the confusion head F_c and randomly put them into image I_2. This step takes advantage of the cluttered background limitation. Note that none of the copies should occlude the key face regions including eyes, nose, and mouth. Second, we now have $M + 1$ regions in the image, where M of them come from F_c and one from F_h. Let Avg(m),

Figure 11.19. Image generated at Stage 3, denoted as I_3.

$m = 0, \ldots, M + 1$ be the average intensity of region m. We next remap the intensities of each region m such that $\{\mathrm{Avg}(m)\}_{m=0}^{M+1}$ are uniformly distributed in $[0, 255]$ across the $M + 1$ regions (i.e., some of the regions become darker and others become brighter). This step takes advantage of the lighting limitation. Third, for each of the $M + 1$ regions, randomly select a point within that region that divides the region into four quadrants. Randomly select two opposite quadrants to undergo further intensity changes. If the average intensity of the region is greater than 128, the intensity of all the pixels in the selected quadrants will decrease by a randomly selected amount; otherwise, it will increase by a randomly selected amount. This step takes advantage of both the face symmetry and the lighting limitations. An example I_3 image is shown in Figure 11.19. Note in the image that (i) the average intensities of the $M + 1$ regions are uniformly distributed (i.e., some regions are darker while others are brighter), and (ii) two of the quadrants undergo further intensity changes.

Step 8. Final ARTiFACIAL test image I_F generation: Make N copies of the facial feature regions in F_h (e.g., eyes, nose, mouth) and randomly put them into I_3 to generate the final 512×512 ARTiFACIAL test image I_F (Figure 11.20). This process takes advantage of the cluttered background limitation to design the HIP test. Note that none of the copies should occlude the key face regions including eyes, nose, and mouth.

These eight steps take the four face feature detection limitations into account and generate ARTiFACIAL test images that are very difficult for face detectors

Figure 11.20. Final image I_F. (See plate section for color version.)

to process. Rui and Liu [184] used the previously described procedure and generated 1,000 images for both user study and bot attacks.

There were 34 participants in the user study. The participants include accountants, administrative staff, architects, executives, receptionists, researchers, software developers, support engineers, and patent attorneys. For each participant, 10 different images generated by the ARTiFACIAL system are presented to him/her, and the participant was asked to click on six face feature points (two eye corners for each eye and two mouth corners) for each image. In average, it takes 14 seconds for a user to identify six feature points for each image. Of all the 340 tests, there was only one wrong detection. For more details on the user study setup and results, the readers are referred to [184]. In summary, the study shows that the HIP test is easy for human users to take.

To succeed in an attack, the attacker (bot) must first locate the face from a test-images-cluttered background by using a face detector and then find the facial features (e.g., eyes, nose, mouth) by using a facial feature detector (also called face alignment). Rui and Liu [184] used three different face detectors and one face feature alignment program to evaluate the difficulty for bot attacks.

The first face detector was developed by Colmenarez and Huang [36]. It used the information-based maximum discrimination (MD) to detect faces. The second face detector was developed by Yang et al. [245]. It used a sparse network (SNoW) of linear functions and was tailored for learning in the presence of a very large number of features. It used a wide range of face images in different poses, with different expressions and under different lighting conditions. The third face detector was developed by Li and colleagues [79, 269] following the Viola–Jones approach [222].

The face feature detection program was developed by Yan et al. [243], which is an improved version of the conventional Active Shape Model. It assumes that a face detector has already found the general location of the face region. It then searches for the facial features in that region.

To evaluate face detector attacks, 1,000 images generated by the ARTiFACIAL images were used as inputs to each of the three face detectors. A detection is considered as correct if the detected face rectangle has 60% or more overlap with the ground truth face rectangle. Among the 1,000 test images, MD face detector has only one correct detection, SNoW face detector has three correct detections, and AdaBoost face detector has zero correct detection.

To evaluate a face feature detector, for each test image, its ground truth face rectangle is used as input to the face feature detector program. The feature detection is considered as correct if the detected points are within twice the average mismatches that human users made. The correct feature detection rate was only 0.2%.

The preceding experiments show that there is still a significant intelligence gap between computer programs and human users in face detection and face feature detection. Therefore face-based HIP seems to be an attractive alternative to the text-based HIP.

Bibliography

[1] L. Ahn, M. Blum, and N. J. Hopper. Telling humans and computers apart automatically. *Communication of ACM*, 47(2):56–60, 1985.

[2] T. Akimoto, Y. Suenaga, and R. S. Wallace. Automatic 3d facial models. *IEEE Computer Graphics and Applications*, 13(5):16–22, 1993.

[3] B. Amberg, A. Blake, A. Fitzgibbon, S. Romdhani, and T. Vetter. Reconstructing high quality face-surfaces using model based stereo. In *International Conference on Computer Vision*, Rio de Janeiro, Brazil, October 2007.

[4] A. Azarbayejani, B. Horowitz, and A. Pentland. Recursive estimation of structure and motion using the relative orientation constraint. In *Proceedings of the Computer Vision and Pattern Recognition Conference*, pages 70–75, New York, NY, USA, 1993.

[5] H. S. Baird and K. Popat. Human interactive proofs and document image analysis. In *Proceedings of Document Analysis Systems*, pages 507–518, Princeton, New Jersey, August 2002.

[6] J. Barron, D. Fleet, and S. Beauchemin. Performance of optical flow techniques. *The International Journal of Computer Vision*, 12(1):43–77, 1994.

[7] R. H. Bartels, J. C. Beatty, and B. A. Barssky. *An Introduction to Splines for Use in Computer Graphics & Geometric Modeling*. Morgan Kaufmann Publishers, 1987.

[8] R. Basri and D. Jacobs. Lambertian reflectance and linear subspaces. In *IEEE International Conference on Computer Vision*, Vancouver, BC, Canada, pages 383–390, 2001.

[9] R. Basri and D. Jacobs. Lambertian reflectance and linear subspaces. *Pattern Analysis and Machine Intelligence*, 25(2):218–233, 2003.

[10] S. Basu, I. Essa, and A. Pentland. Motion Regularization for Model-based Head Tracking. In *Proceedings of International Conference on Pattern Recognition*, pages 611–616, Vienna, Austria, 1996.

[11] T. Beier and S. Neely. Feature-based image metamorphosis. In *SIGGRAPH*, pages 35–42, 1992.

[12] P. Belhumeur, J. Hespanha, and D. Kriegman. Eigenfaces vs. fisherfaces: Recognition using class specific linear projection. *IEEE Transactions on Pattern Analysis and Machine Intelligence*, 19(7):711–720, 1997.

[13] P. Bergeron and P. Lachapelle. Controlling facial expressions and body movements. *Advanced Comptuer Animation, SIGGRAPH'85 Tutorials*, 2:61–79, 1985.

[14] F. Bertails, B. Audoly, M.-P. Cani, B. Querleux, F. Leroy, and J.-L. Leveque. Super-helices for predicting the dynamics of natural hair. *ACM Transaction on Graphics*, 25(3):1180–1187, 2006.

[15] P. J. Besl and N. D. McKay. A method for registration of 3d shapes. *IEEE Transactions on Pattern Analysis and Machine Intelligence*, 14(2):239–256, 1992.

[16] S. A. Bhukhanwala and T. V. Ramabadram. Automated global enhancement of digitized photographs. *IEEE Transactions on Consumer Electronics*, 40(1):1–10, 1994.

[17] I. Biederman and P. Kalocsai. Neural and phychophysical analysis of object and face recognition. In H. Wechsler, P. J. Phillips, V. Bruce, F. Soulie, and T. S. Huang, editors, *Face Recognition: From Theorey to Applications*, pages 3–25, Springer, 1998.

[18] M. J. Black and Y. Yacoob. Tracking and Recognizing Rigid and Non-Rigid Facial Motions Using Local Parametric Model of Image Motion. In *Proceedings of International Conference on Computer Vision*, pages 374–381, Cambridge, MA, 1995.

[19] V. Blanz and T. Vetter. A morphable model for the synthesis of 3d faces. In *Computer Graphics, Annual Conference Series*, pages 187–194. SIGGRAPH, August 1999.

[20] M. Bledsoe. The model method in facial recognition. In *Technical Report PRI 15, Panoramic Research, Inc.*, Palo Alto, CA, 1964.

[21] J. F. Blinn. Models of light reflection for computer synthesized pictures. In *SIGGRAPH*, pages 192–198, 1977.

[22] J. F. Blinn and M. E. Newell. Texture and reflection in computer generated images. *Communications of the ACM*, 19(10):542–546, 1976.

[23] K. L. Boyer and A. Kak. Color-encoded structured light for rapid active ranging. *IEEE Transactions on Pattern Analysis and Machine Intelligence*, 9(1):14–28, 1987.

[24] D. Brainard and B. A. Wandell. A bilinear model of the illuminant's effect on color appearance. In M. Landy and J. A. Movshon, editors, *Computational Models of Visual Processing*, pages 171–186. Massachusetts Institute of Technology, 1991.

[25] M. Brand. Voice puppetry. In *SIGGRAPH*, pages 21–28, 1999.

[26] C. Bregler, M. Covell, and M. Slaney. Video rewrite: Driving visual speech with audio. In *SIGGRAPH*, pages 353–360, 1997.

[27] Q. Cai, Q. Zhang, A. Sankaranarayanan, Z. Zhang, and Z. Liu. Real time head pose tracking from multiple cameras with a generic model. In *IEEE Workshop on Analysis and Modeling of Faces and Gestures, in conjunction with CVPR2010*, San Francisco, June 2010.

[28] D. Caspi, N. Kiryati, and J. Shamir. Range imaging with adaptive color structured light. *IEEE Transaction on Pattern Analysis and Machine Intelligence*, 20(5):470–480, 1998.

[29] J. T. Chang, J. Jin, and Y. Yu. A practical model for hair mutual interactions. In *Symposium on Computer Animation*, pages 73–80, 2002.

[30] K. Chellapilla and P. Simard. Using machine learning to break visual human interaction proofs (hips). In *Advances in Neutral Information Processing Systems 17, Neural Information Processing Systems (NIPS)*, pages 265–272, 2004.

[31] L. Chen, S. Saeyor, H. Dohi, and M. Ishzuka. A system of 3d hairstyle synthesis based on the wisp model. *The Visual Computer*, 15(4):159–170, 1999.

[32] Q. Chen and G. Medioni. Building 3-d human face models from two photographs. *The Journal of VLSI Signal Processing*, 27(1–2):127–140, 2001.

[33] Y. Chen and G. Medioni. Object modelling by registration of multiple range images. *Image and Vision Computing*, 10(3):145–155, 1992.

[34] C. S. Choi et al. Analysis and synthesis of facial image sequences in model-based image coding. *IEEE Transaction on Circuits and Systems for Video Technology*, 4:257–275, 1994.

[35] C. Cohen-Tannoudji et al. *Quantum Mechanics*. John Wiley & Sons, 1977.

[36] A. Colmenarez and T. S. Huang. Face detection with information-based maximum discrimination. In *IEEE Conference on Computer Vision and Pattern Recognition*, pages 782–788, San Juan, Puerto Rico, 1997.

[37] T. F. Cootes, G. J. Edwards, and C. J. Taylor. Active appearance models. *IEEE Transaction on Pattern Analysis and Machine Intelligence*, 23(6):681–685, 2001.

[38] T. F. Cootes, C. J. Taylor, D. H. Cooper, and J. Graham. Active shape models – Their training and application. *Computer Vision and Image Understanding*, 61(1):18–23, 1995.

[39] A. Daldegan, N. M. Thalmann, T. Kurihara, and D. Thalmann. An integrated system for modeling, animating and rendering hair. *Computer Graphics Forum*, 12(3):211–221, 1993.

[40] B. Dariush, S. B. Kang, and K. Waters. Spatiotemporal analysis of face profiles: Detection, segmentation, and registration. In *Proceedings of the 3rd International Conference on Automatic Face and Gesture Recognition*, pages 248–253, 1998.

[41] T. Darrell, B. Moghaddam, and A. Pentland. Active face tracking and pose estimation in an interactive room. In *IEEE Computer Vision and Pattern Recognition*, pages 67–72, 1996.

[42] C. Darwin. *The Expression of the Emotions in Man and Animals*. John Murray, 1872.

[43] P. E. Debevec, T. Hawkins, C. Tchou, H.-P. Duiker, W. Sarokin, and M. Sagar. Acquiring the reflectance field of a human face. In *SIGGRAPH*, pages 145–156, 2000.

[44] D. DeCarlo and D. Metaxas. Optical flow constraints on deformable models with applications to face tracking. *International Journal of Computer Vision*, 38(2):99–127, 2001.

[45] D. Dementhon and L. Davis. Model-based object pose in 25 lines of code. *International Journal of Computer Vision*, 15(1):123–141, 1995.

[46] F. Devernay and O. D. Faugeras. Computing differential properties of 3-d shapes from stereoscopic images without 3-d models. In *IEEE Conference on Computer Vision and Pattern Recognition*, Seattle, Washington, June 1994.

[47] M. Dimitrijevic, S. Ilic, and P. Fua. Accurate face models from uncalibrated and ill-lit video sequences. In *IEEE Conference on Computer Vision and Pattern Recognition*, volume II, pages 1034–1041, 2004.

[48] A. Dipanda and S. Woo. Efficient correspondence problem-solving in 3-d shape reconstruction using a structured light system. *Optical Engineering*, 44(9):1–14, 2005.

[49] G. B. Duchenne. *The Mechanism of Human Facial Expression*. Jules Renard, 1862.

[50] G. B. Duchenne. *The Mechanism of Human Facial Expression*. Cambridge University Press, 1990.

[51] M. D'Zmura. Color constancy: surface color from changing illumination. *Journal of Optical Society of America*, 9(3):490–493, 1992.

[52] P. Ekman and W. V. Friesen. *Manual for the Facial Action Coding System*. Consulting Psychologists Press, 1978.

[53] T. Ezzat, G. Geiger, and T. Poggio. Trainable videorealistic speech animation. In *SIGGRAPH'02*, pages 388–398, 2002.

[54] G. Farin. *Curves and Surfaces for CAGD: A Practical Guide*, 3rd edition. Academic Press, 1993.

[55] O. Faugeras. *Three-Dimensional Computer Vision: a Geometric Viewpoint*. MIT Press, 1993.

[56] G. Felsen and Y. Dan. A natural approach to studying vision. *Nature Neuroscience*, 8(12):1643–1646, 2005.

[57] R. Fletcher. *Practical Methods of Optimization*, 2nd edition. John Wiley & Sons, 1987.

[58] F. Bertails, T.-Y. Kim, M.-P. Cani, and U. Neumann. Adaptive wisp tree – A multiresolution control structure for simulating dynamic clustering in hair motion. In *Sympisium on Computer Animation*, pages 207–213, 2003.

[59] J. Foley and A. V. Dam. *Fundamentals of Interactive Computer Graphics*. Addison-Wesley, 1984.

[60] J. Foley, A. van Dam, S. Feiner, and J. Hughes. *Computer Graphics: Principles and Practice*. Addison-Wesley, 1992.

[61] D. A. Forsyth and J. Ponce. *Computer Vision*. Prentice Hall, 2003.

[62] N. Fraser. *Stage Lighting Design: A Practical Guide*. Crowood Press, 2000.

[63] W. Freeman, E. Pasztor, and O. Carmichael. Learning low-level vision. *International Journal of Computer Vision*, 40(1):25–47, 2000.

[64] W. T. Freeman and J. B. Tenenbaum. Learning bilinear models for two-factor problems in vision. In *IEEE Conference on Computer Vision and Pattern Recognition*, San Juan, Puerto Rico, June 1997.

[65] Y. Fu and N. Zheng. M-face: An appearance based photorealistic model for multiple facial attributes rendering. *IEEE Transactions on Circuits and Systems for Video Technology*, 16(7):830–842, 2006.

[66] P. Fua. Using model-driven bundle-adjustment to model heads from raw video sequences. In *International Conference on Computer Vision*, pages 46–53, Sept. 1999.

[67] P. Fua and C. Miccio. From regular images to animated heads: A least squares approach. In *European Conference on Computer Vision*, pages 188–202, 1998.

[68] P. Fua and C. Miccio. Animated heads from ordinary images: A least-squares approach. *Computer Vision and Image Understanding*, 75(3):247–259, 1999.

[69] F. Galton. Personal identification and description. *Nature*, 38(973):201–202, 1888.

[70] I. Gauthier and N. Logothetis. Is face recognition not so unique after all? *Journal of Cognitive Neuropsychology*, 17(1/2/3):125–142, 2000.

[71] I. M. Gelfand and S. V. Fomin. *Calculus of Variations*. Dover Publications, 1963.

[72] A. Georghiades, P. Belhumeur, and D. Kriegman. From few to many: Illumination cone models for face recognition under variable lighting and pose. *Pattern Analysis and Machine Intelligence*, 23(6):643–660, 2001.

[73] D. B. Goldman. Fake fur rendering. In *SIGGRAPH*, pages 127–134, 1997.

[74] A. Golovinskiy, W. Matusik, H. Pfister, S. Rusinkiewica, and T. Funkhouser. A statistical model for synthesis of detailed facial geometry. *ACM Transaction on Graphics*, 25(3):1025–1034, 2006.

[75] R. Gonzalez and R. Woods. *Digital Image Processing*. Addison-Wesley Publishing Company, 1992.

[76] S. Grabli, F. Sillion, S. R. Marschner, and J. E. Lengyl. Image-based hair capture by inverse lighting. In *Graphics Interface*, pages 51–58, Calgary, Alberta, May 2002.

[77] F. Gray. Pulse code communication. *U.S. Patent No. 2,632,058*, March 1953.

[78] N. Greene. Environment mapping and other applications of world projections. *IEEE Computer Graphics and Applications*, 6(11):21–29, 1986.

[79] L. Gu, S. Z. Li, and H.-J. Zhang. Learning probabilistic distribution model for multi-view face detection. In *IEEE Conference on Computer Vision and Pattern Recognition*, volume II, pages 116–122, 2001.

[80] B. Guenter, C. Grimm, D. Wood, H. Malvar, and F. Pighin. Making faces. In *SIGGRAPH*, pages 55–66, 1998.

[81] S. Hadap and N. Magnenat-Thalmann. Interactive hair styler based on fluid flow. In *Computer Animation and Simulation*, pages 87–100, Interlaken, Switzerland, August 2000.

[82] P. Hallinan. A low-dimensional representation of human faces for arbitrary lighting conditions. In *IEEE Conference on Computer Vision and Pattern Recognition*, pages 995–999, Ft. Collins, CO USA, 1994.

[83] P. Hanrahan and W. Krueger. Reflection from layered surfaces due to subsurface scattering. In *SIGGRAPH*, pages 165–174, August 1993.

[84] R. M. Haralick, C.-N. Lee, K. Ottenberg, and M. Nölle. Review and analysis of solutions of the three point perspective pose estimation problem. *International Journal of Computer Vision*, 13(3):331–356, 1994.

[85] R. M. Haralick and L. G. Shapiro. *Computer and Robot Vision*, Addison–Wesley, 1991.

[86] J. Hardeberg. *Acquisition and reproduction of colour images: Colorimetric and multispectral approaches*. Ph.D. dissertation, Ecole Nationale Superieure des Telecommunications, 1999.

[87] C. Harris and M. Stephens. A combined corner and edge detector. In *Proceedings of the 4th Alvey Vision Conference*, pages 189–192, 1988.

[88] R. Hartley and A. Zisserman. *Multiple View Geometry in Computer Vision*. Cambridge University Press, 2000.

[89] J. Haxby, M. I. Gobbini, M. Furey, A. Ishai, J. Schouten, and P. Pietrini. Distributed and overlapping representations of faces and objects in ventral temporal cortex. *Science*, 293(5539):2425–2430, 2001.

[90] D. J. Heeger and J. R. Bergen. Pyramid-based texture analysis/synthesis. In *SIGGRAPH*, pages 229–238, 1995.

[91] B. K. Horn. Closed-form solution of absolute orientation using unit quaternions. *Journal of the Optical Society A*, 4(4):629–642, 1987.

[92] B. K. P. Horn. *Shape from shading: a method for obtaining the shape of a smooth opaque object from one view*. Ph.D. thesis, MIT, 1970.

[93] B. K. P. Horn. Height and gradient from shading. *International Journal of Computer Vision*, 5(1):584–595, 1990.

[94] B. K. P. Horn and B. G. Schunk. Determining optical flow. *Artificial Intelligence*, 17:185–203, 1981.

[95] T. Horprasert. Computing 3-D head orientation from a monocular image. In *International Conference of Automatic Face and Gesture Recognition*, pages 242–247, Killington, Vermont, USA, 1996.

[96] H. H. S. Ip and L. Yin. Constructing a 3d individualized head model from two orthogonal views. *The Visual Computer*, (12):254–266, 1996.

[97] X. Huang, A. Acero, and H.-W. Hon. *Spoken Language Processing*. Prentice Hall PTR, 2001.

[98] P. J. Hubder. *Robust Statistics*. Wiley, 1981.

[99] K. Anjyo, Y. Usami, and T. Kurihara. A simple method for extracting the natural beauty of hair. In *SIGGRAPH*, pages 111–120, 1992.

[100] L. Itti, N. Dhavale, and F. Pighin. Realistic avatar eye and head animation using a neurobiological model of visual attention. In *Proceedings of SPIE*, pages 64–78, San Diego, CA, USA, August 2003.

[101] J. Xu, R. Lipton, I. Essa, M. Sung, and Y. Zhu. Mandatory human participation: A new authentication scheme for building secure systems. In *IEEE ICCCN*, page 547–552, Dallas, Texas, October 2003.

[102] H. W. Jensen and J. Buhler. A rapid hierarchical rendering technique for translucent materials. In *SIGGRAPH*, pages 576–581, 2002.

[103] H. W. Jensen, S. R. Marschner, M. Levoy, and P. Hanrahan. A practical model for subsurface light transport. In *SIGGRAPH*, pages 511–518, 2001.

[104] P. Joshi, W. C. Tien, M. Desbrun, and F. Pighin. Learning controls for blend shape based realistic facial animation. In *Proceedings of the Symposium on Computer Animation (SCA'03)*, pages 187–192, San Diego, CA, USA, July 2003.

[105] J. T. Kajiya and T. L. Kay. Rendering fur with three dimensional textures. In *SIGGRAPH*, pages 271–280, July 1989.

[106] T. Kanade. *Picture processing system by computer complex and recognition of human faces*. Doctoral dissertation, Kyoto University, 1973.

[107] T. Kanade. Computer recognition of human faces. *Interdisciplinary Systems Research*, 47, Birkhauser Verlag, Basel, Switzerland, 1977.

[108] M. Kass, A. Witkin, and D. Terzopoulos. SNAKES: Active contour models. *The International Journal of Computer Vision*, 1:321–332, 1988.

[109] M. D. Kelly. Visual identification of people by computer. In *Technical Report AI 130, Stanford University*, Palo Alto, CA, 1971.

[110] T. Y. Kim and U. Neumann. A thin shell volume for modeling human hair. In *Computer Animation*, pages 121–128, Philadelphia, USA, 2000.

[111] T. Y. Kim and U. Neumann. Interactive multiresolution hair modeling and editing. *ACM Transaction on Graphics*, 21(3):620–629, 2002.

[112] M. Kirby and M. Sirovich. Application of the Karhunen–Loeve procedure for the characterization of human faces. *IEEE Transactions on Pattern Analysis and Machine Intelligence*, 12(1):103–108, 1990.

[113] W. Kong and M. Nakajima. Hair rendering by jittering and pseudo shadow. In *Computer Graphics International*, Geneva, Switzerland, June 2000.

[114] E. Land and J. McCann. Lightness and retinex theory. *Journal of the Optical Society of America*, 61(1):1–11, 1971.

[115] J. Lasseter, E. Ostby, W. Reeves, C. Good, and G. Rydstrom. *Tin Toy* (film). Pixar, 1988.

[116] A. M. LeBlanc, R. Turner, and D. Thalmann. Rendering hair using pixel blending and shadow buffers. *The Journal of Visualization and Computer Animation*, 2(3):92–97, 1991.

[117] Y. G. Leclerc and A. F. Bobick. The direct computation of height from shading. In *IEEE Conference on Computer Vision and Pattern Recognition*, Maui, Hawaii, June 1991.

[118] J. Lee, B. Moghaddam, H. Pfister, and R. Machiraju. A bilinear illumination model for robust face recognition. *International Conference on Computer Vision*, II:1177–1184, 2005.

[119] K.-C. Lee, J. Ho, and D. Kriegman. Nine points of light: Accquiring subspaces for face recognition under variable lighting. In *IEEE Conference on Computer Vision and Pattern Recognition*, 357–362, Kauai, HI, USA, 2001.

[120] S. P. Lee, J. B. Badler, and N. I. Badler. Eyes alive. In *SIGGRAPH*, pages 637–644, 2002.

[121] Y. C. Lee, D. Terzopoulos, and K. Waters. Constructing physics-based facial models of individuals. In *Proceedings of Graphics Interface*, pages 1–8, Toronto, Canada, 1993.

[122] Y. C. Lee, D. Terzopoulos, and K. Waters. Realistic modeling for facial animation. In *SIGGRAPH*, pages 55–62, 1995.

[123] L. Lepetit and P. Fua. Monocular model-based 3d tracking of rigid objects: A survey. *Foundations and Trends in Computer Graphics and Vision*, 1(1):1–89, 2005.

[124] J. P. Lewis and F. I. Parke. Automatic lip-synch and speech synthesis for character animation. In *Graphics Interface*, pages 143–147, Calgary, 1987.

[125] H. Li, P. Roivainen, and R. Forchheimer. 3-D motion estimation in model-based facial image coding. *IEEE Pattern Analysis and Machine Intelligence*, 15(6):545–555, June 1993.

[126] S. Z. Li and L. Gu. Real-time multi-view face detection, tracking, pose estimation, alignment, and recognition. In *IEEE Conference on Computer Vision and Pattern Recognition Demo Summary*, Kauai, HI, USA, 2001.

[127] S. Z. Li and K. Jain. *Handbook of Face Recognition*. Springer-Verlag, 2004.

[128] L. Liang, R. Xiao, F. Wen, and J. Sun. Face alignment via component-based discriminative search. In *European Conference on Computer Vision*, volume 2, Marseille, France, 2008.

[129] P. Litwinowicz and L. Williams. Animating images with drawings. *SIGGRAPH*, pages 235–242, 1990.

[130] Z. Liu, Y. Shan, and Z. Zhang. Expressive expression mapping with ratio images. *SIGGRAPH*, pages 271–276, 2001.

[131] Z. Liu, Y. Shan, and Z. Zhang. Image-based surface detail transfer. *IEEE Computer Graphics and Applications*, 24(3):30–35, 2004.

[132] Z. Liu, C. Zhang, and Z. Zhang. Learning-based perceptual image quality improvement for video conferencing. In *IEEE International Conference on Multimedia and Expo*, Beijing, China, July 2007.

[133] Z. Liu and Z. Zhang. Robust head motion computation by taking advantage of physical properties. In *IEEE Workshop on Human Motion*, pages 73–77, Los Alamitos, CA, USA, 2000.

[134] Z. Liu, Z. Zhang, C. Jacobs, and M. Cohen. Rapid modeling of animated faces from video. In *Proceedings of Visual 2000*, pages 58–67, Mexico City, Mexico, 2000.

[135] Z. Liu, Z. Zhang, C. Jacobs, and M. Cohen. Rapid modeling of animated faces from video. *Journal of Visualization and Computer Animation*, 12(4):227–240, 2001.

[136] C. Loop and Z. Zhang. Computing rectifying homographies for stereo vision. In *Proceedings of the IEEE Conference on Computer Vision and Pattern Recognition*, Colorado, June 1999.

[137] L. Lu, Z. Zhang, H.-Y. Shum, Z. Liu, and H. Chen. Model- and exemplar-based robust head pose tracking under occlusion and varying expression. In *IEEE Workshop on Models versus Exemplars in Computer Vision, in Conjunction with CVPR'2001*, pages 58–67, Kauai, Hawaii, 2001.

[138] S. Ma and Z. Zhang. *Computer Vision: Fundamentals of Computational Theory and Algorithms*. Chinese Academy of Sciences (in Chinese), 1995.

[139] T. M. MacRobert. *Spherical Harmonics: An Elementary Treatise on Harmonic Functions with Applications*. Dover Publications, 1948.

[140] N. Magnenat-Thalmann, N. E. Primeau, and D. Thalmann. Abstract muscle actions procedures for human face animation. *The Visual Computer*, 3(5): 290–297, 1988.

[141] S. Marschner, H. W. Jensen, M. Cammarano, S. Worley, and P. Hanrahan. Light scattering from human hair fibers. *ACM Transaction on Graphics*, 22(3):780–791, 2003.

[142] S. R. Marschner and D. P. Greenberg. Inverse lighting for photography. In *IST/SID Fifth Color Imaging Conference*, Scattsdale, Arizona, USA, 1997.

[143] S. R. Marschner, B. Guenter, and S. Raghupathy. Modeling and rendering for realistic facial animation. In *Rendering Techniques*, pages 231–242. Springer, 2000.

[144] S. R. Marschner, S. Westin, E. Lafortune, K. Torance, and D. Greenberg. Image-based brdf measurement including human skin. In *Rendering Techniques*, pages 139–152, Granada, Spin, 1999.

[145] A. McAdams, A. Selle, K. Ward, E. Sifakis, and J. Teran. Detail preserving continuum simulation of stright hair. *ACM Transaction on Graphics*, 28(3):62:1–62:6, 2009.

[146] G. Messina, A. Castorina, S. Battiato, and A. Bosco. Image quality improvement by adaptive exposure correction techniques. In *IEEE International Conference on Multimedia and Expo (ICME)*, pages 549–552, Amsterdam, The Netherlands, July 2003.

[147] G. Miller and C. Hoffman. Illumination and reflection maps: Simulated objects in simulated and real environments. *SIGGRAPH 84 Advanced Computer Grpahics Animation Seminar Notes*, 1984.

[148] J. T. Moon and S. R. Marschner. Simulating multiple scattering in hair using a photon mapping approach. *ACM Transaction on Graphics*, 25(3):1067–1074, 2006.

[149] J. T. Moon, B. Walter, and S. R. Marschner. Efficient multiple scattering in hair using spherical harmonics. *ACM Transaction on Graphics*, 27(3):31:1–31–7, 2008.

[150] J. More. The Levenberg–Marquardt algorithm, implementation and theory. In G. A. Watson, editor, *Numerical Analysis*, Lecture Notes in Mathematics 630. Springer-Verlag, 1977.

[151] P. Moreno, C. Joerg, J. M. V. Thong, and O. Glickman. A recursive algorithm for the forced alignment of very long audio segments. In *IEEE International Conference on Spoken Language Processing*, pages 2711–2714, Sydney, Australia, 1998.

[152] G. Mori and J. Malik. Recognizing objects in adversarial clutter: Breaking a visual captcha. In *IEEE Conference on Computer Vision and Pattern Recognition*, pages I:134–141, 2003.

[153] H. Murase and S. K. Nayar. Visual learning and recognition of 3-d objects from appearance. *International Journal of Computer Vision*, 14(1):5–24, 1995.

[154] J. F. Murray-Coleman and A. M. Smith. The automated measurement of brdfs and their application to luminaire modeling. *Journal of the Illuminating Engineering Society*, 19(1):87–99, 1990.

[155] R. Newman, Y. Matsumoto, S. Rougeaux, and A. Zelinsky. Real-time stereo tracking for head pose and gaze estimation. In *Proceedings of the Fourth IEEE International Conference on Automatic Face and Gesture Recognition (FG 2000)*, pages 122–128, Grenoble, France, 2000.

[156] K. Nishino, K. Ikeuchi, and Z. Zhang. Re-rendering from a sparse set of images. In *Technical Report DU-CS-05-12, Drexel University*, 2005.

[157] K. Nishino, Z. Zhang, and K. Ikeuchi. Determining reflectance parameters and illumination distribution from a sparse set of images for view-dependent image synthesis. In *International Conference on Computer Vision*, pages 599–606, Vancouver, BC, Canada, 2001.

[158] M. Noar. Verification of a human in the loop or identification via the turing test. *Unpublished notes*, September, 13 1996.

[159] J. Noh and U. Neumann. Expression cloning. In *SIGGRAPH*, pages 277–288, 2001.

[160] E. Owens and B. Blazek. Visemes observed by hearingimpaired and normal-hearing adult viewers. *J. Speech and Hearing Research*, 28:381–393, 1985.

[161] S. Paris, H. M. Briceno, and F. X. Sillion. Capture of hair geometry from multiple images. *ACM Transaction on Graphics*, 23(3):712–719, August 2004.

[162] F. I. Parke. Computer generated animation of faces. In *ACM National Conference*, New York, NY, USA, 1972.

[163] F. I. Parke. *A parametric model of human faces*. PhD thesis, University of Utah, 1974.

[164] F. I. Parke and K. Waters. *Computer facial animation*. AKPeters, 1996.

[165] A. Pearce, B. Wyvill, G. Wyvill, and D. Hill. Speech and expression: A computer solution to face animation. In *Graphics Interface*, pages 136–140, Calgary, Alberta, Canada, 1986.

[166] B.-T. Phong. Illumination for computer generated pictures. *Communication of ACM*, 18(6):311–317, 1975.

[167] L. Piegl and W. Tiller. *The NURBS Book*. Springer, 1995.

[168] F. Pighin, J. Hecker, D. Lischinski, R. Szeliski, and D. H. Salesin. Synthesizing realistic facial expressions from photographs. In *SIGGRAPH*, pages 75–84, 1998.

[169] F. Pighin, D. H. Salesin, and R. Szeliski. Resynthesizing facial animation through 3d model-based tracking. *International Conference on Computer Vision*, pages 143–150, Kerkyra, Corfu, Greece, 1999.

[170] S. Platt and N. Badler. Animating facial expression. *Computer Graphics*, 15(3):245–252, 1981.

[171] M. Proesmans, L. V. Cool, and A. Oosterlinck. Active acquisition of 3d shape for moving objects. In *International Conference on Image Processing*, Lausanne, Switzerland, Sept. 1996.

[172] H. Pyun, Y. Kim, W. Chae, H. W. Kang, and S. Y. Shin. An example-based approach for facial expression cloning. In *Symposium on Computer Animation (SCA'03)*, pages 167–176, San Diego, CA, USA, 2003.

[173] L. Qing, S. Shan, and W. Gao. Face recognition with harmonic de-lighting. In *Asian Conference on Computer Vision*, volume 2, pages 824–829, Jeju, Korea, 2004.

[174] L. Qing, S. Shan, W. Gao, and B. Du. Face recognition under generic illumination based on harmonic relighting. *International Journal of Pattern Recognition and Artificial Intelligence*, 19(4):513–531, 2005.

[175] G. Qiu. From content-based image retrieval to example-based image processing. *University of Nottingham Technical Report: Report-cvip-05-2004*, May 2004.

[176] R. Ramamoorthi. Analytic pca construction for theoretical analysis of lighting variability in images of a lambertian object. *IEEE Transactions on Pattern Analysis and Machine Intelligence*, 24(10):1322–1333, 2002.

[177] R. Ramamoorthi and P. Hanrahan. An efficient representation for irradiance environment maps. In *SIGGRAPH*, pages 497–500, 2001.

[178] R. Ramamoorthi and P. Hanrahan. A signal-processing framework for inverse rendering. In *SIGGRAPH*, pages 117–128, 2001.

[179] E. Reinhard, M. Ashikhmin, B. Gooch, and P. Shirley. Color transfer between images. *IEEE Computer Graphics and Applications*, 21(5):34–41, 2001.

[180] T. Riklin-Raviv and A. Shashua. The quotient image: Class based re-rendering and recongnition with varying illuminations. In *IEEE Conference on Computer Vision and Pattern Recognition*, pages 566–571, Ft. Collins, Co, USA, 1999.

[181] R. Rosenblum, W. Carlson, and E. Tripp. Simulating the structure and dynamics of human hair: Modeling, rendering, and animation. *The Journal of Visualization and Computer Animation*, 2(4):141–148, 1991.

[182] P. Rousseeuw and A. Leroy. *Robust Regression and Outlier Detection*. John Wiley & Sons, 1987.

[183] A. Roy-Chowdhury and R. Chellappa. Stochastic approximation and rate-distortion analysis for robust structure and motion estimation. *International Journal of Computer Vision*, 55(1):27–53, 2003.

[184] Y. Rui and Z. Liu. Artifacial: Automated reverse turing test using facial features. *Multimedia Systems*, 9(6):493–502, 2004.

[185] M. A. Sagar, D. Bullivant, G. D. Mallinson, P. J. Hunter, and I. W. Hunter. A virtual environment and model of the eye for surgical simulation. In *SIGGRAPH*, pages 205–212, 1994.

[186] F. Saitoh. Image contrast enhancement using genetic algorithm. In *IEEE International Conference on SMC*, pages 899–904, Amsterdam, The Netherlands, October 1999.

[187] J. Salvi, J. Pages, and J. Batlle. Pattern codification strategies in structured light systems. *Pattern Recognition*, 37(4):827–849, 2004.

[188] Y. Sato and K. Ikeuchi. Temporal-color space analysis of reflection. *Journal of Optical Society of America A*, 11(11):2990–3002, November 1994.

[189] A. Saulnier, M. L. Viaud, and D. Geldreich. Real-time facial analysis and synthesis chain. In M. Bichsel, editor, *International Workshop on Automatic Face and Gesture Recogntion*, pages 86–91, Zurich, Switzerland, 1995.

[190] M. Savvides, B. Vijaya Kumar, and P. Khosla. 'Corefaces'-robust shift invariant pca based correlation filter for illumination tolerant face recognition. In *IEEE Conference on Computer Vision and Pattern Recognition*, II:834–841, 2004.

[191] S. M. Seize and C. R. Dyer. View morphing. In *SIGGRAPH*, pages 21–30, 1996.

[192] Y. Shan, Z. Liu, and Z. Zhang. Image-based surface detail transfer. In *IEEE Conference on Computer Vision and Pattern Recognition*, volume II, pages 794–799, 2001.

[193] Y. Shan, Z. Liu, and Z. Zhang. Model-based boundle adjustment with application to face modeling. In *International Conference on Computer Vision*, pages 644–651, Vancauver, BC, Canada, 2001.

[194] A. Shashua. *Geometry and photometry in 3D visual recognition*. Ph.D. thesis, MIT, 1992.

[195] C. Shi, K. Yu, J. Li, and S. Li. Automatic image quality improvement for video-conferencing. In *IEEE International Conference on Acoustics, Speech, and Signal Processing (ICASSP)*, Montreal, Quebec, Canada, 2004.

[196] J. Shi and C. Tomasi. Good features to track. In *IEEE Conference on Computer Vision and Pattern Recognition*, pages 593–600, Washington, DC, 1994.

[197] T. Sim, S. Baker, and M. Bsat. The cmu pose, illumination, and expression (pie) database. In *Proceedings of IEEE International Conference on Automatic Face and Gesture Recognition*, pages 46–51, Washington, DC, USA, 2002.

[198] T. Sim, S. Baker, and M. Bsat. The cmu pose, illumination, and expression database. *Pattern Analysis and Machine Intelligence*, 25(12):1615–1618, 2003.

[199] M. Sirovich and M. Kirby. Low-dimensional procedure for the characterization of human faces. *Journal of the Optical Society of America A*, 4:519–524, 1987.

[200] M. Song, Z. Dong, C. Theobalt, H. Wang, Z. Liu, and H.-P. Seidel. A generic framework for efficient 2d and 3d facial expression analogy. *IEEE Transaction on Multimedia*, 9(7):1384–1395, 2007.

[201] Spharmonickit. Description retrived from http://www.cs.dartmouth.edu/~geelong/sphere/, April 2002.

[202] J. Stam. *Multi-scale stochastic modeling of complext natural phenomena*. Ph.D. thesis, University of Toronto, 1995.

[203] R. Stokes. Human factors and appearance design considerations of the mod ii picturephone station set. *IEEE Transaction on Communication Technology*, 17(2):318–323, 1969.

[204] R. W. Sumner and J. Popovic. Deformation tranfer for triangle meshes. In *SIGGRAPH*, pages 399–405, 2004.

[205] M. Sun, Z. Liu, J. Qiu, Z. Zhang, and M. Sinclair. Active lighting for video conferencing. *IEEE Transaction on Circuits and Systems for Video Technology*, 19(12):1819–1829, 2009.

[206] C. T. Swain and B. G. Haskell. Color balance for video conferencing. In *IEEE International Conference on Image Processing (ICIP)*, pages 815–819, Washington, DC, USA, 1997.

[207] D. Terzopoulos and K. Waters. Analysis of dynamic facial images using physical and anatomical models. In *International Conference on Computer Vision*, pages 727–732, 1990.

[208] D. Terzopoulos and K. Waters. Physically-based facial modeling and animation. *Journal of Visualization and Computer Animation*, 1(4):73–80, 1990.

[209] D. Terzopoulos and K. Waters. Techniques for realistic facial modeling and animation. In N. Magnenat-Thalmann and D. Thalmann, editors, *Computer Animation*, pages 59–74. Springer-Verlag, 1991.

[210] D. Terzopoulos and K. Waters. Analysis and synthesis of facial image sequences using physical and anatomical models. *IEEE Transactions on Pattern Analysis and Machine Intelligence*, 15(6):569–579, 2000.

[211] Y.-L. Tian, T. Kanade, and J. Cohn. Recognizing action units for facial expression analysis. *Pattern Analysis and Machine Intelligence*, 23(2):97–115, 2001.

[212] C. Tomasi and T. Kanade. Shape and motion from image streams under orthography: A factorization method. *International Journal of Computer Vision*, 9(2):137–154, 1992.

[213] K. Torrance and E. M. Sparrow. Theory for off-specular reflection from roughened surfaces. *Journal of Optical Society America*, 57(9):1, 1967.

[214] N. Tsumura, N. Ojima, K. Sato, M. Shiraishi, H. Shimizu, H. Nabeshima, S. Akazaki, K. Hori, and Y. Miyake. Image-based skin color and texture analysis/synthesis by extracting hemoglobin and melanin information in the skin. *ACM Transactions on Graphics*, 22(3):770–779, 2003.

[215] A. Turing. Computing machinery and intelligence. *Mind*, 59(236):433–460, 1985.

[216] M. Turk and A. Pentland. Eigenfaces for recognition. *Journal of Cognitive Neuroscience*, 3(1):71–96, 1991.

[217] L. Vacchetti, V. Lepetit, and P. Fua. Stable real-time 3d tracking using online and offline information. *IEEE Transaction on Pattern Analysis and Machine Intelligence*, 26(10):1385–1391, 2004.

[218] M. A. O. Vasilescu and D. Terzopoulos. Multilinear analysis of image ensembles: Tensorfaces. In *European Conference on Computer Vision*, Copenhagen, Denmark, May 2002.

[219] M. A. O. Vasilescu and D. Terzopoulos. Multilinear independent component analysis. In *IEEE Conference on Computer Vision and Pattern Recognition*, San Diego, CA, USA, 2005.

[220] T. Vetter and T. Poggio. Linear object classes and image synthesis from a single example image. *Pattern Analysis and Machine Intelligence*, 19(7):733–742, 1997.

[221] B. Vijaya Kumar, M. Savvides, and C. Xie. Correlation pattern recognition for face recognition. *Proceedingss of the IEEE*, 94:1963–1976.

[222] P. Viola and M. Jones. Robust real-time object detection. In *Second International Workshop on Statistical and Computational Theories of Vision-Modeling, Learning, Computing and Sampling*, pages 149–154, Vancouver, July 13, 2001.

[223] H. Wang, S. Li, Y. Wang, and J. Zhang. Self quotient image for face recognition. In *International Conference on Image Processing*, pages 1397–1400, Singapore, 2004.

[224] H. Wang, S. Li, Y. Wang, and W. Zhang. Illumination modeling and normalization for face recognition. In *IEEE International Workshop on Analysis and Modeling of Faces and Gestures*, pages 104–111, Nice, France, 2003.

[225] L. Wang, Y. Yu, K. Zhou, and B. Guo. Example-based hair geometry synthesis. *ACM Transaction on Graphics*, 28(3):56:1–56:9, 2009.

[226] Q. Wang, W. Zhang, X. Tang, and H. Shum. Real-time bayesian 3-d pose tracking. *IEEE Transaction on Circuits and Systems for Video Technology*, 16(12):1533–1541, 2006.

[227] Y. Wang, Z. Liu, G. Hua, Z. Wen, Z. Zhang, and D. Samaras. Face re-lighting from a single image under harsh lighting conditions. In *IEEE Conference on Computer Vision and Pattern Recognition*, Minneapolis, Minnesota, June 2007.

[228] Y. Wang, L. Zhang, Z. Liu, G. Hua, Z. Wen, Z. Zhang, and D. Samaras. Face re-lighting from a single image under arbitrary unknown lighting conditions. *IEEE Transaction on Pattern Recogniton and Machine Intelligence*, 31(11):1968–1984, 2009.

[229] G. J. Ward. Measuring and modeling anisotropic reflection. In *SIGGRAPH*, pages 265–272, July 1992.

[230] K. Ward, F. Bertails, T.-Y. Kim, S. R. Marschner, M.-P. Cani, and M. C. Lin. A survey on hair modeling: Styling, simulation, and rendering. *IEEE Transaction on Visualization and Computer Graphics*, 13(2):213–234, 2007.

[231] K. Ward and M. C. Lin. Adaptive grouping and subvision for simulating hair dynamics. In *Pacific Graphics*, pages 234–243, October 2003.

[232] Y. Watanabe and Y. Suenaga. A trigonal prism-based method for hair image generation. *IEEE Computer Graphics and Applications*, 12(1):47–53, 1992.

[233] K. Waters. A muscle model for animating three-dimensional facial expression. *Computer Graphics*, 22(4):17–24, 1987.

[234] Y. Wei, E. Ofek, L. Quan, and H.-Y. Shum. Modeling hair from multiple views. *ACM Transaction on Graphics*, 24(3):816–820, 2005.

[235] Z. Wen, P. Hong, and T. S. Huang. Real time speech driven facial animation using formant analysis. In *IEEE International Conference on Multimedia and Expo*, Tokyo, Japan, August 2001.

[236] Z. Wen, Z. Liu, and T. S. Huang. Face relighting with radiance environment maps. In *IEEE Conference on Computer Vision and Pattern Recognition*, pages 158–165, Madison, WI, USA, 2003.

[237] T. Weyrich, W. Matusik, H. Pfister, B. Bickel, C. Donner, C. Tu, J. McAndless, J. Lee, A. Ngan, H. W. Jensen, and M. Gross. Analysis of human faces using a measurement-based skin reflectance model. *ACM Transaction on Graphics*, 25(3):1013–1024, 2006.

[238] T. Weyrich, W. Matusik, H. Pfister, J. Lee, A. Ngan, H. W. Jensen, and M. Gross. A measurement-based skin reflectance model for face rendering and editing. In *Technical Report, TR2005-046, Mitsubishi Electric Research Laboratories*, Cambridge, MA, USA, 2005.

[239] L. Williams. Performace-driven facial animation. In *SIGGRAPH*, pages 235–242, 1990.

[240] G. Wolberg. *Digital Image Warping*. IEEE Computer Society Press, 1990.

[241] D. Wood, D. Azuma, K. Aldinger, B. Curless, T. Duchamp, D. Salesin, and W. Stuetzle. Surface light fields for 3d photography. In *SIGGRAPH*, pages 287–296, 2000.

[242] R. Xiao, L. Zhu, and H. Zhang. Boosting chain learning for object detection. In *International Conference on Computer Vision*, volume 1, pages 709–715, 2003.

[243] S. Yan, M. Li, H. Zhang, and Q. Cheng. Ranking prior likelihood distributions for bayesian shape localization framework. In *International Conference on Computer Vision*, pages 51–58, Nice, France, 2003.

[244] J. Yang, R. Stiefelhagen, U. Meier, and A. Waibel. Real-time face and facial feature tracking and applications. In *Proceedings of AVSP'98*, pages 79–84, Terrigal, Australia, 1998.

[245] M. Yang, D. Roth, and N. Ahuja. *A SNoW-Based Face Detector*. MIT Press, 2000.

[246] R. Yang and Z. Zhang. Eye gaze correction with stereovision for video tele-conferencing. In *Proceedings of the 7th European Conference on Computer Vision*, volume II, pages 479–494, Copenhagen, Denmark, May 2002.

[247] R. Yang and Z. Zhang. Model-based head pose tracking with stereovision. In *IEEE International Conference on Automatic Face and Gesture Recognition (FG2002)*, pages 255–260, Washington, DC, 2002.

[248] L. Yin, X. Wei, Y. Sun, J. Wang, and M. J. Rosato. A 3d facial expression database for facial behavior research. In *7th International Conference on Automatic Face and Gesture Recognition (FGR06)*, pages 211–216, Southampton, UK, April 2006.

[249] J. Yong Noh and U. Neumann. Expression cloning. In *Computer Graphics, Annual Conference Series*, pages 277–288. SIGGRAPH, August 2001.

[250] Y. Yu. Modeling realistic virtual hairstyles. In *Pacific Graphics*, pages 295–304, October 2001.

[251] A. L. Yuille, D. S. Cohen, and P. W. Hallinan. Feature extraction from faces using deformable templates. *International Journal of Computer Vision*, 8(2):99–112, 1992.

[252] B. Zhang, C. Hu, Q. Cai, B. Guo, and H. Shum. E-partner: A photo-realistic conversation agent. In *Second IEEE Pacific-Rim Conference on Multimedia*, pages 261–268, Beijing, China, October 2001.

[253] B. Zhang, Z. Liu, and B. Guo. Photo-realistic conversation agent. In M. K. D. Zhang and G. Baciu, editors, *Integrated Image and Graphics Technologies*. Kluwer Academic Press, 2003.

[254] C. Zhang and Z. Zhang. *Boosting-Based Face Detection and Adaptation*. Synthesis Lectures on Computer Vision, Morgan and Claypool, 2010.

[255] L. Zhang and D. Samaras. Face recognition under variable lighting using harmonic image exemplars. In *IEEE Conference on Computer Vision and Pattern Recognition*, pages I:19–25, 2003.

[256] L. Zhang and D. Samaras. Face recognition from a single training image under arbitrary unknown lighting using spherical harmonics. *Pattern Analysis and Machine Intelligence*, 28(3):351–363, 2006.

[257] L. Zhang, N. Snavely, B. Curless, and S. M. Seitz. Spacetime faces: High resolution capture for modeling and animation. *ACM Transaction on Graphics*, 23(3):548–558, 2004.

[258] L. Zhang, S. Wang, and D. Samaras. Face synthesis and recognition from a single image under arbitrary unknown lighting using a spherical harmonic basis morphable model. In *IEEE Conference on Computer Vision and Pattern Recognition*, II:209–216, 2005.

[259] Q. Zhang, Z. Liu, B. Guo, D. Terzopoulos, and H.-Y. Shum. Geometry-driven photorealistic facial expression synthesis. *IEEE Transaction on Visualization and Computer Graphics*, 12(1):48–60, 2006.

[260] R. Zhang, P.-S. Tsai, J. E. Cryer, and M. Shah. Shape from shading: A survey. *IEEE Transaction on Pattern Recognition and Machine Intelligence*, 21(8):690–706, 1999.

[261] Z. Zhang. Iterative point matching for registration of free-form curves and surfaces. *Internal Journal of Computer Vision*, 13(2):119–152, 1994.

[262] Z. Zhang. Motion and structure from two perspective views: From essential parameters to euclidean motion via fundamental matrix. *Journal of the Optical Society of America A*, 14(11):2938–2950, 1997.

[263] Z. Zhang. Determining the epipolar geometry and its uncertainty: A review. *The International Journal of Computer Vision*, 27(2):161–195, 1998.

[264] Z. Zhang. On the optimization criteria used in two-view motion analysis. *IEEE Transactions on Pattern Analysis and Machine Intelligence*, 20(7):717–729, 1998.

[265] Z. Zhang. A flexible new technique for camera calibration. *IEEE Transactions on Pattern Analysis and Machine Intelligence*, 22(11):1330–1334, 2000.

[266] Z. Zhang and O. Faugeras. Determining motion from 3D line segment matches: A comparative study. *Image and Vision Computing*, 9(1):10–19, 1991.

[267] Z. Zhang and O. Faugeras. Estimation of displacements from two 3D frames obtained from stereo. *IEEE Transactions on Pattern Analysis and Machine Intelligence*, 14(12):1141–1156, 1992.

[268] Z. Zhang, Z. Liu, D. Adler, M. Cohen, E. Hanson, and Y. Shan. Robust and rapid generation of animated faces from video images: A model-based modeling approach. *International Journal of Computer Vision*, 58(2):93–120, 2004.

[269] Z. Zhang, L. Zhu, S. Li, and H. Zhang. Real-time multiview face detection. In *International Conference on Automatic Face and Gesture Recognition*, pages 149–154, 2002.

[270] W. Zhao and R. Chellappa. Illumination-insensitive face recognition using symmetric shape-from-shading. In *IEEE Conference on Computer Vision and Pattern Recognition*, pages 286–293, Hilton Head, SC, USA, 2000.

[271] W. Zhao and R. Chellappa. *Face Processing: Advanced Modeling and Methods.*
       Acamedic Press, 2006.
[272] Q. Zheng and R. Chellappa. Estimation of illuminant direction, albedo, and shape
       from shading. In *IEEE Conference on Computer Vision and Pattern Recognition*,
       pages 540–545, Maui, HI, USA, June 1991.
[273] S. Zhu, C. Guo, Y. Wang, and Z. Xu. What are textons? *International Journal of
       Computer Vision*, 62(1–2):121–143, 2005.

Index